Decision Making at the Top

DECISION MAKING

AT THE TOP

The Shaping of
Strategic Direction

GORDON DONALDSON
JAY W. LORSCH

Basic Books, Inc., Publishers   New York

85050

Library of Congress Cataloging in Publication Data

Donaldson, Gordon, 1922—
    Decision making at the top.

    Includes index.

    1. Decision-making.   2.   Industrial management—
United States.   I.   Lorsch, Jay WIlliam.   II.   Title.
HD30.23.D655   1983   658.4′03   83–70753
ISBN 0–465–01584–0

CONTENTS

Preface   vii

1. Choices for Corporate Survival   3

2. Who Are the Corporate Managers?   15

3. An Inside Perspective on Financial Goals   32

4. How the System Works—Balancing the Supply and

   Demand for Corporate Funds   49

5. The Psychology of Executive Choice   79

6. Maintaining Strategic Equilibrium   110

7. Changing the Fundamentals   131

8. Strategic Choice Under Managerial Capitalism   159

   Appendix A: Methodology   175

   Appendix B: The Diversification Index   178

   Appendix C: Goals and Performance of Research

   Sample Companies   181

Contents

Appendix D: Corporate Managements' Belief
    Systems   184

Notes   196

Index   203

PREFACE

This book grew out of a series of informal and wide-ranging discussions involving ourselves and our colleague John McArthur, who retired from the study to assume additional administrative duties. Rooted in different disciplines, we were struck both by the similarities and by the differences in our perceptions of the forces shaping top management's choice of strategic goals and the means to achieve them. We were also impressed by differences between the literature of our fields and our personal experience with corporate managers. Intrigued by these discrepancies, as well as by the possibilities inherent in an interdisciplinary study of corporate goal formation, we began to think more specifically about the form such a study could take.

Despite the differences in our theoretical perspectives and training, we shared a commitment to clinical research. Believing that the generation of knowledge about business administration can be furthered by a careful study of actual administrative situations, we designed our project accordingly. We chose a limited number of successful, mature companies, and we embarked upon a careful and thorough study of the financial and psychological forces that shaped their top managers' strategic choices.

The nature of this clinical research is described in detail in appendix A. What we would add here are our memories of the people and experiences that were part of the research. As we traveled from coast to coast to visit these companies and interview their most senior executives, we were greatly aided by our research assistants, Carl Kester and James Singer. Both were skillful and dedicated interviewers and investigators. Without their help we could not have completed the arduous program of field research upon which this book is based. In addition, Jim brought the order to our documents that allowed us to classify and compare the companies. Carl provided the diversification index and the financial analyses that appear in the appendixes.

During the numerous trips, we all spent countless hours discussing what we were observing and learning. We formulated working hypotheses and drew tentative conclusions in planes, rental cars, executive reception rooms, and hotels as well as in our offices. Throughout these discussions we were refining our ideas through the stimulation of one another's thoughts. And from them gradually emerged the ideas that are reported here.

In the course of our work we have accumulated many debts. Foremost among them are those we owe to the chief executives and senior managers of the participating companies. We wish to express our deep appreciation to all these men who must, unfortunately, remain anonymous. Without their serious interest, openness, trust, and commitment of personal and corporate time and energy, this study would have been impossible.

We are likewise indebted to the many scholars who have shared their knowledge and experience with us. Initially we produced two separate but related manuscripts as we sought to record our individual interpretations of the data. Numerous colleagues at Harvard and elsewhere read all or parts of these early drafts, and their responses prompted us to rethink and rewrite. We are particularly grateful for the detailed critiques provided by Professors Richard Caves, Alfred Chandler, Raymond Corey, William Fruhan, Robert Glauber, John Kotter, Paul Lawrence, Henry Mintzberg, David Mullins, Malcolm Salter, and Michael Spence. The shortcomings that remain do so despite their best advice, and we claim full responsibility.

We are also grateful to those who contributed to the creation of this manuscript in other ways. Under the leadership of Professor Richard Rosenbloom and, later, Professor Raymond Corey, the Division of Research at the Harvard Business School provided vital encouragement and financial support. From Steve Fraser, our editor at Basic Books, we received the insightful counsel that led to the joint manuscript we had long envisioned. His comments and suggestions were the catalyst that enabled us to bring our separate manuscripts together in one volume. In achieving that task we were also assisted by Nan Stone, editor for the Division of Research. As we reshaped our individual insights and diverse styles into one harmonious whole, we relied heavily on her dedication, skill, and good humor.

Finally we wish to express our appreciation for the patience and dedication of our secretaries, Janet Norman, Jodie Raduziner, and Annmarie Fennelly, who suffered through interminable drafts, and for the work of the Business

School Word Processing Department, under the direction of Rose Giacobbe, which produced the final manuscript.

To all of those mentioned, as well as to our families, who have had the forbearance to allow us to lock ourselves in our studies, we offer our heartfelt thanks.

GORDON DONALDSON

JAY W. LORSCH

Decision Making at the Top

CHAPTER 1

Choices for
Corporate Survival

Three Decisions

On a wintry New England day in the early 1970s, the chief executive officer of a large electronics company sat with his immediate subordinates around a walnut table in their boardroom. They faced a major decision: Should they expand their entry into the computer industry? The management of the division responsible for the company's computer business had raised the issue in a strategic plan it had developed. The heart of the proposal was the division's request to develop, produce, and market a mainframe computer with a capacity larger than anything the company had attempted before. According to pro forma projections, a favorable decision should lead to shipments of $300 million within three years and an operating profit of $75 million.

Although this was the first formal presentation of the proposal to senior corporate management, the executives had discussed the idea often. Despite the division's rosy projections, the senior managers had reservations about proceeding. For one thing, the economy was in a mild recession. For another, the proposal would bring them into direct competition with IBM and other large mainframe producers. As such, it would require a marketing effort exceeding, in both dollars and sales effort, anything they had tried before. In fact, the millions of dollars needed for marketing dwarfed the projected estimate of $10 million required to complete development of the new model's hardware and software. Further, the managers were aware that encouraging this development would move them away from familiar business applications toward the more technical applications of process control in such industries as chemicals and petroleum. Finally, they had to weigh the impact of a negative decision on the morale of the division's engineers and managers, who had brought the project to this stage and who were committed to going ahead.

As the discussion progressed, the senior managers identified three alternatives. They could continue the program, sacrificing short-term earnings in order to gain potential long-term profit growth. They could modify the program, by slowing down research and development and by tailoring marketing expenditures to fit the economic situation. Or they could cancel the entire project.

At about the same time, in a twentieth-floor office overlooking Lake Michigan and the Chicago skyline, another chief executive sat with his four principal subordinates. The top management of a major consumer products company, they faced a different—but equally complex—problem. They had just received an offer of $250 million in cash for their one industrial products division. Should they accept it?

Their problem was not the idea of the sale. They had been committed to getting out of this business for several years, because it did not fit their vision of themselves as a consumer products firm. Toward this end, they had assigned one of their most capable general managers to the division to improve its profitability and make it a more attractive candidate for divestiture. The offer they had received was the best to date, but it still fell short of what several in the room had hoped to realize. They wondered whether it might not be wiser to turn down the offer and wait for another. After all, the division was now generating a return comparable to the average of the corporation's other businesses. Others disagreed. They argued that this offer was the best they were likely to get. Further, it would finance a long-standing company goal—the acquisition of a small chain of retail outlets and their subsequent expansion nationwide. Such an acquisition could be made in any case, of course. But it would require borrowing or an exchange of stock, which management preferred to avoid.

Regardless of where they stood on these issues, the executives shared a concern for their employees. If they were to accept the offer, would the division's personnel find the acquirer a good employer? As one of the executives asked, would the acquiring company provide a "hospitable home for its managers and other employees"? The question was important not just for the employees in question but also for the company as a whole. What would the sale signal to managers and employees in other divisions about top management's commitment to them and their careers?

Almost one thousand miles to the south, another group was debating its own complicated issue. These executives of a forest products company were committed to modernizing the papermaking machinery at their major manufacturing site. Their problem was financing: How could they provide the $90 million required over the next three years? Cash flows from current operations were not nearly large enough. Given the low price earnings ratios of the industry in general and their company in particular, they felt that new equity was inadvisable. Cutting dividends also seemed inadvisable because of the negative impact it would have on the price of their stock.

As the discussion continued, the chief financial officer (CFO) reiterated his belief that the only option was to increase the company's long-term debt. Others in the group resisted the idea because traditionally they and their predecessors had financed expansion and modernization from current earnings. They supported their position with forceful arguments: Too much long-term debt was unwise given their industry's cyclical ups and downs. More debt might lower their credit rating. It might also make short-term debt more expensive.

In response, the CFO was persistent and insistent. In an inflationary period it made economic sense to borrow. The company had sufficient earnings and equity to allow this much debt, and more. The new debt would increase the company's return on equity as the modernization program paid off. In turn, this increase would be favorably reflected in the price of the company's stock.

As the chairman listened to the sometimes heated discussions, several points were in the forefront of his thinking. There was no doubt that the modernization program was needed to maintain the firm's competitive position and to assure the employment of its work force. Borrowing did seem to be the only economically viable solution; but long-term debt was not something with which he was comfortable. His predecessors had managed to avoid it. Shouldn't he? In addition, it was clear that each major choice was related to others. Maintaining the firm's competitive position meant modernization. But if this led to long-term debt, all the company's other financial goals would have to be reexamined.

The Myths and Reality of Strategic Choice

Such decisions are typical of those being considered daily in the executive suites of large, mature industrial corporations across the United States. They are complex choices about corporate goals and the means to achieve them, choices that outline the strategic direction of the company.* They define the rate at which companies may grow in size and profits. They determine how earnings will be divided between dividends for shareholders and funds to be retained for future internal investment. They define the products and markets in which the company will compete: whether and how to enter new business domestically; how much to spend on research and development; whether to expand internationally; whether to grow and diversify through acquisition.

Obviously such decisions have a major impact not only on the individual corporation and the industry in which they operate but also on the United States' economy as a whole.† Yet in spite of their importance to employees, investors, and the public at large, the forces that shape these decisions have not been wholly understood. Moreover, a number of popular myths exist that stand in stark contrast to the realities as we have come to understand them through our systematic study of twelve mature, successful industrial companies.

Those realities begin with the fact that there are important constraints on the choices the corporate managers of these companies can make.‡ Contrary

---

*Following Kenneth R. Andrews (*The Concept of Corporate Strategy*, rev. ed. [Homewood, Ill.: Dow Jones-Irwin, 1980], pp. 18–21) and Henry Mintzberg ("Patterns in Strategy Formation," *Management Science* 24 (1978): 934–948), we define corporate strategy as the stream of decisions over time that reveal management's goals for the corporation and the means they choose to achieve them. As such, a strategy may be explicitly stated or may be only implicitly understood by the decision makers.

†For example, in 1979 *Fortune* 500 companies accounted for 61 percent of the United States' gross national product, 87.6 percent of the total United States' manufacturing profits, and 16.7 percent of total United States' employment.

‡The term corporate manager refers to the chief executive officer and those who report directly to him. The terms top management, corporate executives, and corporate leaders will be used interchangeably to refer to the same individuals. In the companies studied all these corporate managers were male.

to popular myth, these top executives do not have great latitude in their strategic choices. Instead the constraints on their choices are several, and they are both psychological and objective.

Similarly, it is widely assumed that corporate managers change companies often and that corporate leadership is transitory. In reality, however, these managers are long-service executives who are deeply committed to their companies and identify closely with them.

This abiding commitment underscores another sharp contrast between myth and reality. It is commonly believed that the primary goal of these corporate managers is the maximization of shareholder wealth. But we have found, in contrast, that their primary goal is the survival of the corporation in which they have invested so much of themselves psychologically and professionally. Therefore, they are committed, first and foremost, to the enhancement of *corporate* wealth, which includes not only the firm's financial assets reflected on the balance sheet but also its important human assets and its competitive positions in the various markets in which it operates.

Those who argue that management strives to maximize shareholder wealth have also argued that management's strategic decisions are subject to the discipline of the capital market. From their perspective management's choices are guided by the corporate rate of return on investment compared to the cost of that capital in the public markets. But we have found that the top managers in these large, mature companies seek to minimize their dependence on the external capital market. They work to make their companies financially self-sustaining. Thus their goals reflect the characteristics of an internal capital market in which the demand for funds reflected in growth objectives must be balanced against the available supply provided primarily by retained earnings and secondarily by that borrowing available on a truly arm's length basis.

Further, these corporate executives do not concern themselves solely with investor reactions and expectations, as the conventional wisdom would suggest. Instead they reach choices that also assure that they will maintain or enhance their position in their product markets as well as meet the expectations of their fellow employees for stability and growth in career opportunities.

Recently some critics have argued that these corporate managers are overly influenced in their decision making by short-term considerations. They believe that this short-term orientation has led to the competitive inferiority

7

of many American companies. Again our evidence suggests otherwise. Although there are clearly some pressures on management for quick results, corporate executives are primarily concerned with long-term corporate survival. In those instances where they have failed to adapt their company's strategy to a changing competitive environment, the explanation lies not in a short-term focus but rather in their inability to read environmental trends accurately or in their adherence to traditional beliefs about consumer preferences and competitive practices.

These beliefs are often a major barrier to strategic change because top executives have become so emotionally committed to them that they are unwilling—or unable—to alter practices that have been successful in the past. Events that transform the conditions under which a particular industry or firm operates are therefore difficult to accommodate. As the 1970s have shown, these challenges can come in many guises, including vigorous foreign competition and the dramatic rise in raw materials costs. Companies and even entire industries can experience a period of stagnation, as their corporate leaders struggle with the constraints of their beliefs to fashion strategies that will promote recovery. Consequently, we argue that the ability to manage these psychological constraints is an important key to the success of individual companies and to the economy as a whole.

Another popular misconception concerns the place of diversification in corporate strategy. Most typically, it is associated with "go-go" conglomerates or with corporate takeovers. Hence it tends to be thought of as antithetical to good management practices, particularly in companies with a strong sense of industry identity. But the facts are often different, and diversification can be an essential part of good corporate strategy. All but one of the companies studied had undertaken some diversification into different industries. Moreover, many of these firms had moved into new international markets as well. In both cases, the logic behind such decisions is the same. In the main these choices reflect top management's clear recognition of the organizational vulnerability created by excessive dependence on single products, markets, or technologies. Such choices seek to assure that the corporation will survive even as industries mature and die.

There are also striking differences between the common view of the way in which strategic choices are made and the actuality. Usually it is argued that strategic choice is and should be an entirely rational matter: Managers weigh the economic factors in a decision and make a logical choice. From this perspective major changes in strategy are effected easily and rationally, in one fell swoop. But once again we have found a very different picture. Major shifts in strategy do not occur suddenly or rapidly. On the contrary, the process of strategic change is basically an incremental one, and each step is relatively small. Thus it takes many years for the management of a company to achieve major strategic changes. Moreover, strategic decisions are not the product of simple economic logic alone. Because these decisions often depend on forecasts of future events, they involve considerable uncertainty and ambiguity. To analyze these complexities top managers draw upon their experience and judgment—judgment that has been shaped by the shared beliefs passed on to them by their predecessors. Thus to some extent, their decisions always reflect nonrational considerations, because they have been filtered through their belief systems.

With this reminder about the importance of corporate executives' beliefs, we come full circle to the psychological and objective constraints on their strategic choices (see figure 1.1). Those constraints and their implications will occupy us on the pages that follow.

Corporate leaders' desire to assure the survival of their company, discussed in chapter 2, provides the driving force for their initiatives and strategic choices. To accomplish this corporate immortality these executives must make choices within two sets of objective constraints. They must meet the

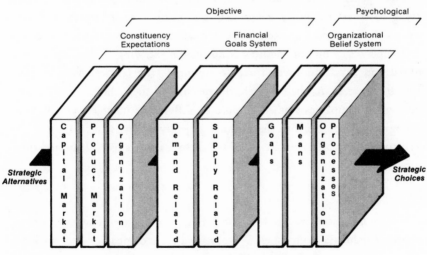

Figure 1.1   Constraints on Strategic Choice

expectations of their three primary constituencies—the capital market, their product markets, and their organization. And they must simultaneously manage the internal system of financial goals so that the demand for funds balances the supply. Chapters 3 and 4 delineate the more precise nature of these objective constraints.

As top managers work within these objective constraints to choose goals and strategies to accomplish them, they also encounter a psychological constraint—their own beliefs. These beliefs, which evolve into an interrelated system throughout the history of each company, provide the managers with a shared commitment to a vision of their organization's distinctive competence, the risks they are willing to take, and the degree of self-sufficiency they desire. As a result, these beliefs are themselves a powerful constraint on the options the executives will consider and the decisions they make, as chapter 5 makes clear. In fact, these beliefs can be so powerful a constraint that top management may miss opportunities presented by actual or potential changes in the objective constraints. This is the major reason that the process of strategic change is so long and problematic, as is amplified in chapters 6 and 7.

Operating within the limits of their unique belief system, corporate managers strive, with varying degrees of urgency, to relax the objective constraints imposed on them: to minimize the potential for dominance by major constituencies; to increase the potential for managerial discretion; and to assure personal and corporate success. Pragmatically, this means they are trying to be as financially self-sufficient as possible to reduce their dependence on the capital market. They are seeking diversification to reduce their dependence on one industry. And they are striving to develop a committed and loyal employee force to minimize the chance of dominance from this quarter. As shall be seen, the specifics of these choices vary among the twelve companies studied because of differences in objective and psychological constraints. But the ultimate objective is the same: to assure the perpetuation of the enterprise to which these managers have dedicated their lives.

The Companies

These conclusions are derived from an empirical study of twelve mature, successful industrial companies. We observed these companies in close detail over an extended period of time. We analyzed their corporate documents. We spoke with their top managements.* The companies themselves represent an impressive cross-section of American industrial corporations. Based in different industries, each firm has its own particular character. Some were founded during the nineteenth century. Others were started as recently as World War II. All have become major forces in their respective industries, despite occasional setbacks. (This is, in fact, our operational definition of success.) In 1979 they ranged in size from sales of $900 million to sales of over $10 billion; thus they fell within the range of the upper half of the *Fortune* 500 list.

These companies produce a variety of products, and they were selected to represent a range of product/market diversity. At one extreme is a single-commodity company; at the other, two firms that characterize themselves as conglomerates and that students of business strategy would characterize as unrelated diversified firms.[1] (See appendix B.)

For purposes of disguise and simplicity, we have categorized the companies into four types: high technology, commodity products, consumer products, and conglomerates. Although they were based in different specific industries, the three high-technology companies all had large research and development staffs. Throughout their histories their scientists' and engineers' innovations had stimulated the growth of these firms. Their products were sold primarily to other manufacturers. The three commodity-products companies all manufactured undifferentiated producer goods. Their manufacturing processes were capital-intensive. The three consumer-products companies produced and marketed branded nondurable items. Both conglomerate firms operated in a wide range of unrelated industries. They differed in one important respect, however. One had completely abandoned its original business, while the other had built its unrelated diversification on the foundation of its base business.

The twelve companies were also selected to represent a spectrum of ownership patterns. In five the common stock was controlled in varying degrees by management and/or founding families. Of these five, one was still entirely privately held, while the others were publicly traded although management or the founding families exercised practical control. In the other seven companies the common stock was owned by a broad base of public shareholders and financial institutions. However, as we shall elaborate later, the basic pattern of our findings did not vary significantly because of differences in ownership patterns.

---

*Appendix A contains a complete account of the research methodology.

The Work of Corporate Managers

We use the term corporate manager to refer to the senior executives in the companies regardless of their specific titles. Typically the chief executive officer (CEO) headed this group. The senior executives who reported to him had a variety of titles—president, vice chairman, executive vice president, chief financial officer, and group vice president were typical. In some companies those holding such positions were formally constituted into an "office of the chairman" or designated as an executive or management committee. In others the group received no such explicit designation.

In some of these companies the CEO made almost all decisions himself, after listening to the advice of his subordinates. In other firms the decisions were more clearly the result of a consensus among the senior officers. Yet in all these companies we found a core group of about six to eight senior managers involved in working together and with the CEO to shape corporate direction.

In focusing on these corporate managers we do not suggest that others cannot affect corporate strategy. Subordinate managers, board members, major stockholders, and past senior officers are all consulted from time to time, and they do have an impact. However, the corporate managers are the men who have the final say.

Several historical trends have led to the emergence of corporate management as distinct from subordinate levels of operating general managers. One was the establishment in most large companies of a multidivisional organization structure. This organizational form had its genesis in strategies of diversification and geographic expansion that date back fifty years or more. As separate divisions were created, a corporate office also became necessary. It consisted of those we have labeled corporate managers as well as various corporate staff groups.[2]

Subsequent developments have sharpened the need for a separate corporate office. Although at one time top management could often stay close to individual businesses, this has become more difficult of late. For one thing, the trend toward diversification outside the original core business has been much more pronounced during the past two decades.[3] In fact, when selecting firms for this study, we tried to locate several that operated in one business only. But after a careful search, we learned that relatively few such firms existed among companies of this size. Ultimately we were able to include two companies that fit this category; however, even one of them had tested diversification through an acquisition during the period of the study.

An additional factor has been the increased international activity of many American firms over the past two decades. As these firms have diversified their businesses and spread their activities around the globe, their strategic business units have come to represent entire countries as well as particular divisions or products. Consequently it has become increasingly difficult for top managers to have the knowledge—and time—essential to make important operating decisions. As one CEO told us: "It's beyond the capability of anyone, even a small group at the head of a diversified company, to really understand the trends, all the implications, all the competitive forces." Thus corporate management has had to delegate operations to subordinates and concentrate its own attention on the broader issues of corporate strategic direction.

Another reason for the development of a separate corporate office has been the ever-more complex and time-consuming relationship between business and government in the United States. Senior managers have found themselves increasingly involved in dealing with various government agencies (legislative and executive) to influence legislation and policy and to assure their own compliance with government regulations. For example, several of the CEOs interviewed indicated that they spend as much as 30 percent to 40 percent of their time dealing with such issues. Similarly, The Conference Board reports that more than one-third of 185 CEOs they surveyed spend 25 percent to 50 percent of their time on such activities.[4]

Together these trends have led to the increased importance of the corporate level of general managers. With rare exceptions, corporate managers in the twelve companies studied do not engage in running the corporation's existing business activities. Instead they deal with the issues of broader corporate strategy that are our focus, and they are involved in business and government relations. They also devote significant amounts of their time to the selection and development of subordinate levels of management, especially their own potential successors. Further, they are concerned with the issues that relate to management development—questions of organizational structure, compensation, planning, and measurement systems. In these activities, as well as in their direct evaluation of individual business results, their intent is to motivate others to implement the corporate strategic direction they have chosen.

Upon his appointment as CEO of RCA, Thornton Bradshaw summarized his view of his job: "In my concept of the job as chief executive of Atlantic Richfield and RCA, the first and foremost goal is to develop with others where the company is going. Second, it is the care and feeding of people who have to get there; and third, it's the financial health of the company." Our study included neither Atlantic Richfield nor RCA. But Mr. Bradshaw captures well the work of corporate management as we have come to know it. In chapter 2 we shall present some of his peers.

CHAPTER 2

Who Are the Corporate Managers?

Corporate managers' working days start early—often with breakfast meetings—and they usually continue for ten or twelve hours. Many, if not most, of those hours are occupied by unending series of meetings with colleagues and subordinates. Such breaks as occur come from the need to attend to other responsibilities: meetings with government officials, phone calls and mail, speeches to employee audiences or trade associations. Nor do the evenings and weekends provide much respite from these responsibilities, for corporate issues follow the managers home in the reports and memos that fill their well-stuffed briefcases. Thus throughout their demanding days, the strategic choices that are our focus are never very far from these executives' minds.

Who are these corporate managers? Two complementary descriptions provide an answer. First, we shall examine these executives in terms of their personal and career histories as well as current life status (e.g., age, family situation, income). Second, by building on these data, current psychological knowledge, and our interviews with the men themselves, we shall describe their current psychological concerns in choosing financial goals and the strategies to achieve them.[1] In addition, we shall focus especially on the CEOs, because our data clearly indicate their preeminence in establishing goals and making the specific decisions to attain them. These CEOs vary, of course, in terms of how they relate to their immediate subordinates and how much influence these subordinates have on decisions. But, to borrow Harry Truman s phrase, "the buck stops here" in all these companies. Moreover, the CEOs are representative of the men who are the corporate managers in the companies studied. Their immediate subordinates are quite similar.

The Demographics of Corporate Management

The CEOs

Like their counterparts in other *Fortune* 500 companies, the twelve CEOs studied had diverse experiences and educational backgrounds.[2] They were raised throughout the United States—in New England, along the Great Lakes, in the South, on the West Coast, and in New York City. They represent a range of ethnic backgrounds, although they are predominantly Protestant, and all are white males. Several had no formal college education. Others attended large state universities. A few attended prestigious private ones. They also rose to their current positions through a variety of functional routes: two are lawyers; others came up through marketing and sales; still others have an engineering or manufacturing background.

Having achieved their positions, however, these twelve CEOs are remarkably similar in three important respects (see table 2.1). First, all are in their fifties or sixties. Second, all save one have spent almost twenty years or more with their current company. Eight have served for more than twenty-five years, six for more than thirty years. Third, all appear to be financially well off. They receive large amounts of current compensation, and they have also accumulated a considerable personal investment in their company's stock.*

In these characteristics, too, our CEOs resemble their peers in other *Fortune* 500 companies. The 1976 *Fortune* survey indicated that 22 percent of the CEOs were fifty to fifty-four years old, 34 percent were fifty-five to fifty-nine, and 26 percent were sixty to sixty-four. This means that over 80

---

*There is some variation regarding shares owned due to the fact that four of the firms were closely held. In some of these closely held firms the CEOs were substantial owners. In others they were not.

TABLE 2.1

The Twelve CEOs

Age	Length of Service with the Company	Total Compensation (thousand $)	Market Value of Shares (million $)	% of Total Shares
50	24	Privately held—Not available		
52	28	$340	$3.8	4.0
56	22	425	.3	.8
56	31	400	.6	—[a]
60	38	270	.6	.1
61	12	450	1.1	.2
62	35	160	1.0	.4
63	35	391	.7	.3
63	25	500	.4	—[a]
64	43	390	2.3	.4
64	19	345	.8	.1
65	39	250	500.0	21.0

SOURCES: *Who's Who*, biographical statements, and company proxy statements. All data have been altered to disguise the individuals and companies without altering the basic facts and relationships. All figures are as of fall 1979. Thus financial data are usually for the calendar or fiscal year 1978.
[a] Indicates a fraction of less than .1 percent.

percent of the *Fortune* 500 CEOs are over fifty, while all twelve CEOs in our companies had passed this age. Length of service is more difficult to compare directly, because the *Fortune* survey reports the number of employers for whom their CEOs had worked rather than their current tenure. However, over two-thirds of the *Fortune* 500 CEOs had switched companies only once. If they were like the CEOs in this study, most made these changes very early in their career. Finally, the compensation range for our twelve corresponded to that for the whole group, when we allow for the effects of inflation from 1976 to 1978. The 1976 range was $172,000 to $344,000 for all CEOs; in 1978 our twelve earned from $160,000 to $500,000. Stock ownership among the CEOs was also comparable, if we allow for the privately held companies in our study. Thirty percent of the *Fortune* 500 CEOs owned $1 million or more in their firm's stock. Another 29 percent owned between $100,000 and $500,000.

In the popular view, it is often said that men of such age, experience, and wealth are unlikely to take risks. We shall present evidence that disproves this truism. As these CEOs lead their subordinates in making strategic choices, they are quite willing to be innovative. As one corporate manager noted in describing his CEO: "[The CEO, who was in his sixties] is a broad thinker.

17

A real risk-taker. He is an exception to the idea that as people age, they become more conservative. Everyone wanted to kill [a specific business]. He wouldn't, and now it's a big winner. If I can think as far ahead as he does at the end of my career, I will be pleased with myself." A corporate manager in another company made a similar point: "He [the CEO] is sixty-five and very conservative in ways, but very interested in growth—profitable growth. He insists on integrity. He's set the direction of the company for the fifteen years I've been here. He's willing to take a risk. It was he who pushed the [Asian] acquisition."

This is not to say that these corporate managers are unaffected by their years of experience in their specific company. Clearly they are. As we shall demonstrate, their tenure builds strong personal commitment to their company and strongly influences their thinking, for good or ill.

Other Corporate Managers

The other corporate managers in this study closely resembled their bosses, with a few predictable differences. They were slightly younger, with an average age of 56.2 (see table 2.2). Their average tenure of 26.2 years was slightly less than that of the CEOs. Both their annual income and their ownership stake were somewhat smaller than their CEOs.

Like the CEOs, these executives differed in terms of their geographical and family origin and their education. However, as a group they tended to have had more formal business training than their superiors. While only two of the CEOs had MBAs and only one had attended a lengthy executive edu-

TABLE 2.2

Characteristics of Non–CEO Corporate Managers

Mean age	56.2 years
Age range	44–70 years
Mean length of service	26.3 years
Service range	4–38 years
Mean salary	$204,000
Salary range	$36,000–$336,000
Mean value of shares owned	$780,000
Range of value of shares owned	$90,000–$5,400,000
Mean % of shares owned	.18%
Range % of shares owned	Less than .1%–.6%

SOURCES: *Who's Who*, biographical statements, and company proxy statements. Data are as of fall 1979.

cation program in a graduate business school, many more of their subordinates had had such experiences.

In terms of their functional backgrounds, the broader set of corporate managers showed the same diversity as their leaders. However, each company's traditional business thrust did have an impact on the kind of expertise most represented in corporate management. For example, in the commodity companies, manufacturing expertise was well represented. As the CEO of one of these companies said: "The emotional appeal of [our industry] is drama. Big furnaces, noise and flame, the danger. We all feel emotional about our industry. We feel our top management must have among its members some from engineering and manufacturing who understand this." Similarly, in the high-technology companies, managers with extensive technical education and experience were very much in evidence. An executive in one of these firms pointed this out: "Keep in mind most of our senior management has a technical background, and they get fascinated with technology, but it helps them in thinking about new business opportunities coming from the labs." And in the consumer-product companies, not surprisingly, there were a large number of executives with extensive marketing experience. Again, the rationale was the same. Such experience equipped these men to deal with the decisions they had to make about the scope of their business activities and to evaluate the performance of the product market managers reporting to them.

Our findings about these corporate executives are consistent with those in a recent survey of 1,700 senior managers in *Fortune* 500 companies. The executives in the larger study had an average age of fifty-four. They had been with their companies an average of nineteen years, and 31 percent had tenure of twenty-five years or more. In fact, like our corporate managers, many had never worked for another firm since graduation from college. Their average cash compensation was $116,000 per year. While this figure is lower than the one we developed, the discrepancy reflects the fact that the larger study included executives one or two levels below those we have defined as corporate managers.[3]

An Overview

Demographic facts such as these give us one description of the corporate managers. They are men in their fifties and sixties who have spent most, if not all, of their career with the company they now lead. They have risen to their current position along diverse career paths, although in any given

19

company their predominant functional experience reflects the firm's most important functional emphasis. Their current cash income is typically in the range of $150,000 to $250,000 a year. While they are not dominant shareholders of their company, their investment in the company's stock is probably an important part of their personal fortune. In and of itself, such a description suggests why these men are so committed to their company—long experience and success build this identification. Yet demographics alone cannot adequately explain what personal forces cause these men to shape their company's strategies as they do. To understand more of their personal motivation in making decisions, we must supplement these data with other information.

One source is the work of psychologists, particularly those who deal with the stages of adult development. Another is the executives themselves, as they reflected on their personal goals and aspirations during our interviews with them. From these sources we shall try to understand who these corporate managers are, in a psychological sense. Obviously, as in any group of people, there are many individual differences. But what concerns us here is the common psychological perspective that these executives share.

The Psychology of Corporate Management

Monetary Motivation

> You have pride. [The president] and I are professional managers. We get our kicks out of running the business efficiently. I'm not here to accumulate wealth. We're here to do a good job. It's the Maslow thing—self-fulfillment. We have high achievement needs, my wife keeps telling me. It's a need to create tangible things. It's "what makes Sammy run."

Conventional wisdom and most economic theory assume that top managers are motivated primarily by financial incentives. But this comment, by one of the corporate managers who was in his late forties, challenges that assumption. Moreover, this view is typical of those expressed by his peers as they spoke about the relative unimportance to them of personal financial gains. Thus it seems that behavioral scientists are right to question the role of financial rewards in personal motivation and, in particular, to ask whether more money will make people work harder.

Some behavioral scientists say no. According to this view, financial rewards are only important because employees will become dissatisfied if they receive less than they believe fair. Others disagree, finding money an important motivation if—but only if—the employee can see a clear connection between his or her efforts and the financial remuneration received. Both points of view have been developed from research done with employees at lower organizational levels, primarily blue- and white-collar workers, salespeople, and so on.[4] However, the latter perspective implicitly underlies the executive incentive compensation schemes that existed in all the companies studied. Whether the reward was cash or stock, whether the relevant measure of performance was the after-tax profits return on shareholder investment or return on net assets, these plans assume that top executives see a connection between their efforts and the desired performance goal, and that the financial incentive will motivate them to work toward this goal.

Given this fact, it seems surprising at first glance that most of these executives said that personal financial stakes were not a major factor in their decisions. In only one company did the executives mention personal financial gains as a factor in their strategic thinking. And even in this firm the reference was very general. As the CEO put it: "We feel if we, as top managers, want to be paid well compared to managers in other companies, we have to do well for our shareholders in comparison to those of similar companies."

Moreover, we found that none of these executives was very concerned about the current market value of his company's stock. To some extent this was a function of the depressed state of the stock market during the time of our study. However, far more important was their conviction that what really mattered was the long-term health of the company, a consideration not necessarily reflected in the current market price of the company's shares. This is a point we shall expand upon shortly.

We did not discuss personal finances with these executives, hence we can only speculate about their lack of concern for their personal fortunes. Possibly those who argue against money as a motivator are correct. However, we prefer an explanation that grows out of our demographic portrait of these executives. Given their age, their major family financial responsibilities are probably behind them. They have been earning large cash incomes for a number of years, and many have accumulated large estates in their company's stock, not to mention other investments of which we have no knowledge. At this stage of their lives, additional financial income probably is not a primary concern.

21

By this conclusion we do not imply that attention to executive compensation plans is worthless or unnecessary. These plans can be very important for the younger executives who manage each company's businesses. And how these junior managers are paid in relation to their corporate bosses could raise important issues of equity, if the senior managers perceived that they were not fairly compensated compared to their subordinates. Similarly, if the corporate managers felt that they were unfairly paid compared to their peers in other companies, they would also be unhappy. But because they perceive their plans as fair, and because of their current life situations, these corporate managers do not give primary weight to the impact of their decisions on their personal finances. Therefore we must look beyond money—to other psychological factors that affect their decisions.

The Drive to Excel

In listening to these executives, we heard many variations on a theme that reveals a great deal about their psychological motivation. The CEO of a diversified, publicly held consumer-products company said: "My own personal goal was to make us achieve a greater growth rate than [a well-known consumer products company]. I picked them because they were the premier marketers in the world." The president of another consumer products firm made a similar point: "This business is war games. We don't mind losing a battle, but we hate to lose the war. Deep down in every marketing guy is the urge to compete. To do that, you must be profitable; you must grow." A member of the founding family of a commodity company, who has recently retired as its chairman, observed: "My personal goals are to do a good job, to be profitable, to have high-caliber people around you, and to be concerned with how you are viewed by the customers, the stockholders, and the community. My objective is to be number one, to do as well or better than anyone else."

All these men suggest that deep within them lies the desire to excel, to do better than others. Their definitions of excellence may differ. One will aim to be the best in meeting the demands of his constituencies, while another will strive to match the performance of his competitors and other similar-size companies. But they all wish to excel. No one put this more colorfully than an executive who was nearing retirement from yet another consumer-products company: "I hate to pick up a paper every day and see [a competitor] getting bigger than we are. It makes me madder than hell. If the doctor would let me, I'd still go out and do something about it. It's crazy. It doesn't mean a thing to me financially with all the money I've got in my pocket." Here is a man in his sixties, with major health problems, telling us how much he still wants to beat his rival, a firm against which he has competed for thirty-odd years. As he states, it is not personal financial gain that motivates him. It is the drive to win or excel. Moreover, this drive persists despite sustained setbacks. As we heard from the CEO of the firm that was encountering the most persistent business problems:

> One thing I've done here is clean up messes. It may have been rebuilding things, but it is negative. The second thing I've done is sponsor the increasing R&D. Whether that will work I don't know, but I think it will.
> I'd like people to say "He turned it around, given all he had to work with." It's a humdrum company, but I'd like to make a success of it. I'd like to make as much of it as I can.

At times this desire to win and excel takes the form of an almost personal comparison with peers and friends who are the CEOs of other companies—the men met at conferences, at board meetings, and at clubs. As one executive noted in describing his CEO: "He is highly competitive versus others in the *Fortune* 500. It's a matter of stature with his peers."

While all these comments were made by men in their sixties, the younger corporate managers had similar feelings. The desire to excel cuts across all ages. In addition, this desire characterized management in every type of company—whether privately held or publicly owned, single industry or diversified. A comment from an executive in one high-technology firm illustrates this: "[One competitor] was somebody we really had to look at because the security analysts had put us up there next to them all the time. They were seen as the smart ones who had rapidly increased prices ahead of costs and we weren't smart because we hadn't."

While the managers in this company ascribed their concern with this competitor to the comments of financial analysts, our own impression was that they protested too much. That competitor had recently surpassed them in important performance criteria. Given a long tradition of being at the top of their industry, this hurt in a clearly personal way, which they found difficult to admit. Thus it was easier to blame such comparisons on the financial community. But as we listened to them, the underlying themes of pride, competition, and excellence arose, with them as with other corporate managers.

In the more diversified companies, where no precisely comparable companies were available, the managers turned to a broader standard of comparison. The CEO of one consumer-product company described his thought process: "We said where are we compared to other companies, we said we wanted to be in the top 25 percent of the *Fortune* 500. We feel this is important if we want our managers to be well paid."

This CEO worked in the one firm in which managers spoke about a connection between their company's performance and their own compensation. But in this company, as in all the others, managers also seemed to have deep psychological reasons for their desire to be number one. Few executives spoke explicitly about this subject. But one who did give us an important clue:

> We're the classical case of the competitive businessman. We don't like losing. Even if you have a fantastic opportunity you don't want to give up on your problem children. . . .
>
> I believe we business school-type guys are trying to prove something to ourselves. My wife thinks I'm terribly interested in this. . . . I was raised by two women, my mother and grandmother. My mother put three of us through college and two of us through graduate school on her $6,000-a-year salary as a school teacher.

This executive was one of the more introspective interviewed. He seemed to be suggesting that his (and others') desire to excel had its roots in a need to prove himself to persons who had been significant to him in his early years. In his case, it was his mother and grandmother. For others, it was the expectations of a father who had founded the business. For still others, the key to these feelings remains unknown.

In the absence of detailed biographies, we prefer not to speculate about the source of these drives. Still, our introspective executive's comments mesh with current theories of personality development. It makes sense that executives, like any individuals, are trying to live up to an idealized view of what parents and other early role models taught them they should become.[5] In any case, on the basis of our discussions with corporate managers, we feel confident that one of the important forces shaping their decisions is the desire to win against some standard of excellence, however it is defined operationally. As these men think about corporate goals, their judgments are influenced by this desire, whether they measure their performance against similar companies or a standing in the *Fortune* 500.

The Impact of Age

This conclusion accords with Maccoby's study of American managers. In that study he identified four character types: craftsmen, jungle fighters, company men, and gamesmen. All four were competitive individuals, but each typically defined competition in a different manner. In "the newer corporate executive," Maccoby found the gamesman's traits combined with those of the company man.[6] The corporate managers in our study, too, were gamesmen in that they were motivated by a competitive desire to win the game they were playing. However, the game itself had changed over the years. When they were younger, in their thirties, striving to reach the top, the rules of the game had been defined by reward and measurement schemes in their company. In addition, their competition was internal as well as external. As they strove to win the reward of promotion to senior management, their peers within the company provided one standard of comparison, while other companies in the industry provided another.

Now in their fifties and sixties, these men have reached the top. They differ from the younger managers—and from their younger selves—in several important respects. The most obvious is that they largely measure themselves against other companies rather than peers inside the organization. It is in this sense, as Maccoby has pointed out, that they have taken on aspects of "companymen"—those who closely identify with their company. This happens for two reasons. First, as already stated, long service has led them to develop a deep commitment to their firm—an identification with it. A senior executive expressed it this way: "[Another executive vice president] and I have worked for [company name] more than twenty-five years. It's become a part of our lives." An executive in another company made a similar point about his CEO: "You can imagine that a man like him who has spent forty years in the company would like to see the company maintain its identity and not be taken over." Thus they begin to feel that company success equals personal success. Second, they have reached the narrowest part of the company's hierarchical pyramid. There is only one CEO, and those who work directly with him must somehow accept the fact that, at their age, the internal competitive game has ended. They have reached the pinnacle of their career without climbing the last rung on the ladder. They must reconcile their earlier dreams with the reality of what can be accomplished, a reconciliation all adults must make.

Several recent studies of adult development have illuminated the psychological processes by which such changes in personal goals come about. A brief description of this work will enrich this psychological perspective on corporate managers. Until the 1950s most personality theorists believed that the individual's personality was fully shaped by the late teens or early twenties. This view was consistent with Freud's formulations. Since that time, however, a number of scholars, most notably Erik Erikson, have challenged that view. They argue that personality development is a lifelong process, lasting from birth until death. Consequently, adults must resolve a series of psychological dilemmas as they grow older. In each instance successful resolution demands a new balance between the pressures of the inner self and the external reality. Several recent studies of American males (including a number of business executives) support and elaborate these ideas.[7]

For our purposes, the work of Levinson and his colleagues is particularly useful. These researchers have found a predictable pattern of stages, or "seasons," to an adult male's life. By applying these stages to a corporate manager's life line, we can understand his current psychological perspective more fully. While we do not know that every executive in our study followed this pattern precisely, we believe that most, if not all, would recognize themselves in Levinson's progression.

The patterns begins with the young man's dream about what he wants to be. He draws the dream from his biological makeup and preadult experience, and it defines his conscious and unconscious goals. In his twenties, the young man works to establish a life structure that will enable him to pursue this dream. To do so he must deal with the two basic life issues identified by Freud: love and work. He tries to establish an intimate relationship with a spouse and begin a family. He also chooses a career. However, he is still experimenting, trying various options to find those most consistent with his dream.[8]

As a manager enters his thirties, he begins the process that Levinson labels "settling down." Important decisions about love and work have been made for the present, and his emphasis falls on commitment to a career and to the building of a family. Levinson's phrase is not entirely descriptive, however, since settling down could convey an image of being at rest. The thirty-year-old manager is clearly not at rest. Rather he is running a race to attain his dream. This is Maccoby's young manager, who is playing the game, trying to win, so that he can move up the organizational ladder. Presumably the corporate managers in our study went through this phase in their career, competing against rivals inside the company and winning the competitive game in their product markets at the same time. By their late thirties, they would already have achieved some degree of success in the company.

In his early forties, the corporate manager must have passed through the stage Levinson labels "the mid-life transition."* While each corporate manager will go through this transition in his own unique fashion, given his dream and his previous experience, we can speculate about certain common themes in this period, because to some extent all the executives we studied were winners in the race of the thirties.

During their early forties, these managers were still in the race to move up in the organization. But the pyramid was narrowing, and they and their families were growing older. Consequently they would also be engaged in the important psychological work of the midlife transition. First, they would be trying to sort out any hiatus between their dream and their experience. Second, they would be working to accept their own mortality. If they had exceeded their career expectations, they would be asking "Was the effort worth it?" If they had still higher career goals, to be the CEO, they would be reworking their aspirations on the basis of the possibility of achieving them in a narrower pyramid, against peers who had different or perhaps better qualifications. All of these career-related issues would be considered, along with their feelings about wives and children. Had they devoted too much time to the work side of their life? Had they missed opportunities to develop family relationships? Or had they achieved a balance appropriate to their dream? All this would be considered amid the growing realization that they had only a finite amount of time left. Was the past path the same one they wanted to continue? Was an adjustment in commitments and activities called for?

We do not know how each of our executives resolved these issues. But we do have some evidence that in two important respects they entered their late forties, fifties, and sixties with a perspective similar to that of the men who were the subjects of the adult development studies. First, our corporate managers had concluded that they enjoyed the work of being an executive for its own intrinsic satisfaction. Work was no longer most important because it was a means to the end of a higher position. It was an end in itself. As an executive in a consumer product company said: "We all have a

*This stage has been termed the midlife crisis in the popular press, but we prefer Levinson's term transition since it emphasizes the normal developmental process.

self-fulfillment need. We work for ourselves but we are constrained by investor needs."

This same theme was developed by the sixty-four-year-old CEO of another company as he described his ascension to that office:

> When I became chief financial officer, I wanted to do something which was important to the company and the people in it. My goal was to do a good job. My ambition was to be chief operating officer, but I didn't articulate it. At that time I was number two on the list to be COO. I was happy doing what I was doing.
>
> I became COO much sooner than I expected. I had a marvelous time working. It was a period of growth and excitement.
>
> As CEO, my term will be short enough so that my goal is to assure the board and the shareholders that we have in place the best management in our business. I have also worked hard to make it more effective. The better the organization is, the better the company.

This CEO mentions the second theme that is most important for understanding how these managers' psychological state affects their strategic decisions. Like most adults past middle age, he and other executives interviewed had become concerned with the next generation. Through the midlife transition they had accepted the fact of their own mortality in a deep psychological sense. Out of this realization came a concern for future generations.[9]

Again, we do not know how this concern affected our executives' families or community relationships, but as they talked about personal goals in their work, it represented their most persistent theme. Here are a few of their comments:

> The highest priority with me is perpetuation of the enterprise. I'd like to leave this joint in better shape than when someone passed me the baton. I have to take care of shareholders in this, but I don't sweat the shareholders too much. Most investors in our industry are passive.

> I want to leave the company as a better company than when I came in. It was a good company when I came in, and I want it to be better.

> From the beginning, as CEO I had two basic goals for myself:
> 1. To leave behind when I retire one of the best organizations in the country;
> 2. To turn a good company into a great company.

Nowhere was this concern for the next generation more clearly evident than in the closely held companies. The CEO of one of them described his ideas and his father's:

> This overseas expansion is important for my grandchildren. My father made all his decisions with the next generation in mind. When you do that, the tough decisions become easier. I'm a dedicated internationalist. . . .
>
> When my father died, he did not own one share of stock. This was a great sacrifice for the sake of retaining private ownership which was passed on to the children.

Other officers of this same company made the point succinctly. According to one: "[Our CEO's] dominant interest is the family. By far his strongest motivation is the dynasty thing." Another said: "The number-one principle is to stay private." And a third said: "When [the CEO] turns the reins over to his progeny, he'll be able to give them something they can relate to."

Corporate managers in other companies, both public and private, recognized that they, as well as their CEOs, were also most concerned with perpetuating the company:

> [The chairman] might go to [a board member] and say, "We're having trouble with [a new business]." Then [the board member] who represents the family interests says, "What do you mean you're having trouble? It's the future of the company." So now [the chairman] has this input to plug in and think about.
>
> The consistent theme in our decisions is what represents the future of [company name].
>
> [The CEO's] goal has been to perpetuate the company, not himself.
>
> As a management, we want to survive. If you don't have vitality and growth, you won't keep healthy. Part of our responsibility is to have a healthy company to turn over to the next generation.

Comments such as these also demonstrate the corporate managers' recognition that a concern for perpetuating the company must include a concern for the younger managers who will succeed them. These senior managers are no longer absorbed in themselves and their own careers. Instead they have begun to care about the next generation, in a personal, not just an institutional, sense. As studies on adult behavior might lead us to expect, they have become more concerned with their subordinates' development as individuals. (In fact, Erikson labeled the crucial dilemma of the forties and fifties "generativity versus self-absorption.") Thus their concern now is with developing managers and employees to perpetuate the company.

These executives' showed an apparent lack of interest in exercising power over others. In this context this makes a great deal of sense. While others have suggested that the appeal of exercising power is an important motivating force for top managers,[10] these executives hardly mentioned it at all. In addition, although their management styles varied considerably and some were quite autocratic, we found only one older CEO whose decisions were motivated by his unwillingness to give up his personal power. Indeed, in the other companies the opposite seemed to be true. The older CEOs actively worked to develop their successors and to turn the reins over to them.

These observations do not necessarily mean that those who argue that power is a dominant theme in the lives of executives are wrong. However, in the companies studied, the corporate managers had reached a stage of life at which such concerns were subordinate to their concerns for generativity and organizational survival. In fact, the realization that he will soon have to step down is one hallmark of the mature corporate manager. In most of the companies studied this recognition is institutionalized by an orderly succession process managed through the board of directors. When an older executive does want to hold on to the reins, it indicates an unresolved psychological issue on his part as well as a failure on the part of the board of directors.

Corporate Executives and Corporate Survival

As we listened to these executives discuss their desire to perpetuate their firms, we realized that the psychological motives we have been describing were resonating in their statements. Their concern for competitive success and excellence, their desire to do a "good" job, their interest in the next generation, and their desire to "take care" of shareholders—all these contributed to the strength of their conviction that "survival was the name of the game."

However, their comments also indicated some of the challenges that had to be met if they were to achieve the corporate survival they desired. Perhaps the most obvious of these was the need to maintain their independence from interference by dissident stockholders and avoid unfriendly takeovers. As one executive in a closely held firm noted, this need for independence was closely allied to personal drives: "I think [the CEO] does have another motivation. Some of his cousins hold some stock. He wants to run the company so well they leave him alone. He doesn't need [their interference]. I *know* it's a motivation." But it also went well beyond individual ends, as another CEO pointed out: "Our goal is to do the most with what we've got. That's the offensive goal. The defensive goal is putting ourselves in a position where we can't be taken over. The guys who think of taking over think of dollars. They don't think of jobs and people."

As this last comment indicates, these managers also closely tied survival to the vitality of their organization. Some focused specifically on growth—and the need to keep growing:

> The important thing about growth beyond just the financial is that that's how you get the best people. It's more exciting for the organization. Excited people do a better job.

> Everything you do forces you to grow. You're out there hiring bright young people. They're aggressive. They want to be with someone who grows. They will make it grow to provide themselves with an opportunity.

Another expressed his concern that the capital market failed to consider human needs and corporate history:

> One of the things I worry about is that people [i.e., investors] are too financially oriented. They look at the company's portfolio. They have no sense of the business and its history, how it was started. It's more than financial. It's the history, people generating things and the value that makes the company a successful generating unit.

A third emphasized the way in which superior products contributed to the company's long-term health and survival:

> The financial side is one of the necessary supports. It is not an end in itself. The end is the building of the institution. But I want to be careful. Building an institution could be misconstrued. It is not as if we want to be a big, important company. That's a by-product of where we got, not the objective. The objective was to make a contribution by building better products. This tended to make the company a fun place to work and caused a lot of creativity.

As all these comments make clear, these corporate managers see their companies as more than financial entities. For them they are people, ideas, and products—all of which are worth perpetuating. Thus their goals for the firm to excel mesh with their personal concerns to make long-term corporate survival their single most important objective. In the following chapters we shall explain how they set about achieving this objective through their financial goals and other strategic decisions.

CHAPTER 3

An Inside Perspective
on Financial Goals

For many years the corporate managers of a large and successful manufacturing company, operating in an energy-intensive industry, had allocated capital in a highly decentralized manner. Divisional managers were encouraged to accept responsibility for their own investment decisions, and they usually obtained whatever funds they requested from top management. Profitability was such that all funding requirements could be met with very little dependence on long-term debt. Management took pride in the company's AA credit rating, and the company was widely regarded as an outstanding example of the best in managerial principles and practices.

Suddenly and quite unexpectedly, the OPEC crisis flared up in 1974 with the now-familiar consequences for profits and for investment in energy-dependent companies. In one year working capital requirements increased by three quarters of a billion dollars. At the same time profits were sharply reduced. For the first time in the current managers' memory, there was a major threat to corporate solvency and continuity. The immediate and only practical response to the threat was a sharp increase in debt, an action that deeply disturbed the conservative instincts of management at all levels. The company's prized credit rating was in danger of being lowered—a severe blow to corporate pride, should it occur. The margin of safety was gone.

In the aftermath of this event, top management conducted a sweeping re-examination of the financial principles under which the company had lived comfortably for decades. The laissez-faire budgeting system was an early victim of the changed circumstances. Control was quickly pulled into the corporate center, and divisional managers suddenly realized that they had lost their financial autonomy. Investments that they considered vital to their market strategy were being rejected or deferred. The illusion of affluence had vanished. Five years later the shockwaves of this event were still reverberating through management's financial plans and strategic choices.

This episode was particularly dramatic, more so than most. Nevertheless, it highlights a critical need all corporate managers share, if they are to achieve the corporate survival they desire: the need for strategy and action to be consistent with economic and financial reality. To operate successfully, management must appraise the economic environment accurately. And, as important, management must be objective and realistic in choosing goals and means that are consistent with the corporate environment as it is—not as it has been, might be, or ought to be.

Public Image and Private Reality

What are the objectives top managers pursue, as they set their corporate goals and strategy? Like their critics, businessmen themselves have debated this subject for many years. At one extreme are those who maintain that their only objective is the pursuit of profit to increase shareholders' wealth. At the other are those who see themselves as statesmen, reconciling public and private interests for the common good. Unfortunately, it is difficult if not impossible to separate sincere convictions from empty rhetoric in these speeches. Whether corporate managers are appealing to shareholders, financial analysts, or the public at large, their own self-interest and that of their audience necessarily color these public or semipublic statements.

Management's financial planning records provide a more reliable source of evidence of real intent, however. In essence, these documents allow us to listen to the private communications of trusted colleagues as they discuss one of the most sensitive elements of corporate achievement—the management of scarce financial resources. Explicit and detailed, these documents reveal top management's objectives clearly, while the figures and projections they contain establish a firm link between management's corporate goals and strategic decisions.

What we have observed in these records leads us to challenge those who argue that corporate managers consider only the bottom line and the shareholders associated with it.[1] These executives may not always be evenhanded statesmen; but neither are they single-minded. Concerned, above all, with the long-term survival of their enterprises, they cannot afford to be parochial in their views. Instead they must balance the demands made on them by three competing constituencies whose cooperation is vital for their firms' success. These are the capital market, the product market, and the organization.

As shall be discussed, each of these constituencies has its own perspective on the corporate enterprise as well as its own set of priorities. Because top managers respond to these competing priorities as they plan, their true financial goals are considerably more complex and comprehensive than outsiders are accustomed to think. In addition, those goals constitute a hierarchy of sorts, because at any given time top managers assign a higher priority to some constituents' goals than they do to others. Why they assign the priorities they do is discussed in detail in later chapters. For now it must be recognized not only that these hierarchies exist, but also that they reflect the objective economic and financial constraints within which corporate managers operate as well as the psychological constraints of their belief systems.

The Nature and Functions of Financial Goals

Ordinarily the term financial goal is used in one of two ways. It may refer to a specific objective, such as a desired credit rating or an increase in earnings per share, which represents an improvement over current performance and which is obviously desirable on its own merits. Or it may include every objective defined in monetary or financial terms that guides the management decision-making process. However, for the purposes of this study, we must be more comprehensive in our definition, so that all corporate goals, quantified or not, that have significant financial implications can be taken into account.

We do place certain limits on our expanded definition of financial goals. For example, because we focus on internal financial goals, we have included only those aspects of financial management or performance over which corporate managers have substantial control and for which they can reasonably be held accountable. In reality these issues are matters of degree, of course, because there is no such thing as absolute control or absolute accountability. But convention does help to determine which objectives to include. Thus, even though a particular credit rating reflects the judgment of an external rating agency, management is usually held accountable if that rating slips because the rating is measured by certain known standards of financial performance. The same holds true for earnings per share, even though aspects of earnings performance, such as the state of the economy, are clearly beyond management's control. However, we have not included target price–earnings ratios as part of the study's formal financial goals because management is not normally held accountable for them. Given the many external and emotional forces at work in the stock market, managers would be foolhardy to take on specific commitments of this sort, and, in reality, none do.

In addition, we have been particularly concerned with the ways in which managers answer funds flow questions: What funds are available, when, and in what form? How should funds be invested in working assets or cycled through the firm? These are critical questions, and goals and guidelines can make a major difference in terms of managerial action and accountability. Yet they cannot be answered by financial goals narrowly defined. They involve the entire management team, and they must include the myriad management decisions that have an impact on financial performance.

Thus we have been led to lengthen customary lists of financial goals. For example, most companies consider growth in the volume of business transacted an important goal, and they reflect that fact in a target growth rate. However, while their list may well stop there, ours does not. Our list goes on to include the target growth rate in assets or investment that follows necessarily, given the fact that the ratio between sales and assets is defined by operating realities which are relatively stable over time. Similarly, our list would also reflect the fact that a goal which measures competitive standing in terms of market share ties the corporate growth rate to the industry's growth rate and has undeniable implications for the flow of funds. Hence our working definition of financial goals recognizes this scope, for we say that they are that subset of corporate goals for which management can be held accountable, and which is concerned with the financial condition and performance of the corporate entity and with the related decisions and actions of management involving the acquisition, custody, and disposition of corporate funds.

However, this comprehensive definition does not mean that all management's hopes or expectations are meaningful financial goals. On the contrary, management's expectations must satisfy several important criteria if they are to serve as meaningful financial goals. They must be specific, clearly understood, and widely shared among key decision makers. They must persist over time and become embedded in the firm's planning and decision-making process. They must be consistently monitored, so that management's behavior is seen to be consistent with the stated objectives and so that a persistent failure to meet a goal results in deliberate action.

It is also important to recognize that not all corporations include a formal set of financial goals in their management process. Some larger companies still retain an element of entrepreneurial spirit at the top, and in these companies shared decision making is deemed neither necessary nor desirable. Instead the chief executive's mind remains something of a "black box" —unpredictable, perhaps deliberately so. However, even within the more entrepreneurial companies a strong trend toward the use of more detailed and widely shared sets of financial goals clearly exists. Moreover, these goals usually involve all the members of the management team in a negotiated understanding with the CEO and the CFO regarding both immediate and longer term priorities. The plans in which the entire management team is involved serve as internal contracts under which all members agree to operate for a defined period of time. At the end of that time, renegotiation may take place and corporate goals may change. But—in the spirit of "no surprises"—such changes must be understood and shared by all concerned.

Most of the managers included in this study used detailed financial goals directly in the planning and decision-making process. Further, these goals served a variety of corporate purposes, not all of which could be quantified. They established a sense of corporate identity, uniqueness, and legitimacy. They provided unity of purpose across a competitive organization and built consensus. They inspired and motivated management, set targets and deadlines, and provided the bases for rewarding accomplishment. They set boundaries on management's strategic choices and guided new initiatives. They set uniform standards for allocating scarce resources among competing demands. And they were used by vigorous and ambitious leaders to assert their leadership, to signal necessary changes in direction, and to stake out their territorial prerogatives within the firm and outside it. Thus, as this summary makes clear, financial goals cannot easily be separated from more general corporate goals, nor can specific financial goals easily be disentangled from corporate strategy.

The Ultimate Beneficiaries

Having identified accountability as a key concept in our definition of a financial goal, we must now ask, accountability to whom? Traditionally, accountability is a legal concept, derived from the laws governing private property and private enterprise. As a result, the logical answer—as well as the customary one—would seem to be the shareholder. And yet our study of management practice has led us to expand accountability to include all the parties in the corporate enterprise who play an integral part in its activities and who have an enforceable claim on corporate performance. Under this broader definition, such claims may be enforced by economic, social, or political means as well as by legal ones. They derive from the power of a particular party to withhold the participation that management deems essential to the future success of the enterprise. This power to withhold stimulates management to ensure that corporate goals reflect the essential needs of each party or group whose cooperation is required for corporate survival.

Corporate goals statements and planning documents clearly reflect present-day management's recognition of its responsibilities to a range of corporate interest groups, or "constituencies." In addition to the usual references to shareholders, corporate goals statements often specifically cite the company's obligations to its customers, employees, and society at large. Of these, all save the last are directly involved in the enterprise. "Society's" involvement is indirect, and its disciplinary powers are vague. Corporate social goals statements tend to reflect these conditions, as the following quotation from one company's goals statement illustrates:

> We recognize the important role that businesses such as ours should play in improving the social, economic, and environmental quality of life in the countries in which we do business. We demonstrate this recognition by a commitment of resources to endeavors directly related to this goal and the understanding that its business activity must be consistent with the social good.

According to this statement, management clearly wishes to contribute to society's well-being; yet progress toward that end cannot be measured objectively. Statements such as this one embody desires or expectations, rather than meaningful financial goals. Consequently, even though we do not doubt management's good faith and genuine concern, we have excluded "society" from our list of corporate constituencies.

This deletion leaves us with the three major parties directly involved in every firm's operations. The first of these is the capital market constituency, which includes both the shareholders and the major suppliers of the firm's debt capital. The second is the product market constituency, composed of the firm's primary customers as well as the unions that represent the work force, the firm's suppliers, and its host communities—in short, all those who benefit most directly from the moderating influence of primary competitors. Third and last is the organizational constituency, which consists of all the career employees including top management.

Each of these primary constituencies expects corporate management to satisfy an objective unique to its special interests. It would be misleading to suggest that these broad constituency groups have uniform needs and expectations. Even among subgroups, such as shareholders, this is not so. However, the capital market constituency does tend to share a perspective on the enterprise that differs in significant respects from those of the other constituencies and that leads to a potential conflict of constituency interest.

Expressed in its most fundamental form, the capital market constituency expects corporate managers to preserve and enhance the private wealth that it has placed, at risk, under their use and control. Because they have the opportunity to impose their expectations through their loan covenants, lenders have greater assurance that their wealth will be returned intact. Shareholders, on the other hand, must rely more heavily on management's discretion and ability to represent their interests appropriately. Their wealth is directly enhanced or diminished by actual transfers of funds under management's control. They are affected indirectly by changes in investor expectations based on corporate performance in relation to market value. In brief, they benefit from maximizing the increase in personal wealth per unit of corporate investment consistent with a defined level of risk.

The product market constituency is more difficult to define as a coherent interest group. Customers demand reliable products and services, at the lowest possible price, from known sources. The union officials who represent the work force care about secure jobs with the best possible working conditions and compensation package. Suppliers look for assured customers willing to pay the highest sustainable prices. Host communities want long-term employers who will provide jobs and tax revenues with minimal demands for public services and minimal environmental damage. Generalizing, we may fairly say that the product market constituency will be best satisfied when the corporation's profit margin provides the lowest acceptable return to investors.

The organizational constituency includes the corporate managers who organize and direct the complex, day-to-day process of producing and delivering a product or service to a mass market as well as their employees. Their principal goal is the preservation of a secure, dynamic, stimulating, rewarding career environment. Normally this means the continuity of the existing organizational power structure and chain of command as well as freedom from outside interference or control—that is, the preservation of the organization as they all know it. In addition, it also implies continuing growth to improve job security and provide upward mobility for all employees who seek it. Unlike the product and capital market constituencies, which tend to view any single business as one of several, or many, vehicles for satisfying their needs, the organizational constituency is more likely to have an exclusive commitment to the long-term future of the enterprise—whatever that future may hold.

The Return on Investment (ROI) ratio gives us a useful, if somewhat simplistic, way to characterize the interests and differences among these three primary constituencies. Maximizing R and minimizing I best serves the goals of the capital market, particularly the shareholders. Conversely, maximizing I and minimizing R best serves the goal of the product market, particularly the customers. Maximizing both R and I best serves the organizational constituency, particularly career administrators, since they benefit from increasing both profits and investment. This double impetus allows them to identify with the goals of each of the other two constituencies, but it also creates in them a certain ambivalence concerning financial goals, as we shall explain later.

The success of any enterprise depends on the active cooperation of all three constituencies. Therefore, the ultimate disciplinary power of any constituency lies in the threatened or actual withdrawal of its cooperation. In practice, however, each constituency's disciplinary power works in a distinctly different way. The lenders' power is primarily explicit and contractual, although the big stick of direct intervention is rarely used. Lenders' funds are available for finite periods of time, and these funds may not be resupplied or increased unless the lenders are satisfied with the company's performance relative to the terms of their contract.

In contrast, stockholders cannot withdraw funds already invested without management's cooperation, and they may even find it difficult to refuse to make further investment if called on to do so. But well-organized stockholders can put pressure on management in other ways. They may express their displeasure by selling the stock, thereby depressing the market value. They may choose to stay and fight, by initiating a stockholder suit in order to try to change management behavior. Most ominous of all, they may prove willing to cooperate with an outside individual or corporation in a takeover bid or a vote to change the composition of the board as a means of changing top management.

The needs of the product market are well known to management, for their day-to-day cooperation is vital, and management is highly sensitive to evidence of dissatisfaction. Customers, suppliers, union members—all can choose to end their association with the enterprise at any time, limited only by contractual commitments, if any. However, this option does depend on the existence of more attractive alternatives. Thus the product market's primary discipline lies in the existence of active competition to the firm's activities and the firm's need to match or exceed the competition in quality, price, wages, and all other terms of production or service. In this context nothing in an enterprise is more powerful, persistent, or persuasive than its standard of performance relative to its most successful competitor.

In considering the organizational constituency, this study does not distinguish sharply between employees and the members of top management. At times their priorities may differ, particularly if a new chief executive officer makes significant changes in the company's direction. However, most CEOs and other corporate executives are long tenured, as we have seen, and they share a strong bond of self-interest with the organization as a whole. Speaking generally, therefore, top management's own self-interest lies first and foremost with the organizational constituency, even though the managers' position requires that they arbitrate among *all* constituent priorities.

If and when it is needed, the organization's primary discipline on corporate priorities exists in the threat that good people will leave, to work for the competition or elsewhere. Corporate managers works hard to attract and hold the very best talent they can. Job continuity, increased opportunity, and appropriate recognition and reward are the means used. If the organization fails to provide working conditions at a level equal or superior to its competitors, its quality and effectiveness will begin to erode, with serious consequences for all concerned. Thus corporate goals must, and do, reflect organizational priorities that go well beyond top management's immediate self-interest.

A Hierarchy of Financial Goals

As corporate managers respond to the demands of these three constituencies, they must make choices among them. These choices, and their associated priorities, are increasingly apt to be reflected in the company's financial goals statements. As we shall explain, this was not always the case. The broad statements of corporate purpose customary in the past made it difficult, if not impossible, to distinguish management's priorities. But today clear and comprehensive sets of financial goals are an integral part of the financial planning and resource allocation process in most large industrial companies. As a result, they can provide a window on management's priorities and strategic choices.

Two documents illustrate the evolution and scope of corporate goals statements. The first was drawn up over thirty years ago by the top management at Commodity Products II. Known within the company as "the ten commandments," these goals were clearly intended to provide a company-wide code of behavior, and they bear the unmistakable stamp of a former CEO. They have been endorsed, unchanged, by all subsequent chief executives, and they are preserved to this day as the company's official statement of purpose.

In a brief preamble, the company explicitly recognizes its responsibility to several constituencies by speaking of "stockholders, employees, customers, and the general public." Some priority seems to be given to shareholders, mentioned first, over the general public, which is mentioned last. Yet the actual goals statement rearranges this hierarchy when management promises to "inform our employees, stockholders, customers, and the public fully and regularly regarding our plans, our progress, and our problems." By this reordering, management suggests a certain ambivalence about its priorities, as well as a willingness for that ambivalence to be perceived.

The document as a whole heightens this ambivalence. Its first three goals refer directly to the quality of management and to the organizational environment. They discuss recruiting and upgrading personnel, ethical behavior and affirmative action, the "quality of life" in the workplace, and the proper rewards. Goals four through six relate to the company's competitive position. They promise to lower costs while preserving quality, to increase market share, and to increase production and product line capacity consistent with an undefined criterion of financial soundness. Finally, goals seven through nine relate to the company's social responsibilities. They encourage employees to be civic-minded and to support their host communities, and they promise to keep the outside world fully informed.

Only in its tenth "commandment" does this company recognize the need for financial performance goals in a form that investors would be able to relate directly to the issue of shareholder wealth. In that goal management promises to "make an annual return on our sales and our invested capital as good or better than any other company in the industry." Whether the position of this goal accurately reflects management's actual priorities cannot be known from the statement. But what is particularly interesting here is the qualifying phrase "as good or better than any other company in the industry." The reference to "the" industry suggests both a narrowly defined set of investment options and an acceptance of industry performance as a sufficient standard for the decision to recommit newly generated funds to the same set of real asset investments. In other words, it is a standard defined by the product market, not the capital market.

The broad sweep of issues addressed by these goals, as well as the absence of objectivity (that is, the inability to test for results), may well have contributed to the statement's enduring quality. In contrast, a more recent corporate goals statement contains very specific targets across a broad range of funds flow management issues. Taken from the records of Consumer Products III, this statement is more representative of the companies studied in both its coverage and its contents. It has been edited only to preclude identification.

Corporate Targets
A. Qualitative:
Provide long-term investors with a superior return on capital.
Develop [product market expertise].
Create a balanced portfolio of product lines.
Manage [corporate] money astutely, conservatively.
Make [corporate] identity with people real.
B. Quantitative:
Reach a 15 percent ROI [companywide].
Grow in volume and profitability:
Sales growth 50 percent greater than GNP, inflation adjusted.
Profit growth 30 percent greater than sales growth, inflation adjusted.
Other financial targets:
Debt ratio less than 25 percent of total capital.
Bond rating: AA.

Dividend payout: 33 percent of total earnings.
Market leadership: Be number one in market segment.

One look makes it plain that this company intends to be an above-average performer in above-average industries. The challenge to management is clear and unequivocal. Moreover, it should also be apparent that this is a very different sort of document from that published by Commodity Products II. While "the ten commandments" could be freely shared with an outside audience—and was—these goals are necessarily private. If freely available, this information could aid and abet the product or capital market competition, because it would define levels and boundaries of commitment that could aid a competitor in better defining its own opportunities or areas of vulnerability. More certain knowledge of a key competitor's future financial or operating strategies can provide a significant competitive edge. The more obscure an adversary's intent, the more resources must be deployed to keep one's own options open. Thus management would have little, if anything, to gain by "going public" and presenting its goals as a statement of intent by which it was willing to be judged.

A Classification of Financial Goals

A set of corporate goals such as the ones just discussed brings many questions to mind. Why these particular goals, for this particular company, at this particular time? Where did the numbers come from? Could they really be attained? Were they defined in isolation or as a consistent whole? Who chose them?

To answer these questions, a rational framework for relating one goal to another and all goals to a common organizational or corporate thrust is required. The beginning of such a framework lies in a classification of those elements or dimensions that the various goals have in common. We have identified two such dimensions: one is the constituency that would benefit most directly from the achievement of the goal; the other is the goal's impact on the flow of funds.

These classifications are slippery, because no law says that the benefits from a particular goal need be limited to only one constituency and because the impact on the flow of funds depends to a large degree on the time frame assumed. However, the characterization of constituency self-interest suggested earlier, particularly when coupled with evidence on corporate awareness of constituency needs, allows us to classify benefits credibly, even when they are not necessarily exclusive. At the same time, it is appropriate to classify the near-term funds-flow implications of each goal as it affects either the demand for or the supply of funds.* Table 3.1 presents all the major goals found to be an important part of the financial planning process in one or more of the twelve companies upon which our research was based classified accordingly.

The first set of goals are those associated with the capital market. When corporate managers discuss investor objectives and their own responsibilities to shareholders, they invariably focus on goals that relate, directly or indirectly, to the supply of funds. Shareholders benefit from improvements in earnings and in dividend income that translate into an increase in their wealth. However, absolute increases in earnings or dividends do not, by themselves, necessarily increase shareholder wealth. The improvement must be related to changes in the amount invested and in the associated risk. Financial goals that discipline the corporate flow of funds are, at best, only a partial reflection of the shareholder's interest. However, the common objective of growth in earnings per share reminds management that shareholders benefit from improved earnings *per unit invested* and that improved earnings should not be bought at the expense of a dilution of the equity base.

The classification of dividend payout as a supply-related goal may bother some readers, given the fact that dividends represent an outflow of corporate funds. However, the distinction is largely semantic. Management's primary motive for improving dividend policy is to satisfy the equity investors and encourage them to leave their primary equity investment in place and existing management in control. In this sense the dividend payout is a supply-related goal. In fact, management's true supply-related goal is the complement of the payout ratio—the proportion of earnings retained and reinvested.

Credit limits are universal financial goals, and they are commonly expressed as a percentage of the permanent capitalization from debt and equity sources, as a minimum bond rating, or as both. These limits may derive from existing debt contracts; but for the companies studied they were more likely to be self-imposed. Moreover, the limits the managers observed were gener-

---

*The term demand for funds is used herein to represent an ongoing process of converting liquid financial resources into specialized investment (inventory, credit to customers, plant and equipment, market or product research and development) for the purpose of producing and selling goods or services at a profit. The term supply of funds is used to represent a process of providing liquid resources (cash, credit, or equivalent purchasing power) available for specialized corporate investment. As shall be shown, a near-term demand stimulator may, in the longer term, stimulate the supply of funds.

ally quite conservative—they were designed to assure that the planned sources of funds, including increments of debt, could be counted on even under uncertain economic conditions.

Corporate managers did not always identify various forms of an ROI target (expressed in table 3.1 as Return on Equity) as an investor-oriented goal. However, as noted previously, the professional investor in a publicly traded company who manages a diversified portfolio and whose loyalty begins and ends with performance has no interest in increasing his or her investment in any individual enterprise unless it promises a superior return *per unit* of capital invested when compared with alternatives of comparable risk. Thus an objective classification of goals must be distinguished from a subjective, management-based classification.

Corporate managers are prone to place great stress on loyalty, speaking of loyal customers, loyal employees, and loyal shareholders. In this context, though, "loyalty" means long-term commitment to *this* enterprise—as managers see themselves—through times good and not so good. Those shareholders who are in it "for the quick buck," here today and gone tomorrow, evoke little sympathy from professional management. It becomes quite easy, therefore, for managers to begin to assume that their company is the best or the

TABLE 3.1

Classification of Corporate Financial Goals

		Initial Stimulus to Funds Flows	
		Demand for Funds	Supply of Funds
Primary Beneficiary	Capital Market Constituency (Investors)		–Growth Rate of earnings per share –*Dividend Payout* –Credit Limits –Return on Equity
	Product Market Constituency (Customers)	–Rank in Industry –Share of Market –*Growth Rate of Sales and Assets* (by industry)	
	Organizational Constituency (Employees)	–Absolute Size –*Growth Rate of Sales and Assets* (over-all) –Diversification of revenue Sources	–Growth Rate of (Retained) Earnings –*Return on Net Assets* –*Debt Capacity* –Reserves

NOTE: Italics identify key financial goals referred to in chapter 4.

only place for existing shareholders to invest and that improved earnings, by themselves, redound to the shareholders' benefit. When confronted with these assumptions, managers will recognize the point. But typically they remain unmoved from their emotional bias.

Regarding the goals associated with the product market, the continuing demand for funds is unmistakable. So too is the extent to which these goals are influenced by corporate managers' drive for success and their need to measure achievement against leading competitors. These forces were most apparent at the divisional level, where management was responsible for performance up to the norms of a particular industry, or "strategic business unit," and where they confronted the competitive dynamic on a day-to-day basis. In fact, as the following summary suggests, these pressures may create a sharp distinction between the goals of divisional managers (those close to and strongly influenced by their product market) and the goals of top management.

Corporate Versus Divisional Goals
A. Corporate
   1. Growth rate of EPS
   2. Minimum return on equity
   3. Assured access to capital markets:
      A bond rating
      Maximum debt-to-equity ratio
   4. Dividend payout range
   5. Minimum ROI
B. Divisional
   1. Sales growth
   2. Rank in industry
   3. Increasing market share
   4. New product development
   5. Increasing capacity

Both sets of goals come from the same company, Consumer Products I. Yet top management's goals are primarily oriented toward the capital market constituency and the supply of funds, whereas the divisional goals are oriented toward the product market constituency and the demand for funds.

The driving force in the product market's demand for funds stems from managers' virtually universal belief that competitive strength and profitability correlate directly with rank in industry or share of market. With one noteworthy exception, every company in the study fought to gain competitive ground against its toughest rival. But, given an industry growth rate and the objective of holding or gaining market share, this also meant that the company's target growth rate in sales was externally defined. In turn, target growth rates in assets were also defined by what was going on in the industry, since the relationships between a given sales level and the invested capital necessary to support that level tend to remain stable over time. Productive capacity, production and distribution processes, terms of credit, and other physical, organizational, and institutional relationships normally change gradually and predictably. Few companies are willing to admit to an explicit goal of growth in assets, but that goal is implicit in a share-of-market strategy.

It should also be apparent that any goal which drives the roots of earning capacity deeper into the soil of a particular industry assures a more lasting commitment to that industry's needs, as well as an increased necessity to respond to the industry's competitive discipline on price, quality, and delivery. Other things being equal, the greater the proportion of capital committed to a particular industry, the more dependent on that industry the company becomes for its continuity and well-being and the higher the barriers become to a successful exit. The company cannot walk away from its primary industry, or threaten to do so, without risking a major discontinuity in its funds flows and reported earnings.

The last set of goals are those most clearly associated with the organization. Because managers often tend to argue for the constituency to which they are closest, direct attribution can be more difficult to document here than it is for the other two constituencies. However, every manager has an organizational or personal motive in addition to an administrative responsibility, and the two are usually interwoven in the roles the manager plays. Moreover, because managers identify their primary responsibility in terms of *loyal* shareholders and *loyal* customers, they are apt to assume that what is right for their company must be right for its shareholders and customers, and vice versa.

However, this may not be so. More than anything else, organizational survival and growth are at the heart of every corporate objective because they are so important to the managers who frame them. Survival, of course, means not the mere avoidance of bankruptcy but the preservation and expansion of the economic, competitive, and social roles that current management has inherited. Thus those goals that relate to *corporate* economic mass and growth and that drive the rate of corporate investment clearly promote job security and upward mobility. But they do not necessarily serve the product market or capital market constituencies. The corporation as a whole may grow while individual product market flows are being milked to fund investment in other areas. A successful diversification strategy makes the company more independent of any single revenue source.

Likewise, from an independent investor's point of view, increased investment per se is not inherently desirable. It may even be highly undesirable, if the funds are being used to develop or perpetuate inferior returns on investment or to incur disproportionate risk. Better investment alternatives outside the corporate entity might indicate a need to reduce investment rather than increase it—an idea repugnant to anyone strongly committed to the survival of the individual firm. The same can be said for earnings objectives that do not in themselves contain a strong test of the risk-related benefit to the individual investor per unit of investment. Similarly, goals related to building up cash reserves are inherently part of management's strategy of corporate survival. Yet they may or may not benefit the professional investor immediately, or even in the longer term.

The foregoing classification of corporate financial goals reflects our interpretation of our data and experience. Others might place one or more of these goals in some other part of the table so far as constituency orientation is concerned. Yet several conclusions are inescapable. One is that in each of these firms there exists a complex network of financial goals, created by management's need to respond to its product market and organization as well as to the capital market of lenders and stockholders. Thus as these managers strive to achieve the long-term corporate survival they desire, their perspective encompasses far more than the bottom line. Moreover, none of these goals can be thought of in isolation. A variety of constituency claims stimulates and reinforces each, and each affects the flow of corporate funds in ways that go beyond any immediate effect on supply or demand. Consequently, these financial goals constitute a system or discipline within which managers must operate as they make their choices and establish corporate strategy. What that means for these managers and how this system fits together will be discussed in the following chapter.

CHAPTER 4

How the System Works—
Balancing the Supply
and Demand
for Corporate Funds

In the preceding chapter the fact that the top managers of large industrial firms work within a complex financial goals system was discussed. They do so because they must weigh a variety of financial goals as they formulate their plans and strategy. As we have explained, these goals meet the needs of the three major constituencies whose cooperation is vital to the firms' health and survival. Committed to that all-important goal on a deep personal basis, these managers cannot afford to overlook the legitimate demands placed on them by the capital market, the product market, and the organization of which they too are a part.

Yet these demands are not easily reconciled. On the contrary, top managers must make hard choices and trade-offs among their constituencies' priorities as they strive for the internal consistency the financial goals system requires. In this context a strategy of maximum self-sufficiency proves to be immensely useful. To the extent that top managers can minimize the potential of any single constituency to dominate the goals system, they can create the space for their own corporate goals and plans.

Central to this strategy is management's desire to avoid dependence on the external capital market for the funding of established product markets. Managers choose instead to rely on an internal capital market as the primary source of the funds essential for corporate growth. Yet this choice imposes real constraints on managers, because it cannot be supported unless they succeed in balancing the flow of funds within the firm. Thus the price of capital market independence is the discipline of self-sustaining growth.

The Financial Goals System

The Illusion of Unlimited Resources

The popular notion of the United States as a cornucopian society, in which abundant opportunities and resources await those with native intelligence and initiative, dies hard. People continue to believe that hordes of investors will beat a path to the better mousetrap builder's door. And people conveniently forget the questions that create doubts about the investors' ability to find the path amid the tall grass: Is it truly a better mousetrap? Behind whose door can the best be found? Can the inventor mass produce the trap with adequate quality control? Can those plagued by mice afford it, and will they buy in sufficient quantities to return a profit?

Still, the illusion persists, even within the formal structure of hard-headed corporate financial planning and analysis. The standard analytical approach to bottom-up investment planning and capital budgeting begins with an initial screening process in which each discrete investment is considered on its own merits. Its contribution to the corporate funds flows is evaluated by modern return-on-investment methodology in which a corporate hurdle rate, commonly defined as the corporate cost of capital, possibly adjusted for risk, is the test of acceptability. In the spirit of encouraging investment initiative, this process leads lower-level managers to believe that clearing the hurdle is the major step en route to approval because, like a published interest rate, an established cost of capital clearly implies that money is always available at the right price.

Were this implication valid, corporate managers would be free to pursue all the financial goals listed in table 3.1 simultaneously and without conflict. Growth in one product market would not restrict growth in another. A target return on investment would direct investment opportunities but not restrict them. Dividend payout and debt/equity goals would define the sources from which funds were to be obtained—internal or external, debt or equity—but they would not oblige top managers to make hard choices between investors' objectives and their own.

In fact, choices such as these are one of top management's primary responsibilities. Even though in some companies a combination of limited investment initiatives or opportunities and a strong liquid position could create the impression of unlimited financial resources for a time, such impressions are transitory. Top managers are well aware that they must ration capital carefully, even among the investment projects that have passed their particular corporate hurdle. Thus the fact of limited available funds can be added to other, more familiar limitations senior managers face: limited knowledge of corporate or competitive conditions and capacity; limited ability to predict the future for the industry or the economy; and limited ability to implement investment decisions and to manage the human and financial resource commitments they have agreed on.

The Internal Capital Market

The reality of limited financial resources, for even the largest industrial corporations, stems from senior management's fundamental mistrust of the capital markets, both debt and equity. In particular, these experienced managers are loath to rely on the capital markets as the primary source of the funds essential to achieve vital corporate objectives. Such funds must be available at a time of management's choosing, on terms it considers acceptable, in the amount it requires. However, managers' experience has taught them that investors' judgments and expectations are often out of phase with their own judgments, expectations, and needs. Just when the company's vital financial and competitive interests are at stake, the market's terms may be wholly unacceptable. While the capital market window may never be literally closed, for practical purposes it remains shut because these managers are unwilling to step up to it.

Evidence of this unwillingness can be seen quite clearly in the record of equity financing undertaken by our twelve companies. In the entire group, top management chose to issue stock for cash only twice during the decade of the study. These issues, one in each of two companies, accounted for approximately $100 million in new funds, or about half of 1 percent of the $17.4 billion of new funds added in all companies. Counting the repurchase of equity, the net addition of new equity was zero. Moreover, these managers did not include new equity in the list of variables they considered when they planned for mainstream corporate funding programs. The conclusion is inescapable: financial goal setting and planning for the companies' major long-term revenue sources took place within an environment of limited financial resources.

Yet the need for growth—to retain market share, to meet organizational needs, and to satisfy top managers' competitive drives—was equally inescapable, as these managers acknowledged in their financial goals. Among the nine companies for which complete financial data were available, the managers of seven adopted growth objectives that equaled or exceeded the ten-year growth rate of the related industries, while goals in the other two were only modestly lower. Nor were these vain hopes. As the data on actual company performance reveal, six of the nine outperformed the industry.* How, then, was this growth funded?

When we studied the managers' financial plans, we found that they chose to rely on their firm for these essential funds. Two sources supplied the primary funding for their firms' ongoing needs. One was internally generated funds; the other, a conservative amount of debt. Both were sources that management could rely on, with a high degree of certainty, to be available during the planning period, whatever circumstances might prevail, for whatever use deemed appropriate. Thus they were viewed as *assured* or *plannable* sources of funds, key adjectives in many of the corporate goals statements we examined.

---

*A comprehensive overview of the entire research sample of companies will be found in the statistical record of goals and performance against goals for the period 1968–1979 in appendix C. These data allow the reader to consider the internal consistency of these goals systems as well as compare the goals with the past performance of the company and its relevant competitors.

Within these companies, top managers showed a strong tendency to target one-half or two-thirds of earnings for reinvestment. In fact, the majority favored plans that allotted only one-third of earnings to the shareholders, an objective that differs significantly from the 50 percent share commonly associated with mature companies. Thus these dividend policies reflect the influence of a strategy of self-sufficiency within established product markets as did their complement, the targets for earnings retention. In all but one company, this target equaled or exceeded the industry average performance, while in all the cases the goal equaled or exceeded the company's past performance. There is a strong presumption, therefore, that the managers of these companies were pushing against the limits of conventional earnings retention norms, an observation consistent with aggressive growth objectives as well as with the concept of financial self-sufficiency.

These managers' preference for self-reliance was also evident in their debt policies. In every case they favored a conservative amount of debt, that is, that amount which normally provides a *wide* margin of safety to the lenders and which they are accustomed to lend on a truly *arm's-length* basis. However, because debt limits are customarily defined in terms of balance-sheet ratios of debt-to-equity or earnings coverage ratios, such debt capacity is in essence a direct function of anticipated internally generated funds.*

Management could escape from the limitations of internally generated funds in two ways: through its reserves and through new equity. However, as has already been seen, top managers chose to avoid new equity when they planned because it is not an assured source of funds. Moreover, such avoidance is considered appropriate, given the fact that the cash-flow planning process in all mature corporations is designed primarily to fund the *cash requirements for the maintenance and growth of established product markets.* In this context, new equity is thought of as an emergency defensive or offensive reserve. Were these managers to rely on an unpredictable source of cash to fund the company's existing operations, it would indicate a serious defect in their financial planning and strategy.

When we turn to reserves, we find considerable evidence of their importance as a planning tool. And yet, in the last analysis, reserves are also finite. Consequently these managers had to recognize the need to balance corporate

*As an index of the risk of default, the earnings coverage ratio shows the multiple by which a company's net earnings available for debt servicing exceed the amount of fixed charges associated with outstanding debt contracts.

funds flows. Having chosen to operate within an internal or closed capital market, they had to accept the discipline that choice placed on them in their financial plans and strategy.

A memorandum from one of the companies acknowledges this constraint:

> . . . It is obvious that capital expenditures cannot indefinitely exceed cash flow available for such expenditures unless a sharp increase in future profitability and cash flow is expected. It appears to me that if one is seeking a formula or guideline in capital expenditure planning, he might consider the following equation:
>
> Capital Expenditures = Cash Flow Available for Capital Expenditures, i.e., cash flow from operations less dividends, mandatory debt retirement, and required increases in working capital + Incremental Increase in Borrowing Capacity (based on a targeted debt capital ratio) + Debt Retired in Current Year.
>
> To this equation would be added spillover spending reflecting the large size of the components of a capital-intensive company's fixed asset program. The spillover years would have to be offset by shortfall years if targeted debt capital ratios are to be maintained. Also, if a company were desirous of improving liquidity or building a cash reserve for future opportunities, shortfalls in capital spending versus cash flow available for capital expenditures would have to be planned. . . .

Although this memorandum refers to capital expenditure only, its logic is relevant to all aspects of internal resource management in the mature industrial corporation. Because financial planning concerns real monetary transactions, in which accounts must be balanced and commitments backed by legal tender, the flow of events imposes a strict discipline on managers as they plan. Unless plans and reality match, day to day and year to year, the company's continuity will be jeopardized. Committed funds must not exceed the available supply during the period in which the commitment is to be honored.

Management can, of course, adjust the balance to deal with an unexpected need for funds or an unexpected shortfall in sources. Planned expenditures can be reordered, less urgent discretionary outlays postponed. In some instances, sources planned for future periods can be accelerated. In a diversified company, a surplus of resources generated in one division can be drawn on to fund a deficit in another. However, there are ultimate limits on management's ability to adjust to the unexpected, because there are limits to the total resources available from predictable, reliable sources during any given planning period. Consequently there must be an inherent balance within the overall financial system, and planned outflows must be paced to coincide with expected inflows.

Anyone who has had to balance a checkbook will see the relevance of these comments. For, like the individual, corporate managers must consider their plans and goals as well as their actual expenditures. They cannot undertake projects unless they have the funds to finance them. With this in mind, therefore, we refer you again to table 3.1, which classifies financial goals according to their impact on funds flows. By now it should be apparent that any individual company's set of financial goals constitutes a financial goals system. Further, the aggregate of demand-related goals should not produce a need for funds that exceeds the supply provided by the aggregate of the supply-related goals.

Most of the corporate managers studied openly recognized this interdependence. They tended to talk about it in terms of self-sufficiency. As the following representative quotes from several companies reflect, these managers believe that every established product market position in which the company operates ought to earn enough to fund its own growth.

A calculation [the CFO] presented to the division managers has had a great impact. It [showed] whether the various divisions were supporting their sales growth goals. Not being self-sufficient was a sign of "second-class citizenship."

The concept of "quality of earnings" should be a criterion for all segments of the business: to be or to have the capacity to become "self-financing."

In the [company's] system, the [goals] are figured . . . to be cash sufficient. A common thread is that each business unit, with few exceptions, is expected to operate at [a level] which will produce enough cash to finance its own needs. . . . These self-sustaining performance goals are . . . a necessity.

Whether or not it is appropriate to expect *every* division or product market to be self-sufficient or self-financing, these managers clearly believe that this principle applies to the corporate entity as a whole. Further, by starting with the principle of financial self-sufficiency, they are led by a natural progression to recognize that there must be a balance between those goals that drive the demand for funds and those that drive the supply. The following quotes from six different companies emphasize the widespread acceptance of this discipline within the research sample:

We expect our people to do 6 percent to 8 percent [profit] on sales, in which case we can do our 20 percent growth. If we don't achieve 6 percent to 8 percent on sales, then the pressure is on management to get up to that level of return—not on the financial office to find the funds. We keep the heat on operating management and don't let them off the hook by resorting to other financing.

This company needs to grow at a minimum of 7 percent to 10 percent a year in people in order to maintain upward mobility and excitement. This equals 15 percent growth in sales. . . . Growth versus debt has been the classic conflict: slowing down growth or raising long-term debt . . . growing up in the Great Depression taught us to avoid debt.

There is a continuing dialogue between the office of the chairman and the planning people. We have lots of financial goals, not all of which are compatible. So there is a continuing debate as to aspects of compatibility and which is to be ascendant . . . how rapidly can a private company afford to grow, particularly with a limit on utilization of debt. . . . If we tried to optimize all our goals, we'd have a problem. As it is, we fall into the trap of giving lots of emphasis to goals that do conflict with each other. . . . In the last four years, we've never taken our eyes off the ROI ball. . . . Twenty percent seems to balance our need for funds with what we can get.

Our dividend policy is designed to straddle the need for growth within the company and the needs of the investors and the realities of the market.

It is [the CEO's] opinion now that the company needs a 7 percent net income on gross assets if it is going to sustain the desired corporate growth rate. . . . The growth rate is based primarily on the industry growth rate, adjusted for inflation and translated back into a figure in relation to book investment. The goal is based on a philosophy of staying in the industry and protecting the company's position. What it says basically is that if we earn less than 7 percent on gross assets for any extended period of time, we are going to run into trouble.

The answer to the question of where we got our 15 percent ROI goal is that we backed into it. We started by asking ourselves what we had to invest to achieve the desired growth and then we asked the question what should we be able to earn [based on] our historical record . . . without pulling rabbits out of a hat. . . . We also agreed that we wanted to continue a reasonable but not exorbitant dividend. . . . With respect to debt, we are probably old-fashioned. . . . If you were a fly on the wall of our board meetings, you would realize how conservative we are. . . . We like to have responsibility for our own cash flows and we don't want to put future generations in a dangerous position. . . . Maximum ROI is not our principal goal. We are always involved in a trade-off between growth and ROI.

We would expect to hear comments such as these from the managers of private companies. Seeking to preserve their privacy, they would operate under tight self-sufficiency constraints, and they would be very conscious of the need to balance goals related to the flow of funds. But it is less apparent that the managers of publicly funded companies would be governed by the same belief. It should be noted, therefore, that only two of the six executives just quoted spoke for private companies. In addition, it was the managers of publicly owned (traded) companies who carried the concept to its most precise and objective form.

The Self-Sustaining Growth Equation

Many companies used a mathematical form to express the principle of self-sufficiency or self-sustaining growth in their planning for existing product markets. In fact, as we examined corporate documents, we found six different examples of algebraic equations used in the planning process to test for consistency among financial goals. At first the existence of these formulas surprised us, because we had not anticipated the closed financial goals system we have been describing. But, on reflection, we realized that these formulas provided excellent evidence that the managers of these companies had accepted the discipline imposed by their reliance on an internal capital market.

Although the formulas differed, each recognized the interdependence among management's financial goals by specifying the key variables that affect the rates of inflow and outflow of funds and by defining their precise relationship to one another.[1] Working along the same lines, we have derived an equation that describes such a goals system in its simplest and most basic form, by reducing the list of financial goals presented in table 3.1 to its principal elements (shown in the table in italics). There is only one primary demand-related goal, the target corporate growth rate. The primary supply-related goals are more numerous. They are: (1) the target return on investment; (2) the target dividend payout or earnings retention ratio; and (3) the target debt/equity ratio. To transform these elements into a funds flow equation, we need only add a number that defines the average after-tax interest rate on outstanding debt. Then the relationship among these goals can be expressed by the equation shown in figure 4.1.

To be objectively true, several simplifying assumptions must be made about this statement. However, only one is of concern here—the assumption that the relationship or ratio of sales to assets or investment is relatively stable

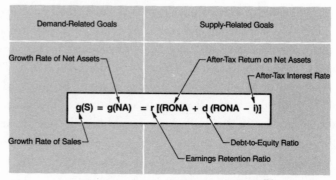

Figure 4.1   The Corporate Self-Sustaining Growth Equation
*A stable sales-to-assets ratio is assumed.

over the one-to-five-year planning horizon. In an inflationary economy this assumption is debatable, but it provides a good—and widely used—first approximation for planning purposes. (In fact, we found that only one of the self-sustaining planning models attempted to incorporate an inflation assumption explicitly into the equation.)

The same relationship can be presented in a nonalgebraic form by drawing a graph of the line defined by the equation. Figure 4.2 represents the demand-supply relationship in its most elementary form, for a company that plans neither debt nor dividends. (The research sample included one such company, Technical Products I.) In this case, the self-sustaining growth equation is: $g(S)$ = RONA = ROE. That is, the growth rate of sales equals the rate of return on net assets equals the rate of return on equity. When

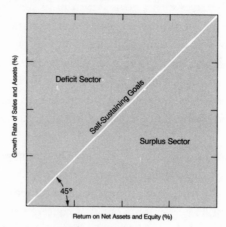

Figure 4.2   Self-Sustaining Goals System for a Company with Zero Debt and Zero Dividends

management's target growth rate of sales and target return on equity represent a point on the line, both the goals system and the planned funds flows will be in balance. If the company's *actual performance* also represents a point on the line—even though a different point—then *actual* funds flows are likely to be in approximate balance. If the company's goals are represented by a point in the area to the left of the line, there is an implicit planned deficit. If the company's goals are represented by a point in the area to the right of the line, there is an implicit planned surplus.

The graph in figure 4.3 represents a more typical, and more complex financial goals system. In this case, the company's goals include both a target dividend payout and a target amount of debt. The dividend drain acts to lower the potential rate of growth for any given return on investment, while the use of debt leverage acts to increase it (*if* the return exceeds the after-tax interest cost).

A Test for Consistency in the Financial Goals System

As has been seen, the statements of top managers clearly imply that they are guided by the principle of self-sufficiency when they formulate their financial plans for established product markets. But did these managers actually follow this principle? This question can be answered by using the self-sustaining growth equation to test the managers' goals systems for internal consistency.

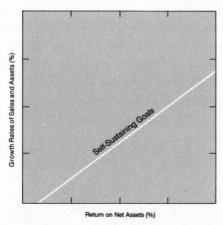

Figure 4.3   Self-Sustaining Goals System for a Company with Normal Debt Equity and Dividend Payout Targets

NOTE: Slope and intercept are defined by targeted debt/equity and payout ratios.

Consumer Products III provides an instance in which management's goals were seriously imbalanced. As you may remember, not all of those goals were quantitatively defined. Management wished to:

Reach a 15 percent (companywide) ROI.
Grow in volume and profitability:
    Sales growth 50 percent greater than GNP, inflation adjusted.
    Profit growth 30 percent greater than sales growth, inflation adjusted.
Other financial targets:
    Debt ratio less than 25 percent of total capital.
    Bond rating: AA.
    Dividend payout: 33 percent of total earnings.
Market leadership: Be number one in market segment.

Viewed in this form, these goals are not obviously incompatible. But when we apply the test of the self-sustaining growth equation, the imbalance becomes evident, because they cannot be reconciled. As the equation indicates, management simply could not finance an 18 percent growth rate through a 15 percent return on net assets:

$$.18 = .67 \left[.15 + .33(.15 - .044)\right]$$
$$.18 \neq .123$$

To achieve self-sufficiency, the managers would either have had to raise their target RONA to 21 percent or have lowered their sights considerably in terms of growth.

Figure 4.4 applies the same test to Commodity Products I. In this case, the results are presented graphically and the figure includes points that represent five years of actual performance against goals. The line drawn defines pairs of growth rate and rate of return objectives that are consistent with management's other financial goals. The line's slope and its intercept are defined by those goals: a target dividend payout of about one-third of after-tax earnings; a target debt/equity ratio of approximately two-thirds; and an average after-tax interest cost of 5 percent.

The point within the triangle represents management's current target growth rate and RONA, and, if achieved, it implies a modest surplus of funds. The point within the circle represents the company's actual five-year average growth rate and RONA, and it indicates a slight deficit in the flow of funds. The company's actual year-to-year results are shown by year within the box. Thus the figure represents a system that is essentially consistent internally. Moreover, the company's actual funds-flow experience within this time

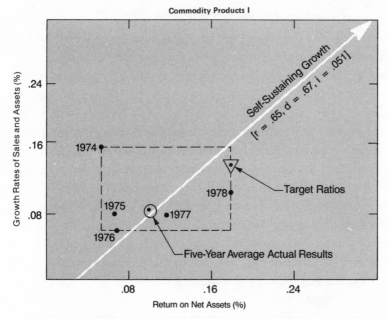

Figure 4.4   Financial Goals: Actual Versus Targets

NOTE: *Data for Period 1974–1978*

Retention Ratio *(r)* Target	.65	Asset Efficiency Sales/	
Actual (Avg.)	.65	Net Sales	
Debt/Equity Ratio *(d)* Target	.67	1974 1.5	
1974 Actual	.42	1978 1.	
1978 Actual	.37		

period has been roughly in balance, even though it has fallen substantially short of management's goals.

The Discipline of the Financial Goals System

What has just been described is the essence of the financial goals system. It captures the basic elements of internal resource management in the mature industrial corporations studied. Founded on the resources most accessible to management's control, the system is designed to ensure that the vital long-term needs of the enterprise will be properly funded at all times. In addition, when the system is properly balanced, it promises to reward management with considerable financial and managerial independence if the goals are achieved. The fact that many of these managers make frequent use of formal models in the planning process testifies to their awareness of the contribution the financial goals system can make to corporate long-term survival. So too does the fact that in five of the nine companies for which we have complete financial data, the goals system was essentially in balance.

When we tested these nine companies for self-sufficiency, we obtained the figures listed in table 4.1. (The table reproduces figures from section B of appendix C.)

As can be seen, in five of these companies, management's target RONA falls within two percentage points of the RONA figure that would be consistent with a self-sustaining goals system. Consequently it can be assumed that the goals systems in these companies were essentially in balance, given that these numbers do not warrant a high degree of precision and that the financial system allows for some operational "wiggle room" by which to achieve a balanced funds flow. Before we consider the implications of this fact, however, we must stop to consider the four companies in which this criterion was not met. Why is it that the discipline of the self-sustaining goals system did not appear to operate in these cases?

Ironically, Consumer Products III would seem to be most in need of such a discipline, because it is a wholly private company that must abide strictly by the self-sustaining growth principle to preserve its independence. Yet its target RONA not only fails to meet that objective but also falls short of both the company's and the industry's past performance. The fact that the company's goals are still treated somewhat independently by the family member whose prerogative they are best explains this inconsistency. Because he does not think of these goals as an integrated system, the test of reconciliation has never been applied. And yet, as the company's performance record

TABLE 4.1

A Test of Goal Consistency

Company	Implicit (Self-Sustaining) RONA (%)	Actual RONA Target (%)
Consumer Products II	12	14
Consumer Products III	18	14
Consumer Products IV	20	19
Technical Products II	17	14
Technical Products III	13	17
Commodity Products I	16	18
Commodity Products III	11	13
Conglomerate I	10	16
Conglomerate II	9	9

shows, in practice managers do balance their internal funds flow, whatever their goals may say.

Technical Products II is a publicly traded company, although the founding family still dominates the organization. In this company top managers were strongly aware of the company's inferior ROI performance, and the 14 percent goal they had set was openly acknowledged to be a challenging target, albeit one consistent with industry performance. In our opinion, however, these managers had yet to recognize the full implications of their aggressive growth and market dominance objectives, and the goal system remained significantly out of balance—a fact they would have to confront in due course.

Investment and funding decisions had long been separated at Technical Products III; hence it was not surprising to find the goals system out of balance. For many years every investment proposal that cleared organizational hurdles had been readily financed, within a very conservative financing strategy. The engineers and scientists rarely, if ever, crossed swords with the finance committee. The capital budgeting process was a dispersed system, with each department or division largely autonomous. However, recent events have put pressure on the company's debt capacity, and management has retreated from its former ultra-conservative debt policy. More centralization and coordination of the funds flow process have been important by-products of this experience, and they seem likely to remain in place, even if management succeeds in reinstating more conservative debt levels. (The current RONA target of 17 percent appears designed to achieve this end by deliberately generating a surplus of funds.)

Last, there is Conglomerate I, a well-run company in which management has strongly identified with stockholder interest in ROI and ROE since the firm's inception. A goal that exceeds the requirements for self-sufficiency, as well as that of company and industry past performance, is not at all surprising, therefore. Surplus funds would fund expansion and diversification.

It should be clear that the goal of self-sufficiency in the funds flows for established product markets imposes certain limits upon those managers committed to it. As we would expect, some of those limits are set by the financial imperative that says that no individual or corporation can spend what it does not have. The demand-related goal of corporate growth must be in balance with the supply-related goals of rate of return, debt level, and dividend payout. Management's aggressive competitive aspirations are doomed to disappointment, therefore, if they outpace the company's ability to earn the complementary rate of return on investment or the managers' own willingness to assume a more aggressive debt posture. Similarly, in a closed funds-flow system, every goal is quantitatively related to every other goal and must be so defined. Goals should not be defined in isolation. Instead each goal—and each related constituent interest—must be reconciled with all other goals and their related constituent interests. Top managers cannot cheerfully respond to shareholders who press for a higher share of current earnings through dividends unless they are also prepared to reduce their growth expectations or unless they expect an improvement in the corporate return on investment, perhaps in conjunction with a more aggressive debt policy. These are simple and inescapable facts of financial life, although they may not always be appreciated by the more intuitive and subjective members of the management team.

What this model of funds-flow planning does not define is the *particular* combination of key demand and supply-related goals managers ought to choose at any given time. If you refer again to the graphs shown in figures 4.2 and 4.3, the relevance of this fact will be readily apparent. As can be seen, the companies' funds flows will be in balance at *any* point on the line, although some goals are obviously more aggressive than others. But the equation says nothing about which particular pair of target growth rate and target rate-of-return ratio management ought to choose to pace corporate activity. In short, the self-sustaining growth equation by itself does not define the corporate goals system. Top managers do.

Moreover, as should also be apparent, they may choose a combination of goals that creates a marked imbalance in the system without challenging its inherent consistency (at least in the short run), *if* they choose targets that generate more funds than their established product markets require. Thus important questions remain about the way in which these corporate managers define particular combinations of self-sustaining goals. However, one important topic remains to be explored before these questions can be addressed: management's perception of risk and the way in which that perception is related to the financial goals system.

The Perception of Risk

For those who live in the world of financial economics, risk is a critical concept. Financial choices are viewed as conscious trade-offs between risk and reward; and invariably some deliberate and objective measurement of risk is associated with every resource acquisition or allocation. Thus it is remarkable that in our extended conversations with senior managers about their financial goals, this topic was seldom touched on. Contrary to what we might have expected, these managers rarely mentioned risk as a major consideration in their choice of specific objective criteria.

Nevertheless, risk is inherent in every aspect of the financial goals system. New product-market investments often pose the alternative of higher return and higher risk against a lower but more certain return. The appeal of a diversified portfolio of income sources over a single market strategy is strengthened by the possibility it holds out for reducing earnings fluctuations and providing the comfort of a positive income stream during good times and bad. The balance between debt and equity contracts reflects a choice between investors who accept a limited but legally enforceable compensation for the use of their money and those who are willing to take a back seat to boardroom priorities in exchange for a full share when their turn comes. Conscious adoption of an aggressive growth strategy that pushes against the limits of the corporate resource base places a high premium on being right and a high cost on being wrong. A more conservative goals system promises more restful nights and fewer rewards. How, then, can we account for the fact that these managers neither discussed the question of risk nor spent much time on its refined quantification and calibration?

One explanation lies in the fact that risk implies the possibility of failure. To speak of danger is to imply weakness or vulnerability, and such implications run counter to top management's responsibility for inspiring and instilling confidence within the organization at large. Thus the managers' failure to mention the topic may well confirm its importance for them rather than suggest that it is insignificant.

Moreover, these senior executives believe that risk can be modified by managerial wisdom and skill. Accustomed to facing economic risks as part of their daily agenda, they are like the early fur traders who knew the risks of the rivers they had to travel and could run the rapids seemingly oblivious to the danger involved. The unacceptable risks were obvious to them, while lesser risks warranted little conscious attention even though wealth—and sometimes life—was at stake. Long-practiced, they could rely on themselves.

Like the traders, these managers' confidence in themselves—and their lack of confidence in available data about future uncertainties—accounts in part for the absence of explicit risk analyses in the formal planning process. The point of diminishing returns may be just beyond a few crude approximations. However, our experience also suggests that the most significant factor lies in the personal and corporate beliefs that will be discussed in the following pages. Through their experiences, managers become familiar with the risks they face. They develop beliefs about those risks that divide acceptable dangers from foolhardy exploits. At times these beliefs are translated into explicit decision rules. More often, however, they remain an unarticulated and intuitive response to the decision of the moment.

Thus the entire financial goals system can be regarded as an extension of management's perception of appropriate risk. If top managers are comfortable with the risk parameters their goals system implies, they will make a decision without having had to ask a question. If they feel otherwise, they will adjust their goals in the appropriate direction—quite possibly finding the words to turn a defensive reaction into an aggressive advantage as they do so.

Constituency Demands

Managerial Choices and the Financial Goals System

By delineating the relationship between top managers' perception of risk and their willingness to establish specific financial goals in this way, we have already begun to answer the question posed earlier: Why do corporate managers choose a particular combination of financial goals? For as these managers define their goals and strategy, they are influenced by two complementary sets of constraints. One set, discussed in chapter 5, consists of the psychological constraints created by their belief system. The other are the objective constraints imposed by the financial and economic environments in which the firm operates and by the managers' need to reconcile conflicting constituency demands. Together these constraints explain the logic that lies behind the particular choices corporate managers make at any given time.

A good way to begin thinking about the objective constraints that limit and define management's choices is to consider the extent to which any single constituency has the potential to dominate the goals system and limit management's self-sufficiency. This possibility is derived from a general theory of dependency, for it can be assumed that management's willingness to pursue goals that best serve a particular constituency will vary in direct proportion to its dependency on that constituency for the health and continuity of the enterprise. Obviously, dependency is a relative term, for no company is totally dependent or wholly independent. But conditions of greater or lesser dependency with respect to each of the three constituencies—capital market, product market, and organization—do exist within these companies' goals systems. As a result, connections can be made between the three constituencies and the goals and strategy most closely connected with each.

Figure 4.5 depicts the conditions for constituency dominance in matrix form. The figure shows the intersection of three dimensional cuts, or surfaces, that separate each constituency according to the primary elements of the goals system that heighten or lessen dependency. The vertical surface from front to back separates relatively self-sufficient companies from those that are substantially and persistently dependent on external capital markets for strategic investment needs. The vertical surface from left to right divides those companies whose key personnel are highly mobile, thanks to a vigorous and attractive external employment market, from those whose key personnel see their only meaningful job opportunities within the organization itself. The horizontal surface divides single-industry or single-industry–dominated companies from those whose earnings stream is substantially diversified.

The resulting eight cubes suggest the potential for dominance by individual constituencies. Product market dominance is illustrated by cube 4, in

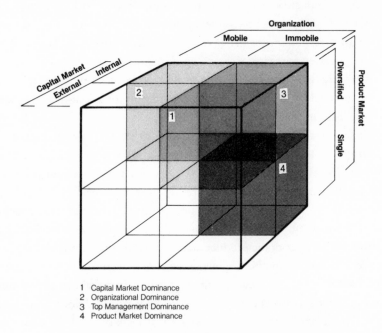

1   Capital Market Dominance
2   Organizational Dominance
3   Top Management Dominance
4   Product Market Dominance

Figure 4.5   The Potential for Constituency Dominance

which the company is dependent on a single industry, financially self-sufficient, and organizationally immobile. Capital market dominance is indicated by cube 1, in which the capital market is external, the product market diversified, and the organization immobile. And organizational dominance is illustrated by cube 2, in which the key personnel are highly mobile, the enterprise is financially self-sufficient, and the product market is diversified.

Cube 3 illustrates top management's ideal—the conditions most likely to promote independent goal setting on their part: a diversified product market, an internal capital market, and highly loyal (immobile) key personnel. The remaining cubes represent combinations of constituent circumstances in which the potential for dominance is indeterminate and the potential for conflict within the goals system greatest.

Product Market Dominance

Product market dominance of the corporate goals system is potentially greatest in the single-industry company that lives or dies by its performance within the economic and competitive realities of one finite product market. Given a large, well-established competitive position and a high degree of financial self-sufficiency, such a company could survive for long periods relatively free from apparent constituency dominance. However, the emergence of industry-related problems reveals more basic realities. Technological change, industry recession, foreign or domestic competition—any one of these quickly demonstrates how vulnerable the financial system is to the demands imposed by the industry as a precondition for a long-term corporate earnings base in that industry.

While it is true that few large companies market only one product, several companies in this study, including Commodity Products II, Commodity Products III, and Consumer Products I, had an income stream dominated by a specific family of products. As a result, their managers had to take particular account of such product market uncertainties as demand, productive capacity, technology, distribution channels, and competitive initiative.

For these companies the product market discipline was imposed by a small number of close competitors against whom they were constantly measured. They had to be fully competitive in every aspect important to the customer, from product quality and innovation to delivery schedules, capacity, and price. To the extent that these corporate managers could differentiate their products so that they were in some degree proprietary, they could relax the discipline of competitors and of the product market. But appealing as the goal of finding and dominating unique market segments was, these managers were also limited in the extent to which they could sustain market segmentation across the entire corporate income stream, because any major component of the income stream inevitably tends to develop more of the characteristics of a commodity market in which vigorous competition sets the tone.

Under these conditions it is difficult to overstate the influence the competitive environment has on the financial goals top managers specify and define. During our interviews their conversations were filled with analogies to sports—particularly team sports. "Winning" by some commonly accepted and widely publicized rules of the game is an ever-present and powerful motive for these competitive individuals. Thus it is not surprising that they usually frame their financial goals in terms that allow easy measurement against the competition, individually or collectively, nor that they derive specific targets from competitors' past performance. Competition against the company's own past performance, and that of predecessors in office, is a natural—and common—extension of this frame of reference.

"Share of market" or "rank in industry" was the measure of competitive performance we found most often in the goals systems of these corporations. In fact, top managers tended to see this standard as the ultimate test of their competitive strength. (Only the management of one high-technology innovator rejected share of market as a meaningful standard; and even so, the company's managers were well aware of where the company stood.) Typically these executives linked share of market to economics of scale and market dominance; but their drive to win—and to be seen as winners—persisted, however vague the economics of scale might be. The related concept of market segmentation revealed top managers' ability to discriminate among profit opportunities, yet even that only transferred their drive to dominate the market to a more specific target.

Ironically, these managers' strong preoccupation with share of market or rank in industry has an unintended consequence: it makes an external factor, the industry growth rate, the driving force in the internal financial goals system. To maintain or improve its share of the market, a company's growth rate must equal or exceed that of the industry. If the industry is growing at a rate of 6 percent compounded, then the company must grow at a rate of 6 percent or lose market share and possibly its rank in industry. In addition, to hold that position management must meet whatever terms the competition sets for price, quality, and delivery, and it must be prepared to invest at a rate that enables the company to match the industry growth rate in sales.

If the managers are also intent on being financially self-sufficient and have modeled the goals system on self-sustaining growth, then the industry growth rate and its competitive environment define the target rate of return on investment as well. It is under these circumstances that the potential for domination of the corporate goals system by the product market environment is greatest—particularly if the company is a single-industry firm.

Figures 4.6 through 4.9 will help you grasp the potential impact of the product market on the financial goals system and compare it with the influence of other constituencies. Figure 4.6 displays the entire network of corporate financial goals as described in chapter 3. The central box contains the key financial goals that are the elements of the self-sustaining growth equation and graph. The double arrow indicates that no one of the goals has inherent dominance over the others, but that all must be in balance. The succeeding figures depict the way this network is affected and defined when one or another of the constituencies dominates the system. Thus Figure 4.7 represents the product market–dominated goals system in a single-industry company. The crucial target numbers originate in the industry growth rate, which defines both the corporate growth rate target and the target return on investment, because of the strategic importance of defending share of market. Moreover, as a by-product, the buoyancy of career opportunities is also defined, because opportunity is linked to growth.

Management could escape from a constant preoccupation with the indus-

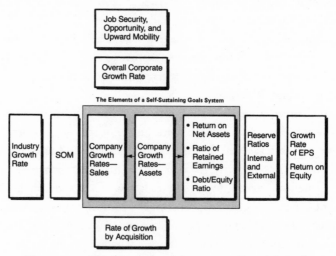

Figure 4.6   The Network of Corporate Financial Goals

try's conditions and norms by one route only: diversification into unrelated and complementary income streams. Many of our managers had chosen just this strategy. By establishing a strong, sustainable earnings base in two or more industries, they could reduce the organizational disruption that took place when any one industry suffered a setback. They could also diminish any one industry's capacity to dictate the amount and timing of corporate investment as a defensive or aggressive response to industry conditions.

Capital Market Dominance

The potential for capital market domination of the financial goals system is increased when the enterprise requires major funding from the external capital market over an extended period of time to support its strategic objectives, as happened at Technical Products III. Such an event may come about because the company has failed to achieve management's goals related to financial self-sufficiency and existing reserves cannot absorb the deficits or tar-

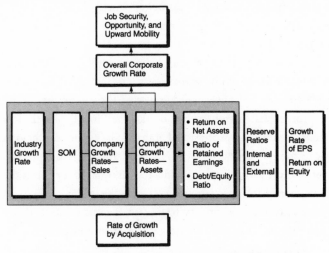

Figure 4.7   Product Market–Dominated Goals System

geted investments cannot be deferred. Or it may occur during a period of diversification through acquisition, when management wishes to exchange substantial amounts of parent equity for the equity of the acquired companies. But whatever the circumstances, management tends to give higher priority to investors' expectations and demands at those times when lenders and equity investors are in the position to assert their power through their preference for particular performance measures.

The potential for dominance by the capital market, and by the equity investors in particular, is also increased when the issue of control, usually dormant in successful companies, comes to the surface. A threatened withdrawal of support for the incumbent management in a proxy battle or ownership raid would obviously heighten management's sense of dependency and make it more sensitive to the stockholder interest. But whether it concerns the supply of funds or control, management's self-interest is best served by an attempt to define the form and level of corporate performance likely to satisfy the independent investors' objectives.

In practice, this is likely to mean that managers will pay particular attention to goals such as dividends and return on equity, which directly benefit the equity investors. This is not to say that lenders' expectations have no effect on management's choices. On the contrary, the covenants debt contracts impose place limits on both demand- and supply-related goals, and they restrict management's freedom of choice considerably. But with the help of these covenants, lenders are prepared to take care of themselves and do, whereas management must take care of the stockholders.

During times of heightened financial uncertainty or stress, managers will be more concerned about dividend payments, because their shareholders may well prefer a larger payout in order to have more direct control over investment decisions. In addition, these managers will also be particularly mindful of the rate of return on investment because of the importance accorded this figure by professional investors. For unlike the "loyal" shareholder whom management prefers, the professional investor in a publicly held company looks first to the rate of return on investment, and he or she prefers to limit investment to those activities that yield a return equal to, or better than, comparable investments in other companies. From this point of view, therefore, the company's growth is secondary to its rate of return, and its share of market is a residual of whatever investment opportunities clear the hurdle.

In academic discussions of corporate finance, these standards have a very precise and technical meaning.[2] But they also have practical, if less precise, counterparts in the targets chosen by the top managers of these firms for such goals as the growth rate of earnings per share and the rate of return on equity. The first of these, though crude, implies that improved earnings on a fixed equity base must be the result of a higher return on investment. Consequently it is also widely believed to produce high price-earnings ratios in the equity market and higher wealth "leverage" for the investors. Management's targets reflect these beliefs.

The second standard, rate of return, is even more reflective of top managers' judgment, for there is no published index of equity returns comparable to the industry growth rate to guide them in responding to capital market priorities. Theorists and investment analysts have developed a "beta" risk factor for estimating the market equity cost of capital; but as an operating corporate discipline this factor has a number of practical problems. At present managers are more inclined to estimate their own target return on equity, and these estimates may or may not capture the real expectations of the dominant shareholder group. Ultimately, of course, the test of the managers' success lies in their ability to obtain essential external funding and run the business without interference.

As figure 4.8 illustrates, the goals system is driven from right to left when it is dominated by the capital market. The target return on equity implicitly defines the target return on net assets, which, in turn, significantly affects the acceptable target rate of growth in assets and sales. (This is so because RONA, coupled with the acceptable earnings retention rate and debt/equity ratio, defines the supply side of the funds-flow equation.) But those matters that concern the organizational and product market constituencies—the buoyancy of career opportunity and the share of market—are an unintended residual of these investor-oriented goals, and such goals can have a negative impact on management's human resource and product market strategies. Consequently it is not surprising that the top managers of these companies chose to limit their reliance on the external capital market by achieving as much self-sufficiency as possible. Only their ability to fund essential investment

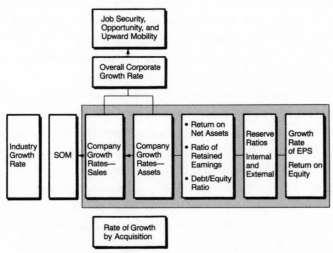

Figure 4.8   Capital Market–Dominated Goals System

requirements entirely from what we have called the internal capital market could reduce or eliminate the need to give precedence to these goals, if other considerations were more pressing.

Organizational Dominance

Finally, there is the organization itself. As we have emphasized repeatedly, top managers and other personnel are primarily concerned with the long-term survival of the healthy, buoyant work environment that attracts superior management and employee talent. Most often they express this concern in terms of the expansion and growth necessary to provide continuing opportunities for individual development, stimulation, upward mobility, and monetary rewards. Hence it surfaces explicitly in the financial goals system through the growth targets top management chooses. However, as table 3.1 also suggests, top managers are equally interested in the goals that drive the supply of funds, since these are essential to support the expanded investment base they desire. Thus, all things being equal, they are likely to choose an earnings retention rate and a debt/equity ratio that are as high as possible, consistent with their sense of financial conservatism. They are also likely to pay careful attention to their reserves, to forestall any sudden vulnerability to the dictates of the external capital market should unexpected needs arise.

Yet unlike other members of the organization, top managers must also respond to the needs of other constituencies. Thus they are likely to be faced with the need to trade off organizational priorities in favor of those of other constituencies. How much freedom management feels it has to make such trade-offs depends in large part on the real or perceived mobility of key organizational personnel. Given a "loyal" organization—that is, one in which key personnel are locked into a career at one particular enterprise without ready access to alternative comparable employment—top managers can afford to be less sensitive to important issues such as upward mobility. Conversely, a vigorous industry or cross-industry market for highly trained professionals—scientists, engineers, lawyers, administrators—requires that top managers pay constant attention to the working conditions that attracted those who are critical to short-term performance and long-term survival.

Assuming a competitive market for professional employees, two conditions are essential if the organization is to dominate the corporate goals system. One is financial self-sufficiency, the other is a diversified income stream. The logic here is straightforward. Financial self-sufficiency is necessary to diminish the influence of the capital market, particularly as it may constrain investment or threaten job security. Diversification is likewise essential to reduce the capacity of any single-product market to define the rate of investment in that industry and thereby limit growth.

As has been shown, most of the firms included in this study met one or both of these conditions. Many of the top managers chose to pursue a strategy of self-sufficiency by emphasizing the internal capital market and balancing their supply- and demand-related goals. And most had also taken significant steps toward the development of a diversified product stream—a strategy we could anticipate, given the fact that they manage mature firms. Top management will be forced to seek out new, more promising growth opportunities if its product market strategy fails to create sufficient growth to satisfy organizational needs—as is likely to be the case, sooner or later, in mature companies confined to a single industry.

The diversification process itself tends to increase the company's capital market dependency at least temporarily, because the relevant time frame often leaves management no choice but to diversify externally through an exchange of equity (thereby heightening its concern for market values and shareholder priorities). But if the process succeeds and the newly diversified company settles back into a pattern of financial self-sufficiency, then the organization is in a position to reduce the power and influence of both external constituencies. Figure 4.9 illustrates this situation. The dotted lines indicate two possibilities inherent in the system. One possibility is the temporary capi-

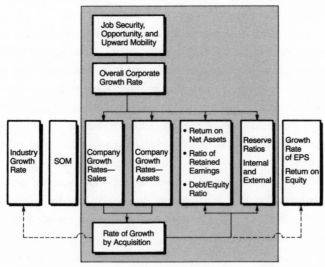

Figure 4.9   Organization-Dominated Goals System

tal market dependency likely while diversification is in progress. The other possibility reflects the fact that once a new product market has been acquired, it begins to assert its own priorities through individual share-of-market strategies. Any constituency's dominance is at best an unstable condition.

Moreover, top managers' behavior, as they choose the financial goals they want to emphasize, inevitably mirrors this instability. The fact that for every target growth rate there is a target return on investment essential to self-sufficiency and independence has already been discussed. Yet the relationship between the growth rate and the rate of return, both of which are essential to corporate survival, is complex. The growth of sales and of investments is a natural prerequisite for organizational opportunities. However, the return on investment may suffer when growth objectives predominate, because investment inevitably precedes full exploitation of profit potential and because growth in sales and market share can be bought at the expense of profit margins. Consequently top managers must shift their emphasis as they struggle to equalize the demand for funds with the supply. As we heard often in our discussions with these executives, a consistent balance among corporate goals is difficult to maintain.

The Boundaries of Top Management Initiative

This empirical study of corporate financial goals systems in action suggests that the Horatio Alger image of the American entrepreneur considerably overstates management's discretionary realm. The demands of competitive strategy and survival in specific product markets dictate a minimum level of rate of investment, which persists as long as the product market remains an integral piece of the corporate income stream. You play by the rules, or you leave the game. The need to attract superior management at all levels will drive the organization into new product markets if the old ones fail to provide a satisfactory rate of growth. Financial imperatives drive management into the external capital market, where money is rationed according to strict rules of reward, whenever the company falls short of financial self-sufficiency. And—over all these intersecting disciplines—orderly funds-flow planning requires that demand- and supply-related priorities be carefully balanced so that management can honor its commitments in the right amounts at the right time, without interrupting the continuity of resource-dependent activity.

Where, then, is the space for independent initiative and for corporate management's own plans and goals? To the extent that it exists, it must be developed and defended; it is not a divine right bestowed with the mantle of executive office. Those managers who choose to set an independent course must adopt strategies to relax the disciplines of the major constituencies. In the capital market, it is the strategy of financial self-sufficiency. In the product market, it is the strategy of diversification of the corporate income stream across industries and/or countries. In the organization, it is the creation of a work environment that produces loyalty and immobility in a talented work force.

Yet each of these strategies has its limitations and its unintended effects. Financial self-sufficiency may not be attainable during a particular phase of accelerated growth or a particular stage of the economy. Diversification may or may not succeed in relaxing the constraints of a dominant industry, and even when it does succeed, it substitutes a new set of competitive disciplines for the old. Building a loyal and dependent work force requires that the organization's priorities be given an appropriate place in the corporate goals system.

As figure 4.5 indicates, the combination of a diversified product market, an internal capital market, and immobile personnel provides top managers with the best opportunity to set an independent standard for their enterprise. But as the figure also suggests, that coincidence of constituent conditions is only one of the many possible combinations likely to obtain in real life. Indeed, managers are much more likely to face a complicated environment in which no one constituency dominates the corporate goals system but all demand their consideration and response.

Management is free, of course, to *assert* any goal it chooses. New chief executives, particularly those new to the company, may signal their leadership intentions with bold new goals. However, unless those goals are consistent with the economic, competitive, financial, and human environmental realities, they will not stand the test of time and credibility. Either they will have to be modified or they will be disregarded by those who must make the company's real day-to-day decisions.

And yet we must reiterate that we have been considering the conditions that create a *potential* for dominance. The conditions are relative, not absolute. The environment in which corporate leaders find themselves at any particular time may allow significant freedom to test an independent course. For example, at a time of diversification and acquisition, top managers may wish to support the market for their company's equity. They may also have evidence that some shareholders would prefer a higher dividend payout.

Nevertheless, they may choose to disregard these signals, and there may be no apparent response from the capital market. Perhaps the shareholder group was unwilling or unable to withhold resources or support. Perhaps the signal was false.

Similarly, top managers may have the power to hold their constituencies at bay and assert alternative priorities, but they may choose not to do so. At times the reasons for these choices seem clear. Thus it is natural that the chief financial officer would tend to be the capital market's self-appointed representative, while the divisional product-line manager would represent the product market. However, the choice made by a chief executive officer follows less automatically and logically, for it is his responsibility to arbitrate among all the constituents' interests and reconcile their needs into a single corporate goals system. Nevertheless, some CEOs appear to have a strong philosophical or emotional identity with their shareholders, while others appear to have the same sense of identity with an industry or with a group of career professionals within the organization. To understand why this might be so, the second set of constraints that limit these corporate executives—the psychological constraints of their belief system—will now be considered.

CHAPTER 5

The Psychology of Executive Choice

Should top managers commit additional resources to a declining business, or should they "milk" it? Should they commit more funds to a promising but still uncertain research project or terminate it? Does added long-term debt make sense to finance plant modernization in a mature industry? Should division general managers be involved in corporate strategy, or should management impose its choices from the top down?

As corporate managers grapple with complex questions such as these, their decisions are limited by the objective constraints of the financial goals system and constituency demands. However, a more elusive set of constraints limits them as well—the psychological constraints of their own beliefs. Among the corporate managers in each of the companies, we found a distinctive system of beliefs.*[1] These interrelated beliefs act as a filter through which management perceives the realities facing its firm. Thus they serve two essential and significant functions. One is to simplify: to translate a world that can

---

*We use the word belief in its common meaning—"a conviction or persuasion that something is true." We must emphasize that persons (even senior executives) often have a deep emotional attachment to such convictions.

be overwhelmingly complex and ambiguous into comprehensible and familiar terms. The other is to provide continuity and stability when change threatens to undermine the lessons of experience.

Further, although these beliefs are influenced by and interact with the objective constraints of constituency pressures and the financial goals system, they exist apart from them. Indeed, as we shall explain more fully later, a key issue for corporate managers is their ability to balance the psychological constraints of the belief system with the more objective pressures they face. An example of this, which we encountered in several firms, involved the amount of long-term debt that management ought to incur. In several instances management chose to balance the financial goals system without increasing long-term debt, despite strong objective pressures to do so, because more debt would violate important and deeply held beliefs.

Central to each belief system is management's vision of the company's distinctive competence. In its managers' minds, this vision defines what the company's economic, human, and technical resources can—and cannot—accomplish: the kinds of economic activity the firm should undertake and how this activity is to be conducted. In essence, therefore, it shapes the strategic means they select. Moreover, by leading management to select specific product markets and competitive environments, the belief system is ultimately responsible for the particular parameters of the demand side of the funds-flow equation and the financial goals system. Thus management's subjective beliefs about individual competence and comparative advantage lie behind the objective realities of the firm's economic and financial environment.

The issue of diversification illustrates well the impact of managers' vision on their strategic choices. In some of these firms, managers had a very narrow view of the company's distinctive competence, and they chose to stay in activities closely aligned to its traditional focus. In others, top managers were willing to diversify because they believed that they and their organization could operate successfully in a wider sphere of activities.

Top management's vision of the firm also includes beliefs—powerful and persistent convictions—about the sources of funds and the conditions under which the financial goals system remains in balance. A related set of beliefs conditions the way in which reality is perceived for every major objective consideration in the financial goals system. Those that concern self-sufficiency, or the necessary degree of independence from key constituencies, including the primary sources of funds, are particularly significant. So too are the beliefs, critical to the financial goals system and the management of funds flows, that concern the trade-off between risk and reward, for these are deeply personal judgments about the margins of safety necessary to assure financial continuity, competitive success, and organizational survival.

Unless corporate managers' beliefs about the distinctive competence of their firm, including themselves, are understood, neither their propensity to take risks nor their appraisal of corporate self-sufficiency can be understood. A venture that seems risky to one group of managers will look quite safe to those in another firm. Similarly, a decision to borrow up to the lender's limit will raise fears of capital market dependency for some managers but create none for others. To an outside observer, one group of managers might seem more risk-prone than another, or more concerned with self-sufficiency. But one must be cautious of such judgments, because from the perspective of the managers themselves, they are not necessarily so.

The themes of distinctive competence, acceptable risk, and self-sufficiency provide one way to categorize management's beliefs about corporate goals and strategy. Top managers' own tasks in choosing and implementing corporate strategy provide another, for these beliefs take specific form as corporate managers fulfill their responsibilities. The essential point, however, is that all of the beliefs in each company are a tightly interrelated system in which specific choices are guided by three overriding beliefs (see table 5.1).

As an executive in one of the companies observed:

> It is a closed loop. You can make the argument that in the beginning of the company [the founders] wanted to make certain products, which led to a certain organization, which in turn led to our way of managing, which reinforced our products. It all hangs together. It isn't the result of any intellectual process but it

TABLE 5.1

The Dimensions of the Corporate Management Belief System

Specific Choices About	Overriding Beliefs		
	Vision of Distinctive Competence	Beliefs About Risk Preference	Beliefs About Self-Sufficiency
Establishing Goals			
Establishing Means			
Establishing Internal Management			

evolves. The pattern of principles which emerges out of a lot of individual decisions is totally consistent, and it is a fabric which hangs together and leads to success.

For descriptive purposes, this "fabric" may be categorized. But all our research strongly indicates that these beliefs do not exist in isolation as discrete principles. Rather they are closely interwoven in managers' thought processes; there are no clear boundaries between them.

In spite of this systemic nature, however, it is useful for analytical purposes to divide these belief systems into categories according to the dimensions of managerial responsibility that have been examined: the establishment of financial goals; the establishment of means designed to achieve those goals; and the establishment of internal management practices intended to achieve strategic ends and means. (See appendix D.) Other categories might be equally useful, but we prefer these because they correspond to the way in which corporate managers actually talked about their beliefs. Indeed our words are theirs, as far as possible without revealing company identities. Additionally, we have recorded only those beliefs that were widely shared among the corporate managers in each firm and that they indicated had affected their decisions.

We shall begin by describing the beliefs in each of these areas and illustrating the interrelationships among them. Then we will demonstrate more fully the significant impact they have on managers' strategic choices.

As we describe these belief systems, it will become apparent that despite some similarities in specific beliefs, the character of each firm's system is unique. Why this is so is a matter discussed fully in the next chapter. For now we simply point out that these belief systems are shaped by each group of managers' personal experiences in making successful decisions in the past, as well as by their understanding of similar lessons learned by their predecessors. Thus it should be obvious that the conclusions they draw from their own experience, and from history, are also shaped by the objective constraints they and their predecessors have encountered.

Beliefs About Establishing Goals

A perusal of these belief systems makes it clear that each group of corporate managers has convictions about many, if not all, of the elements in the financial goals system (see appendix D, column 1). To consider long-term debt: as just mentioned, each management held convictions, which varied considerably, about the correct level of long-term debt. At one extreme are those managers who viewed it with suspicion. In Technical Products I, for example, management believed that "we must stay on a pay-as-you-go basis." No long-term debt was deemed appropriate, therefore, and management refused to borrow long term. A similar bias existed in Technical Products II, although here management accepted the use of minimal long-term debt. According to one top manager there: "We must be conservative financially. There are not more good opportunities than we have generated funds internally."

At the other extreme are the corporate managers who believed that their company should be heavily leveraged. Consumer Products I provides an example. Here management agreed that "you have to grow to survive and be prepared to issue equity and long-term debt to grow." As a result, the company carried a substantial amount of long-term debt. Between these extremes are the firms in which management pursued some middle course. At Commodity Products II corporate executives were willing to accept debt up to a level that would not jeopardize their credit standing. They wished to "maintain [X] credit rating by keeping debt less than [X percent] of capital." Similarly, Technical Products III's managers believed that "we must maintain a conservative financial structure," yet their definition of conservatism was influenced by another deeply held belief that "flexibility for the future is needed more than financial safety now." Consequently their practice included some use of long-term debt, with a healthy reserve for future contingencies or opportunities.

Turning to growth, a similar congruence can be found between managers' beliefs and their goals. In some companies the belief was simply a conviction that growth was a generally desired end. A manager at Technical Products II, for example, put it this way: "We must grow in volume and ROI"; one at Commodity Products I said: "We want a high sustained growth in EPS. . . ." In other firms management's beliefs involved a specific reference to competitive standards; for example, at Technical Products III, we were told: "We must grow as fast as the industry, plus the rate of inflation." There was even one firm, Consumer Products III, in which growth was downplayed in preference to quality: "We don't have to be the biggest company in the world, but we must be the best." Again, these beliefs were reflected in the numerical goals managers set for growth. The more desirable growth seemed, the more ambitious the targets set.

Beliefs about financial goals such as these are complemented by beliefs about nonfinancial goals, which often are closely related to the managers' beliefs about both means and internal management. In fact, one of the striking characteristics of these belief systems is that the means to financial ends often become ends in themselves. For as corporate managers strive to balance the demands of their three constituencies, they come to recognize that the ends of serving the product market and the organization are legitimate and must be met if the company is to survive. Thus these beliefs provide management with a logical way to balance their relationships with their constituencies, prevent domination by these constituencies, and assure corporate survival.

The examination of a few examples can provide a flavor for how beliefs about means become ends in themselves. In Technical Products I, management was committed "to do a good job by making technically superior products." In Technical Products II, technology was also given top billing: "Our mission is technology, profit, and market [in that order]." But in this company, as in several others, the corporate managers' desire to excel was also reflected in their beliefs about goals in a more general sense. They wished "to be measured against the best. To be at the top of everything." In Consumer Products III, the belief about general purpose was even more sweeping: "We must make the world a better place for us having been here by: improving or maintaining the quality of life for employees and enhancing the quality of life for [the host community]." This commitment to excellence was also evident in the belief that "we don't have to be the biggest company in the world, but we must be the best."

It is important to emphasize the long-term perspective these beliefs reflect. In some firms managers referred directly to the importance of long-term corporate survival. Technical Products III provides an example: "We must take a long-haul view and worry about the integrity and survival of the corporation above all else." Similarly, at Consumer Products III, a closely held firm: "We must preserve the company as a private concern for the next generation." And at Commodity Products III, management's conviction was equally explicit: "We must grow at an [X percent] per annum rate to survive and get the best people."

It was unusual to find statements like that of Commodity Products III, which explicitly tied beliefs about financial goals to beliefs about other corporate ends. However, the relationship described was not at all unique. On the contrary, in every company we found an interrelationship among all these beliefs about corporate ends. Two factors account for this. One is the nature of the human mind, which seeks internal consistency in its beliefs.[2] The other is the interrelationship among the elements of the financial goals system, which is mirrored in management's beliefs about these goals.

We can demonstrate the interrelationship among beliefs about goals by examining the corporate goals at Technical Products I. While this interconnection could be seen in any of the firms studied, we have chosen this example because the company's goals were explicitly stated in its brochures.* The goals were:

1. Do a good job; make a genuine technical contribution, not just "me too" products.
2. Keep [the company] on a "pay-as-you-go" basis; grow through our own resources.
3. Make [the company] a stimulating, fun, and secure place to work.
4. Don't be a hire/fire company.
5. Make a profit to benefit the shareholders.

How these beliefs relate to one another and to the other elements of the financial goals system not explicitly mentioned can be understood by "listening" to these managers describe their convictions. A statement by the second-ranking executive in the company reflects the relative importance of these goals in management's minds:

Our most important goal is to do a good job. We don't have a specific growth target, but what we want to do is to make a contribution. Not just a "me too" thing, but to develop technically superior products. Another goal is to earn our way, to grow from our own resources. A third goal is to make this an interesting and satisfactory place to work. The fourth goal . . . there must be a fourth goal. I mentioned it also in a speech at [a nearby university]. Oh yes, the fourth goal is to make a profit.

As another senior executive explained, this did not mean that they ignored the capital market constituency:

If you take care of the other things, the shareholders get taken care of. You can grow for growth's sake and that takes care of the shareholders. You can do these other things (as we do) and not stress growth in earnings per share, per se, but the shareholders will also benefit.

*Although the explicit statement of goals was practiced in ten of these firms, their circulation to a broad group of employees and the public was unusual.

But two fundamental principles had shaped Technical Products I's direction. As another corporate manager observed: "Self-financing and stable employment have shaped the strategy and the organizational philosophy of the company."

To do a "good job" in technological innovation, talented and innovative engineers and scientists are needed. The best way to attract and hold such people, management believed, was to offer them stable employment, as other employers often did not. But retaining and motivating these skilled employees was also facilitated by growth, and the rate of growth was constrained by the no–debt tenet. Therefore, as one executive pointed out: "We say we will grow as fast as internal funds will allow. We adjust the demand for funds by deferring projects to meet the supply. When the growth of the company has slowed, we have increased the R&D expenditures to assure growth." The strength of the company's no–debt conviction was emphasized by two other corporate managers: "We are not fanatics about not borrowing. We do have standing credit lines for short-term financing"; "At one point we did have over $100 million in short-term debt. But our general attitude is, what do you do with borrowed dollars? I think most of us believe something unwise." Clearly they believed that borrowing was too risky a way to finance long–term growth. For one thing, it could threaten the stability of earnings that allowed management to meet its commitment to stable employment. For another, they felt that the refusal to borrow kept pressure on management to utilize assets effectively and thereby achieve an improved return on investment. As an executive said:

> If I list the near-term concerns, self-financing has to be high on the list. We're growing fast, and we are faced with providing cash needs at a time of growth and for investments that has caused us to say we can't afford all these things. We do short-term borrowing, but basically we don't undertake things beyond our means. It's a good discipline. It forces us to look at inventories and accounts receivable.

Even though ROI and growth targets were not assigned specific quantitative values, therefore, they were ends to be sought within the constraints of management's other beliefs. Similarly, dividends are not mentioned in the beliefs yet the beliefs have clear implications for the company's dividend policy. Given management's commitment to finance growth from retained earnings, dividends, while paid, were a secondary concern, as investors were believed to understand. Thus here, as in all these firms, top managers' beliefs about financial and nonfinancial goals fit together into a consistent and related pattern and, as we shall demonstrate, meshed with their beliefs about strategic means. This pattern determined to an important extent the decisions they made about the quantitative targets assigned to their financial goals and the choices they made about strategic means.

Beliefs About Establishing Means

As pointed out earlier, management's vision of the firm's distinctive competence is at the heart of the belief system. This is so because it defines the strategic means management will use to pursue its goals. Nowhere is this more evident than around the question of diversification. While a diversification target is an important element in the financial goals system because of its impact on the supply and demand for funds, questions about diversification also involve strategic means: what specific businesses to enter; whether such businesses should be acquired, developed internally, or both; whether the company's businesses should all be related to a common strategic focus, or whether they should be unrelated to each other. All of this obviously defines the specific product market constituency with which management chooses to engage. Beyond this, the vision and related beliefs also shape the specific means management chooses to use in relation to customers and competitors.

As corporate managers make decisions about diversification, they must address two fundamental issues. First, what is their vision of their organization's distinctive competence—and their own? Second, are the risks inherent in a venture commensurate with the financial gains to be achieved by pursuing it? For when all the market and financial studies have been completed and debated, the final choice in such matters depends on the judgments of these senior executives. As one CEO put it: "What is really needed is a clear idea of the future prospects of whatever is being proposed. It's not clear from the figures alone."

Obviously such a "clear idea of the future prospects" depends on how management assesses the future in various product markets. But it also depends on the managers' vision of their organization's unique capabilities. (See appendix D, column 2.) Convinced that their firm can successfully perform particular activities, managers perceive their options about strategic means differently than they do when they are otherwise persuaded.

To illustrate this we have compared these twelve firms across company types and within each type in terms of the extent of their diversification.*

*The diversification index is found in appendix B.

As we make this comparison, we shall also be examining managers' beliefs about how to compete within their chosen product markets as well as presenting evidence of the way in which these beliefs about means are related to those about goals. However, our focus will be on the corporate managers' vision of their company. In choosing this emphasis, we do not ignore the fact that each firm faced real environmental conditions that encouraged or constrained diversification. But we also recognize that this reality is always filtered through each corporate management's belief system.

In Conglomerate I, corporate managers believed that they could operate a wide range of businesses, and their decisions to diversify reflected and reinforced this belief. They were the most diversified among the companies (diversification index .97). But even in conglomerates, corporate managers' willingness to enter certain businesses was limited by their vision. We see this clearly in Conglomerate II (diversification index .71), even though the consensus among corporate managers about beliefs was less cohesive here than in the other companies described. Committed to continuing operations in their original business, corporate managers believed that they should "run [their] business as a conglomerate but stay out of electronics." This limitation was self-imposed, and it grew from the difficulties the company had faced several years earlier when it had tried to enter the electronics business. But other beliefs about means also reinforced the managers' conviction that this was the proper course. In contrast to Conglomerate I, where corporate managers believed they must be number one in each market to be successful, these executives believed they could succeed in industries where they did not have the leading market share. To do this, however, they had to develop superior products through research and development. While they felt that they could accomplish this in many industries, they believed it was impossible to compete with the technological strength of firms exclusively engaged in electronics.

In contrast, in Commodity Products II management was convinced that major diversification outside of the base industry was not within its distinctive competence. Thus it was the second least diversified company (diversification index .22). This vision, like the commitment to stay out of electronics at Conglomerate II, had been heavily influenced by an unsuccessful diversification attempt. To the current corporate managers, then, the lesson was clear: "No more of that. [The base industry] has been good to us and [the diversification attempt] was a fiasco." Guided by this belief as well as by their other convictions, these corporate managers developed a perspective on the future of their base industry sufficiently optimistic to make strategic decisions about capital and product development expenditures that tied their company's future exclusively to that industry.

Commodity Products I, (which had a diversification index of .36) was slightly more diversified than Commodity Products II, and its management was committed to "diversify the portfolio of business, but keep it balanced in cash flows and cash needs." Such diversification was important, top executives believed, so as not to "be too dependent upon [a particular] industry." But their vision limited diversification "to noncapital equipment," and they stayed "away from high-technology and capital-intensive products" because they believed that their company lacked the capacity to succeed in such industries.

Like Conglomerate II, Commodity Products III was a company in which there was less consensus of beliefs. Corporate managers shared a conviction that success in the core industry was essential. However, a strong minority also believed that some diversification was necessary to meet the company's growth and return-on-investment objectives. With a diversification index of .40 it was more diversified than the other two commodity products companies; but the diversification had to be consistent with management's vision of the company's basic strengths—"manufacturing and distribution." As one executive said in discussing an acquisition: "We weren't frightened of their business. [Commodity Products III] is a manufacturer with marketing and distribution expertise. It's the biggest in the field. It has the contacts. It knows the key wholesalers in the country and provides them with products. . . . These managers had made several acquisitions, all related to this vision, and the company was more diversified than many of its competitors in its base industry.

Consumer Products III provides yet another example of how corporate management's beliefs shape diversification decisions. Here the executives' belief that they were skilled at marketing branded consumer products, combined with their belief that the company had to grow for the next generation, led them to a modest degree of diversification (diversification index .48). To support a series of new consumer-product businesses, Consumer Products II was following a very similar, if slightly wider, diversification strategy (diversification index .51). In this instance, however, corporate managers believed that diversification was necessary to achieve growth and earnings stability, but that diversification had to be consistent with their belief that the company's strength also lay in branded consumer products. Relying on this vision, these managers had recently divested a major, nonconsumer business with which "they were not comfortable."

In marked contrast to their counterparts in the other two consumer products companies, the corporate managers at Consumer Products I did not believe in product diversification, and they were the least diversified of the twelve companies (diversification index .12). Their vision told them that they could manufacture and market a superior product to consumers *around the world*. While Consumer Products II and III were diversifying their product lines within the United States, therefore, these corporate managers had decided to compete with a single product on a worldwide basis.

Interestingly, Consumer Products IV, with a diversification index of .32, offers yet another perspective. Throughout its early history, this firm had grown by expanding its American consumer business, by selling its raw material to other domestic industrial users, and by expanding its consumer products and industrial business overseas. Corporate executives believed that their goals could best be met by sustaining the current balance between consumer and industrial, United States and international business. Their motto was the "pursuit of our basic strengths." As a result, they were opposed to any further diversification. Over the past decade the company had made only one acquisition, another branded consumer product. Current managers saw this decision as a clear departure from tradition. It had been consummated at a transition point, when one CEO was giving way to another, and the current CEO felt he had no choice but to approve it, since his predecessor, urged by several other corporate managers, had committed to make it.

In contrast to their peers in the other types of companies, none of the technical products executives was very committed to acquisition as a strategic means. In fact, there was unanimity on the subject of diversification across all three companies. Management believed in expanding its business base as long as such expansion could be brought about through the basic technological strengths that were its organization's distinctive competence. Even the rare acquisition had to build on this strength. As an executive in Technical Products III put it: "The research laboratories are the heart of our company. When you gamble on technology, you are always convinced that the next breakthrough is just around the corner, and this is a motivation for pursuing investment sometimes beyond what seems like reasonable limits in retrospect." Given such a vision, the only limit on diversification was the company's ability to develop its technological strengths profitably. These three companies ranged in diversification from .42 (Technical Products I) to .58 and .59 (Technical Products III and II, respectively). This range was partially the result of the possibilities for new products inherent in the technology in which each had its strength. But it also reflected the beliefs each management held about the best means of using its technological competence in relation to its product market constituency.

In Technical Products I, management believed that it was important to "compete with many unique products." This meant that the company should "innovate in bite sizes" and that each innovation should be based on relatively small, up-front expenditures. This practice was consistent with the managers' belief in financing growth without long-term debt. It was also consistent with their conviction that their organization's greatest strength rested in technology: "Be innovative in technology but conservative in marketing." Technologically innovative products directed at smaller market opportunities built on this perceived strength. They also enabled the company to avoid confrontations with competitors with greater marketing strength.

The top management at Technical Products II held somewhat different beliefs. While these executives also believed that their competence lay in technological innovation, they aimed to "develop unique technical solutions to large market needs, or . . . find the large market to fit the technology." Thus they believed in major long-term research and development efforts. They "bet on the long ball." Further, while the managers of Technical Products I preferred a market position in which their technology would give them a long-term competitive advantage ("compete with many unique products," "don't buy a market share," "products should show a profit from the start"), Technical Products II's managers believed in seeking high-volume customers so that they could reduce manufacturing costs, even if this involved profit sacrifices in the near term. According to one: "After solving the technical problems for high-volume users, we must work down the learning curve and keep others from integrating backward."

At Technical Products III, the senior managers held beliefs very similar to those in Technical Products II. They were committed to "follow new technology and stick with potentially big technological breakthroughs." They believed in introducing a new product to gain market leadership at the outset, even if this meant losing money initially: "Get the strongest leadership position in each business and hold it even in the short run." And they also held the conviction that product costs had to be reduced to make money, even when the product reached a mature state. In the words of one executive: "Today one must ride technology-based products longer rather than letting competition have it as soon as it becomes commoditylike."

A closer examination of the belief systems in Consumer Products II and Commodity Products II illustrates more fully how beliefs affect corporate managers' thinking about diversification in particular and means in general. Presented with a similar possibility, the two managements responded quite differently. Thus they provide an interesting contrast of the way in which beliefs shape strategic means.

As just pointed out, Consumer Products II was among the more diversified of the companies, while Commodity Products II was the second least diversified. At Consumer Products II, top management placed a high value on earnings stability in all phases of the economic cycle as well as on growth. As one executive noted, "We are trying to construct a strategy where we are an all-weather growth company."

But management also had convictions about how it wished to achieve these objectives: "We decided we didn't want to be a conglomerate. Why not? We wanted to have a strategy people could identify with and understand. If our strategy is to grow, you look for growth opportunities. The things we were in that got divested were not rewarding, not growing, or not in a good position." Not wanting to be a "conglomerate" stemmed from a desire to build commitment in the organizational constituency. But it also meant that top management had to develop a concept of what types of product markets the company could deal with. This choice was directly related to the managers' vision about the firm's distinctive competence. As one top manager remembered: "We said our real know-how was marketing consumer goods on which a brand could be created—things that evolved around the homemaker and the family. We knew how to communicate to them." Decisions to acquire new ventures had to be consistent with this principle. Therefore, as a second executive explained: "The [acquired] business was seen as a good adjunct to our [core] business. There was a certain comfort level for us. Also it seemed an exciting business at the time."

But management's vision of the firm's distinctive competence also limited its choices insofar as it indicated opportunities that did not seem appropriate. One executive put it this way: "We're more comfortable with U.S. expansion rather than international. We've not been successful buying companies overseas. There's not a commitment to growing a part of our business overseas."

Together these beliefs led to a strategy best summarized as stable but growing earnings through expansion into U.S. consumer products businesses. The specific means top executives chose to accomplish this strategy were also based on their convictions. Acquisitions were felt to be the best way, but they had to have certain characteristics, as this manager told us: "Our philosophy was to get a little one and make it big with the same management. We'd anchor them in with an incentive compensation plan." Further, only certain types of acquisitions made sense, as one of his colleagues explained:

—Get into consumer versus industrial.
—We must see substantial growth potential.
—Our management must be comfortable with it—consumer and marketing is a significant way of doing business for us.
—We want to be fully competitive. We are not anxious to be number five or six.
—We wanted strong continuous management, not turnaround situations. This has worked well for us, by the way.
—We wanted to be able to use our cash flows and leverage. In other words, we would just finance the growth and add a few controls.

Finally, management was convinced that success depended on its willingness to divest businesses that were not making the desired contribution and/or did not fit its vision. Two executives pointed this out: "We're willing to get out of businesses that are not successful. You must keep yourself current by getting out of things as quickly as you can"; "The parts of the company fit a long-term strategy. If it doesn't, it becomes a candidate for divestiture." In this company, then, management's beliefs about financial goals included beliefs about the desirability of diversification. But to be a feasible option, this diversification effort had to be consistent with management's vision of the company's competence.

At Commodity Products II there was a similarly close relationship between beliefs about goals and company capabilities, but these beliefs were a marked contrast to those at Consumer Products II. In the commodity-products company, management's central tenet was to "be the strongest, top-ranked participant in the [industry]." As one senior executive put it:

Our goal here is to stay in [our industry] and not make any major diversification out of it. We survived the fiasco in [our one diversification attempt], but we're reluctant to look at diversification again. Although I might argue that if we are going to diversify, we should do it now when we really don't have to and not

93

wait until we're pushed into it. Now we are emphasizing diversifying our line in our basic products somewhat.

Having failed several years earlier in one attempt to diversify through acquisition, these corporate managers were now convinced that they should stay in their industry and be the best. But staying in their industry was a tenet derived from historical forces that predated this one failure. Two managers expressed this fact slightly differently:

> The guys were [core-industry] oriented. They never were dedicated to making the [acquisition] work. We didn't put any substantial effort into it. We really couldn't. We were too lean. We didn't have the time.

> We thought we were getting into a good industry when we got into the [acquisition]. It wasn't all of our own doing, but we should have been smart enough to see it. In our company there has been a strong sentiment toward [the industry] for many years. It's been good to us, so one of the things we've decided is we aren't smart enough to do well in industries which don't fit our capabilities: to do engineering, to move large amounts of materials, to know our customers. Our problem is to try to figure out where we can go from there. We could go into [raw materials] and have just done so.

Thus management's commitment to no diversification was clearly tied to its vision of the company's distinctive competence—"to do engineering, to move large amounts of materials, to know our customers."

This vision also tied the company to the risks of a single product market. Top executives had to accept its cyclicality, its growth rate, and the returns on investment possible in it. Further, to be the best required improved manufacturing facilities. Thus they also believed in maintaining a level of long-term debt sufficient to improve their plants and to achieve the low-cost, high-quality products and services they felt were necessary to achieve top rank in the industry. In fact, as this manager explained, the importance of these capital programs was another reason for not diversifying: "We are not looking to expand at this time out of [the industry]. One of the reasons is we have enough capital programs on the horizon. We have another capital program on the horizon as big as the one we are finishing. We have to get this done to be the best in our industry."

Not surprisingly, several of these executives were critical of their competitors who were diversifying out of the industry instead of investing in it. They felt that their capital program would give them a competitive edge.

For example, one said: "What [the number-one company in the industry] is doing by not investing in new plants suggests to us that we are going to be an ever-growing factor in the industry over the next years and they are going to be less so."

Finally, commitment to their industry meant that these corporate managers, unlike their counterparts in the more diversified companies, were quite involved in product market decisions.* They were firmly convinced that they knew how to succeed with this constituency. Several executives described these fundamental beliefs:

> Our strategy has been to offer service superior to the competition, which is really quality and delivery. We have skills to grow with our major customers.

> Customers give business to those who are expanding in the industry. We are able to run more efficiently than our competitors because of our better computer systems. We have all kinds of systems, and we have as a result more stable relations with the customers who pay our prices. We do not cut our prices like our competitors. They pay our prices because we are a reliable supplier and have done as much as anyone in the industry to develop new products. We think of ourselves as a dynamic young company with young, dynamic managers who are going to burn up the roads.

> The relations between manufacturing and sales are really bottom-line oriented. But you've got to maintain penetration [share of market] because the volume leverage is so big. You get these as a base; then upgrade profitability.

> The variable I watch is penetration. We also watch ROI and contribution margin. However, if you go too far in penetration, your price structure goes to hell, and you lose money. But if we know we have good costs and are a strong seller with little discounting, it's axiomatic that with good market share we'll have the best profits.

> We are insulated from foreign competition by our location. We are so far away from their source of supply. We have the largest plants in the U.S. Therefore we must be efficient. We also have better relations between the sales end of our business and manufacturing. Our biggest plants are in the best markets in the world.

As the last comment indicates, this management found several other reasons to support its commitment to its industry and its narrow strategic focus.

---

*In fact, one can make the generalization that the more diversified the company, the less corporate managers become involved in decisions about how to compete in a particular product market. They simply do not have the time, information, or experience to do so.

The executives believed that their geographic location gave them a unique competitive advantage, and they perceived a similar source of strength in the good working relationship between their sales force and their manufacturing people. Their beliefs about internal management were intertwined with their convictions about competitive means and financial goals.

Beliefs About Internal Management

Just as top managers' beliefs about strategic means importantly shaped the nature of their product market constituency and their ways to deal with it, so their beliefs about internal management shaped the decisions that dealt with the organizational constituency: how to keep their employees committed, motivated, and loyal; and how best to utilize their talents.

On specific issues of internal management, particular convictions varied considerably. Illustrating this is the extent to which—and when—subordinates were involved in decisions. We found the strongest commitment to delegation in the more diversified firms and the high-technology companies.

Technical Products I:	We are all one big interactive team of 40,000 people.
Technical Products II:	Compensation alone won't build commitment. It takes management team building.
Technical Products III:	Don't shove targets down people's throats. Leave initiative with the bottom. Let top management respond to what people say.
Conglomerate I:	We allow divisional autonomy except in control of cash flows.
Conglomerate II:	People have identified with their individual businesses. It's hard to build a corporate identity.
Consumer Products II:	We believe in a lot of participation in planning. We want each operating manager to sponsor his own effort.
Commodity Products I:	We must be willing to delegate responsibility to separate businesses. We allow managers to act and don't overcontrol.

In these companies corporate managers were overseeing businesses in rapidly changing environments and/or a variety of industries. Therefore they believed it necessary to permit such delegation, because the information relevant to make specific product market decisions existed at lower managerial levels.[3] This fact points up an interesting characteristic of the two conglomerates. As Conglomerate II's statement suggests, there seemed to be more disparate beliefs at the divisional level in the two conglomerates than in the other firms. Allowing such heterogeneity of beliefs may have been an important reason for their success with diverse product market constituencies.

Corporate managers in the companies with more stable or less diverse businesses believed less strongly in delegation. Some, such as the executives in Consumer Products I and III, were silent on the issue. In Consumer Products IV, managers believed that major decisions should be left to the CEO. And in Commodity Products II and III, the dominant theme was to "keep the managers in the [basic industry] happy." In practice this meant that while corporate managers did not delegate as many major decisions, even about product and market issues, they did recognize the necessity to make decisions that would keep this important part of their organizational constituency satisfied.

Given this particular pattern of decision making, it is interesting to note that in both these commodity products companies, members of senior management had had extensive experience in the core industry. They had the experience to make such choices. In fact, at Commodity Products II there was even an explicit conviction that "top management must include one person who understands manufacturing operations and processes."

Corporate managers also had strong beliefs about what psychological contract it was appropriate to enter into with subordinate managers and other employees. Here too the different companies had different views. In two companies the beliefs centered on the importance of security and stable employment:

Technical Products III:	We believe in hiring the best people and keeping them. We don't believe in firing a manager if he makes a mistake.
Consumer Products I:	Stability [of employment] is a basic employee right. We get good people and keep them.

In two other companies, the beliefs emphasized the creation of a stimulating and challenging work environment through growth:

97

| Consumer Products II: | We need growth opportunities to attract good managers. |
| Conglomerate I: | We want to create an exciting environment for management by growing. |

In three companies, managers were convinced that their organizational constituency wanted a mix of growth and stability:

Technical Products I:	We are not a hire/fire company. We grow to give people a challenge.
Technical Products II:	People [in the local city] have few alternatives for places to work, and therefore should be isolated from some employment fluctuation. People wish to grow with stable careers.
Consumer Products III:	We believe in womb-to-tomb security. Growth is necessary to provide opportunities for employees.

Despite these variations among the firms, in each company corporate managers' beliefs affected the way in which they thought about internal management issues and their relationship to strategic choices. Where employment security was the dominant belief, more attention was paid to stability of earnings and less to growth. Where growth was the major theme, it was emphasized in goal setting. In those companies where employees were believed to want both, the financial goals system had to be balanced accordingly. But all these decisions were derived from a common premise held by the top managers in most of these companies about the importance of the organizational constituency.

Technical Products I:	We don't have holes in the ground that gush oil. Our major resource is our people.
Technical Products II:	I have blind faith in our technical people. . . . We are betting on people. You put the people where you need them to accomplish the results you want.
Consumer Products III:	[The CEO] has come down pretty hard on the good life for the employee.
Commodity Products I:	[The company's] first responsibility is not to the shareholder but to the employees.

Consumer Products II:	We want to grow not only for the shareholders but ourselves as well. If we disappoint the shareholders, we're in trouble fundamentally, but we work for ourselves. We work for the internal dynamics.
Technical Products III:	The primary concern of our managers must be the well-being of their people.

One could argue that such statements are merely lip service to the organizational constituency, or public relations "puff." However, our interviews with these corporate managers revealed a strong commitment to these premises. In addition, four of these companies had no unions and their managements were committed to remaining nonunion.* As has been pointed out, companies that are not unionized have managements strongly committed to recognizing employee interests in their decisions.[4] Such a commitment reduces the employees' needs for the protection of a union. That four of the companies had no unions, therefore, and that a fifth was a leader in encouraging improved union-management relations in its industry, provides supporting evidence that these top managers believed in meeting the expectations of the organizational constituency. Of course, this belief in meeting employee expectations, and thus staying free of unions, is also evidence that these managers believed strongly enough in self-sufficiency to want to prevent any involvement by a formal bargaining agent.

Belief Systems and Strategic Decisions

By now it is obvious that there is an interrelated pattern or system to the beliefs in each company. What top managers believe about one aspect of their work is related to what they believe about other aspects. This belief system provides corporate managers with a framework for thinking about the complex and uncertain choices they must make as they balance the often conflicting demands of their three constituencies. It defines implicitly the distinctive competence of their company, the corporate risks they should take, and the degree of self-sufficiency that is desirable. Thus it sets important limits on the strategic choices these managers are willing to make.

Because they have their beliefs to guide them, corporate managers rarely focus explicitly on these larger issues in the course of their day-to-day activities. More typically, they make specific decisions that, when added together

---

*When we selected the companies for this study, no attention was given to whether their work forces were unionized or not. Our only aim was to select mature, successful companies.

over time, reflect their strategic intent.[5] Therefore, we shall now examine a specific decision in each of four companies and illustrate how it was shaped by top management's beliefs. As we do, we shall stress again the systemic quality of these beliefs, because it is this interrelated wholeness that creates such a powerful psychological constraint on top management's specific choices.

Although we could illustrate the way in which belief systems affect specific decisions in every company studied, for the sake of brevity we have focused on four that are representative of the type, ownership, and diversity of all twelve (see table 5.2).

Consumer Products III

Many years ago, the research and development personnel at Consumer Products III had come forward with a new consumer product. Corporate managers decided to launch the product nationally, even though it was in a different category from their traditional products, with a different application and different distribution channels. Moreover, over almost a decade they made a series of decisions to stick with the product until it achieved the market leadership position they had initially hoped to claim within six months. Why were they so patient?

Their tenacity can only be understood in terms of their belief system. Central to it was their dedication to preserving the company as a privately owned entity that would be viable for the family's next generation. Related to this dominant goal was the executives' conviction that the firm must continue to grow. Growth was seen as important to maintain a vital company and to provide opportunities for employees, including younger members of the family if they joined the management. But growth also required just such a new product, as the demand for their traditional products had softened.

TABLE 5.2

Representative Companies

Company	Diversity Index[a]	Ownership
Consumer Products III	.48	Privately held
Technical Products II	.59	Publicly held with family control
Commodity Products II	.22	Widely held
Conglomerate I	.97	Widely held

[a]Lower number indicates less diversity.

Consequently management was ready to commit to the new product to "spread the risk" and "leave something for the next generation."

The particular new product was consistent with management's vision of the company's distinctive competence in consumer marketing. Furthermore, the product had the "high gross margins" the executives wanted, and initially they thought it could be "launch[ed] for leadership in six months." Such a market share, they believed, would lead to the higher profits necessary to maintain dividends.

This last requirement, of course, was not actually met, but top managers chose to be patient for several reasons. First, they could take time as long as the company was profitable enough to support a commitment to keep the family happy. (Some family members who owned stock were not active in management, and they expected current dividend income.) Long-term debt was acceptable to finance diversification or other expansion, but it was carefully held below a certain level to "keep free of any bank restrictions." Obviously this policy tended to limit growth (as did the company's dividend payouts). But it also meant that management was self-sufficient from the capital market constituency. As a result, the company could stick with a loser, such as this product, as long as other sources of funds provided dividends in the short term.

Moreover, the product was very much the sort in which management had faith. It had true "product pluses," providing consumers with characteristics superior to those of the competitors. And it was "a good, clean, healthy product," fully in keeping with management's commitment to avoid unhealthy products or industries with a reputation for dishonest dealings. Thus the product itself also played directly into management's desire to be "the best."

This desire to be the best extended well beyond the company's commitment to engage in "only good, clean, honest businesses." It was related to the managers' concern for enhancing the life of the "host communities" in which the company operated. It was also related to their commitment to maintain or improve the quality of life for the organizational constituency. Thus being the best meant being people-oriented and providing career opportunities and security for management and employees, and the quality of life included high pay and profit sharing.

Perhaps most relevant here, however, was management's conviction that the best do not admit defeat. They work until they succeed. Or, as the executives admonished themselves, do not "abandon losers [either products or geographic markets]. Stay with them until they become winners." This they did by committing marketing effort and money to this product and by investing in further research and development over several years until other, compatible products could be put on the market. These other products, and the marketing effort on the original one, so enhanced the original product's position with the trade and consumers that it gradually gained the leadership position corporate management sought.

In effect, then, these corporate managers were making a stream of decisions, over almost ten years, about staying with this new product. Their decisions were heavily influenced by a number of their beliefs: in their organization's competence to make the product successful; that the risks inherent in doing so were necessary for the survival of the company; and that this venture would not adversely affect the company's self-sufficiency in the shorter term. Indeed, this corporate management was committed as strongly as any firm studied to being self-sufficient in order to assure company survival. The executives believed in maintaining private ownership, limiting long-term debt, and remaining free of unions. They were willing to take risks to accomplish their financial goals as long as these risks did not reduce their self-sufficiency or violate their vision of the firm's distinctive competence. Taking such risks was necessary to be "the best" company they believed they should be.

Technical Products II

From the CEO of a large customer, two Technical Products II executives learned about his firm's need for a new type of material. They knew that their scientists had already invented a substance with most of the desired characteristics. However, major technical problems remained, including very complex processing ones. If the scientists and their engineering colleagues could solve these, the corporate executives felt that they could obtain the business of this large customer as well as that of other customers in the industry.

Over a period of several weeks these two executives discussed the opportunity with each other and with their colleagues. Finally one of the two, who had extensive research-and-development experience, went on a trip with his firm's CEO. He told the story this way:

> We were caught in this big snowstorm. I was stuck in my hotel room so I was thinking about this, and I walked over to [the CEO's] room. I told him I wanted to go at it [the name of the prior president's] style. He asked me what that style

was. I said, "hammer and tongs," and he said, "Go to it." So we did. At one point we had 25 percent of our lab working on it. We took five or six different approaches and started working on it.

This effort continued for over a year. When asked how much money was spent on the effort, this same executive smiled and said: "I couldn't tell you. I have no idea. The critical resource in such an undertaking isn't dollars. It's your technical people." Eventually this crash program succeeded. The company was rewarded with a major new business serving a number of large customers in a major industry. Why had these managers been willing to take the risk?

Once again the corporate belief system helps us to understand their logic. At Technical Products II, if top management's goal was not so ambitious as to be the best company, it was "to be measured against the best" and to "be at the top" in all measures. For these managers, this meant growth in size and improving return on investment. But if a choice had to be made between current return and future earnings, they believed that they "should run the company for exotic future growth." This research-and-development effort could lead to such growth, and it promised a substantial return on investment.

The effort was also consistent with their premise that "their mission was technology, first and foremost, then profits, and then market performance." And the program fit their vision of their distinctive competence: "Technology is our driving force in fact and in perception. Pay-off will come from invention." While they already had developed the basic invention, they believed their technical people could solve the complex problems that remained.

The particular product was also appealing because it met another related belief: any invention should be suitable for high-volume customers. With a market potential of several major industrial customers, the product could give management the opportunity to establish a major market share and "then work down the learning curve," discouraging both backward integration by customers and market entry by competitors.

Making such a commitment of research-and-development personnel was also consistent with another tenet—"bet on the long ball," or take big technological risks. To do this the executives believed the critical resource-allocation question was "how to use good people effectively." These "good people" would be stimulated by the technological challenge and also rewarded by the growth of the new product, which would provide stable employment in a community where job opportunities were limited.

All this might sound as if this were an easy and obvious choice. However, other convictions made these managers weigh their decisions carefully. They believed that the commitment to growth through technology could lead to too much earnings instability. While they hoped the new product would succeed and lead to increased earnings stability, they wanted to protect themselves against failure "by being masters of our own fate." To maintain this self-sufficiency, they chose a conservative financial policy—"we want plenty of excess debt capacity and liquidity reserves," and "there are not more good opportunities than we have generated funds internally." Thus the decision to go ahead with this program meant that they might have to postpone or ignore other opportunities.

It is impossible to compare in any precise sense the beliefs of these executives with those of their peers in Consumer Products III in terms of self-sufficiency, risk, and distinctive competence. We lack the quantitatively calibrated scales for such a comparison. Yet our description suggests several interesting similarities and differences. Although both groups were convinced that self-sufficiency was important, the executives in Consumer Products III were most strongly committed to this principle because of their company's private ownership. Apropos of risk, at first glance it might appear that the executives in Technical Products II were more risk-prone. But the specific examples described suggest why we must be cautious of such generalizations. From the point of view of the Consumer Products III executives, the risks they were taking, in diversifying and marketing new consumer products, were consistent with their vision of their organization's distinctive competence. Similarly, from the perspective of the Technical Products II managers, making a major commitment to research and development was not unduly risky. Such decisions were quite consistent with their beliefs about the competence of their organization.

Commodity Products II

At a time when their major competitors were engaged in diversification, top management at Commodity Products II strengthened its commitment to its industry. Managers there decided to invest several hundred million dollars to improve manufacturing facilities. The investment was designed to make one of their major facilities "the most efficient and low-cost source of supply in the country" and "keep large, major customers happy." Why did they choose to follow this course?

Central to these managers' decision was their vision, described earlier, of the company as a single industry, first, last, and always. Others might argue that in an industry with intense competition, low profit margins, and a history of cyclical demand, this was indeed a very risky strategy. But given the interrelated beliefs of the Commodity Products II managers, this commitment was reasonable and appropriate. They believed that in this way they could not only perpetuate the company but also perform favorably. They could be both "the strongest, top-ranked participant" in their industry and "in the upper one-third of all manufacturing concerns."

To be successful in the industry meant having a strong management, including in top management a person who had come up through plant operations. Such a person understood the firm's technology and employees and had credibility with the employees who also believed in the industry. Together these practices would provide the best management in the industry, though not one that was capable of diversification.

Commodity Products II's top managers also believed their goals were attainable because of their convictions about their product market position (described earlier) and their ability to capitalize on it. Central here was the conviction that their geographic locations gave them a definite cost advantage over competitors. From this flowed a series of corollary beliefs, one of which was the need for a constant effort to improve profit position through cost reductions. This belief enabled them to set competitive prices as a basis for gaining market share. However, they also believed that it was necessary to offer customers better service than the competition, in both delivery and quality. Better customer service was also related to another conviction about internal management, the need to achieve "good coordination between manufacturing and sales," to serve customers better than their competitors and avoid competing solely on a price basis.

All these beliefs led to a commitment to continuing process and product innovation, requiring major capital commitment for plant modernization, and hence to their specific decision. To finance this program these executives believed in long-term borrowing. But they also believed it important to maintain a high credit rating, to provide a debt reserve as a contingency in their cyclical industry. The importance of maintaining and, when possible, improving dividend payout to shareholders was another important convic-

105

tion, for they felt that their public shareholders expected such dividends from them. In essence, they believed that the capital market constituency thought of their common stock as a fixed income security.

Given these executives' beliefs about product market issues and internal management, their commitment to their goals represented an acceptable risk. "Fostering harmony and preserving a family feeling through all levels of employment" would give them the strongest management (and employees) in the industry. Important members of this family were the unionized skilled workers in their plants, whose commitment to the company the managers saw as critical to success. They also believed that there was a drama to their industry, which stimulated an emotional attachment among managers and employees. To keep those employees happy, they practiced nondiscriminatory hiring, higher than average for the industry, and placed a strong emphasis on employee stock ownership. Consistent with the mature nature of their single industry, these executives believed in minimizing interference from organized labor by seeking harmonious relations with the union.

By comparing the belief system of these executives with those previously described, we see that the executives in Commodity Products II were less committed to self-sufficiency than their peers in Technical Products II or Consumer Products III. They were less concerned about interference from "bankers," and they were willing to undertake the long-term debt necessary for plant expansion and modernization. Their belief in the importance of dividends to their shareholders led them to feel that they would be under no pressure from this constituency as long as dividends were acceptable. And if they were growing by gaining market share and earning a return better than others in the industry, they could sustain the dividend payout to their institutional and individual investors.

When they assessed risk, these executives acted in a manner comparable to that of the top managers in the other two companies. Management in all three firms was convinced that in making a specific choice it was taking risks appropriate to the rest of its beliefs about goals and means, including—most important—its vision of the distinctive competence of its organization. However, the executives in Commodity Products II had a narrower view of their own and their subordinates' abilities than did their peers. They believed that they were only good at managing in one industry. Their beliefs provide an interesting contrast with those of the corporate managers at Conglomerate I, the most diversified of the companies.

Conglomerate I

At a time prior to our study the top managers of Conglomerate I were engaged in the final stages of negotiating the acquisition of a company in a business unrelated to their existing ones. The discussion leading to the decision to acquire focused primarily on the new company's position in its industry and whether it would enhance Conglomerate I's earnings picture. As the managers decided to go ahead, no mention was made of their own lack of experience in the business to be acquired. In fact, over a period of several decades, the company had completely diversified out of its original industry. This process had been the result of numerous acquisition decisions. What was the framework of beliefs in which an acquisition decision was made?

Once again the executives' belief system must be examined to understand their reasoning. Here, however, we will begin with their vision of their organization's distinctive competence, the belief that they could manage successfully in "a wide range of industries." Thus the new company's specific industry was not a major issue. They had the managerial capability to succeed. Through such managerial talent, they felt, they could achieve a higher return on equity than "the better *Fortune* 500 companies" and also attain an above-average growth in earnings and dividends as compared to these same companies.

That the new acquisition added to the company's wide range of businesses was desirable because this diversity provided "a stream of opportunities to be exploited." These, in turn, led to the "stable earnings and capital base" management sought. However, the executives' concern went well beyond the shareholders who would benefit from these financial goals. They also believed that "employees, customers, and society in general" would benefit through "superior performance based on products and service of excellence." And they looked to their growth goals to create "an exciting environment for management" (i.e., themselves and their subordinates). Thus they identified their priorities as "people development, internal growth, and expansion into new areas of opportunity," in that order.

This emphasis on people development is related to the central conviction of the corporate managers at Conglomerate I that their managers "can (and must) successfully operate businesses in a wide range of industries." To do this, it was important to "allow divisions autonomy." However, they constrained such autonomy in the area of cash flows. They believed that corporate management control was necessary there to utilize financial resources most effectively and to balance the financial goals system.

Similarly, management was committed to allowing "each division [to] compete in whatever way is best for it." But top executives also held firm beliefs about the means to be used in this competition among their numerous industries. They looked for "excellence in products and services" in all businesses. They also believed it important to be "dominant in each market segment." To this end, they wanted to be "the most efficient producer" in each industry. The new acquisition met these criteria. Interestingly, they rejected as inappropriate the recommendation of some strategic planning consultants that they label businesses "dogs" or "cash cows." They believed that such an approach could lead to underinvesting in businesses that could be made profitable. Instead they were convinced that it was corporate management's job to allocate funds among divisions.

Compared to the managers in the other three companies just described, these conglomerate executives showed less concern for self-sufficiency. They believed in issuing equity and borrowing to finance acquisitions and internal growth. But they were similar to their counterparts in that they were implicitly convinced that the risks in being involved in many industries were acceptable, given their vision of distinctive competence. Thus they were led to pursue a strategy that carried them into new and disparate industries.

Such visions of their company's capabilities are central to each corporate management's belief system. Moreover, this vision, with all the managers' other interrelated beliefs, becomes an important psychological commitment in its own right as corporate managers make their choices. Their decisions about strategic ends and means, as well as their internal management practices, are subtly shaped by the interrelated fabric of these beliefs, so that all their choices will be consistent both with their vision and with their convictions about risk and self-sufficiency.

Several years ago Thomas Watson of IBM recognized the importance of beliefs in guiding successful corporations.

> Consider any great organization—one that has lasted over the years, and I think you will find that it owed its resiliency not to its form of organization or administrative skills, but to the power of what we call beliefs and the appeal these beliefs have to provide.
>
> This, then, is my thesis: I firmly believe that any organization, in order to survive and achieve success, must have a sound set of beliefs on which it premises all its policies and actions.

Next, I believe that the most important single factor in the corporate success is faithful adherence to those beliefs.

And, finally, I believe that if an organization is to meet the challenges of a changing world, it must be prepared to change everything about itself except these beliefs as it moves through corporate life.

In other words, the basic philosophy, spirit and drive of the organization have far more to do with its relative achievements than do technological or economic resources, organizational structure, innovation and timing. All these things weigh heavily in success, but they are, I think, transcended by how strongly the people in the organization believe in its basic precepts and how faithfully they carry them out.[6]

Our findings offer strong confirmation of Watson's basic argument; but we must differ in one important aspect. In the italicized passage, Watson argues that beliefs must not be changed "to meet the challenges of a changing world." We feel otherwise. Because beliefs are such powerful constraints on management's choices, they must change to deal with a changing economic reality. In the following chapters, we shall expand upon this point, first by studying the forces that create stability in the belief system, then by examining the forces that lead to changes in beliefs and fewer constraints on corporate management's strategic decisions.

CHAPTER 6

Maintaining
Strategic Equilibrium

In the fall of 1978, the chief executive of an industrial products company faced a serious dilemma. One of his divisional presidents had proposed a major marketing program and a related plant expansion to support the introduction of a significant new product. Both the product and the proposed marketing methods were new to the CEO and his corporate management colleagues. Moreover, they were uncomfortable with the proposal, even though the information supporting it looked promising, because it did not mesh with their vision of the company's distinctive competence. Yet the divisional president who was its chief proponent had been brought into the company several years earlier to stimulate the development of just such products. This proposal represented painstaking work on the part of the divisional president and his subordinates. Refusal by top management would be a major blow to them.

After much discussion with his colleagues, the chief executive decided not to approve the proposal: it was simply too foreign to their beliefs about their company. Due to this disappointment, the divisional president resigned within a few months. So did his two key subordinates.

As this example illustrates, corporate managers have a deep emotional commitment to their beliefs. To them these beliefs represent the "right" choices to make. They are the "correct" way to view the external environment and their organization. Most of these executives are strongly attached, almost religiously devoted, to their beliefs. Moreover, these emotional convictions shape in important ways the pattern of decisions that are labeled corporate strategy. Hence it is not altogether surprising that beliefs and corporate strategy are closely intertwined—at times almost indistinguishably so. On one hand, the belief system has an important impact on management's strategic choices; on the other, the results of past strategic choices are an important source of corporate management's current beliefs, as shall be seen.

Nevertheless, beliefs and corporate strategy are not identical, nor should they be treated as such unless management is willing to risk the strong possibility that its strategy will be the captive of its beliefs—a dangerous course for those committed, as these managers are, to corporate survival. Successful strategies must recognize the objective constraints of the environment as well as the psychological contraints that exist within the firm. They must enable managers to appraise their world and themselves accurately.

During the decade prior to this study, most of these companies followed strategies that were successful in this regard. Moreover, those strategies were themselves in a state of dynamic equilibrium. The direction of particular decisions could and did shift slightly, as external conditions warranted. But over time in most of the twelve companies being considered there was a remarkable stability to management's choices. The reason for this stability is deceptively simple: the strategies worked. They allowed management to respond appropriately to changes in the economic and financial constraints under which the firm operated. They also allowed the executives to modify their beliefs through incremental changes that could alter one tenet of the belief system without destroying its basic fabric.[1]

To understand why these managers were able to pursue such strategies, we shall look first at the financial and economic conditions that promote stability through their effect on the firm's financial goals system. Then we shall return to the subject of corporate beliefs to examine their origins as well as the way in which they are transmitted from one generation of managers to the next. Finally we shall discuss why these managers become so strongly attached to their beliefs.

When Financial and Economic Constraints
Promote Stability

Under certain circumstances, the firm's real economic and financial constraints perpetuate stability in the financial goals system that is central to corporate strategy. The first such circumstance occurs when the composition and objectives of management's three primary constituencies remain constant over time. If the existing financial goals system truly represents a balanced response to each constituency's minimum acceptable requirements for continued participation in the enterprise, then external pressure for change is not likely to develop in the absence of some fundamental change in the constituencies themselves.

In the twelve firms studied, such stability was typically the case. The basic characteristics of groups of shareholders, lenders, customers, competitors, and employees tended to change slowly or not at all over the customary five-year planning horizon. In part this continuity was a matter of management perception, for the concept of "loyalty" implies constancy, and, in some degree, management could choose those shareholders or customers or competitors to whom it wished to be responsive. But it is also objectively true that sudden major shifts in institutional affiliations are unusual. Most of the time stability is in everyone's interest. If management has read its environment accurately, therefore, it can harmonize its corporate goals and strategy with that environment's inherent stability.

The requirements of a closed or internal capital market also foster stability and continuity in the financial goals system. As has been seen, such a capital market requires that demand- and supply-related goals be in reasonable balance and that the resultant performance be consistent with this plan—that is, that there be neither a persistent deficit nor surplus of funds. In practice, a balance in actual funds-flow performance may exist and fail to coincide with the balance targeted by the goals system: the goals may anticipate a higher or lower level of performance. However, only if it reflects a persistent deficit in the flow of funds will this gap represent a serious challenge to management's stated goals. Such an event is likely to pose the most serious threat to the stability of existing goals and strategy; but smaller or less frequent failures are acceptable because the firm's "reach should always exceed [its] grasp" by some margin.

Continuity in the condition of the economies and industries in which the firm operates is a third factor conducive to stability in the goals system. Goals reflect expectations, and expectations depend on a perception of what is attainable. Absent clear signals to the contrary, the longer a given business climate persists, the stronger the commitment to a given set of corporate goals designed to fully exploit the opportunities of that climate. This applies whether the climate is the buoyant optimism of the sixties or the pessimistic uncertainty of the early eighties. Consistent experience reinforces management's expectations and its related strategy. It also argues strongly for continuity in the financial goals system, even though history suggests that some form of business cycle is built into our economic system and that, contrary to human intuition, the longer a given phase lasts, the sooner significant change is likely to occur. (In fact, as shall be seen, the revision of corporate goals in response to changes in the economic environment tends to lag behind those events rather than precede them.)

As this last suggests, corporate executives' expectations about the future can also promote stability in their financial goals and the strategy of which these are a part. This is seen at the most fundamental level in the financial planning process, which is designed to minimize disruptive change and make an unknown future more predictable. Working on the basis of an agreed-upon set of "most likely" assumptions about the next one to five years, corporate managers make a collective commitment to their financial goals and the means necessary to reach them. With reputations and egos on the line, they are strongly disposed to make events happen as the plan predicts. Additionally, their goals are, by definition, constants over some extended period of time. Frequent changes in goals, particularly if they are unexpected, undermine confidence in management's judgment and break down consensus within the company.

In this context, too, the record of corporate performance on the dimensions specified by the formal goals system also plays its part in reinforcing stability. Attainability and credibility are essential if any set of corporate goals is to serve as a meaningful discipline on organizational decisions and actions. A goals system cannot be credible unless it is perceived by those who are charged with its achievement to be attainable within some agreed-upon time frame. Therefore, it follows that tangible evidence of progress is essential to sustain this perception. And yet in the real world evidence of progress across a range of important and difficult objectives is often mixed and interrupted by contrary signals—two steps forward, one step back. Thus management will be disposed to give the strategy time to prove itself and be willing to tolerate a shortfall in performance as long as the results are ultimately acceptable. For, as we have noted, once a firm commitment has been negotiated and publicized, there is a strong disposition to make it work, even though the evidence of positive results is slow in coming.

An example will help to make these conditions of goals stability more meaningful. At the same time it will introduce some of the behavioral realities that affect the consistency and stability of both financial goals and corporate strategy. The company in question maintained its goals and belief systems essentially intact for twenty years. Throughout this period the company continued to concentrate its investment and its energies in the same industry. Its group of primary competitors and customers remained essentially the same. The mix of shareholders and their investment objectives did not appear to undergo significant modification. A brief flirtation with diversification, in response to pressure from a surge of acquisitions from outside the industry, was unsuccessful; and the company quickly returned to its instinctive and traditional industry affiliation. Thus the identity of the constituencies and their perceived interests remained clear and constant throughout the period.

As we would expect, the economic and industry climates varied significantly over the twenty years. Further, the period was one of considerable uncertainty and competitive pressure. However, corporate managers were strongly convinced that, with all its defects, this industry was the right setting for their unique technological and managerial skills. They also believed that they performed at a level of excellence well above the industry average. Thus they were motivated to persist through extended periods of competitive and financial strain. Perhaps these managers saw no alternative. If so, this suggests another cause of goal stability: the absence of perceived and viable alternatives.

Throughout the period the company managed to balance its funds flows within the internal capital market and without resort to excessive debt or the interruption of the dividend payments to which they gave high priority. However, period-to-period surges in capital expenditures did force the company to an equity issue on one occasion. This tested the goals system severely since the equity was ultimately sold below book value. A second and more important test of goals stability could have developed on the issue of performance versus goals. In this regard the company failed persistently because of a long period of industry overcapacity and competitive challenge. However, the fact that management's formal goals were largely qualitative, and that relative change or "improvement" could be accepted as proof of progress, minimized the problem. Management set few quantitative goals, and these were not the focus of general attention within the company. Further, the goals system was sufficiently incomplete that a clear test of internal consistency could not readily be applied.

This example leads to a final and obvious comment on goals stability. Such stability may disguise a real need for new goals and strategies in response to changing financial or economic constraints. Unless the company's goals are stated clearly and unequivocally, and unless they are presented to a substantial audience beyond the top management team, those goals may never be seriously tested. The financial goals system must have an objective and measurable bite if it is to serve as a serious discipline to which management can be held accountable. A set of comfortable generalities may persist indefinitely and may even influence management's behavior in undefined ways. But such generalities are unlikely to convince managers of the need to take a new direction.

Yet even when corporate managers do face the external conditions that necessitate strategic change, the constraints of the belief system can and do severely limit their choices, as has been seen. Therefore, how and why these belief systems evolve, and why corporate managers develop their deep emotional commitment to them, must be understood. To do so, three questions must be answered: Where do these beliefs come from initially? Why do corporate managers develop such an attachment to them? Why do they persist in adhering to them? As we answer these questions, we shall also examine how, to what extent, and why these belief systems are modified incrementally to take account of changing internal and external events.

Corporate Belief Systems

The Roots of Belief Systems

With the exception of Consumer Products IV, the twelve companies under consideration shared a characteristic we had not anticipated when we began this study—all had been founded by a dominant individual or individuals. In some cases, even in the companies that today are publicly held, these individuals were members of one family. In other cases they were individuals without family ties who joined together in the company's early years to build it into a major industrial concern. This pattern was equally true whether the company had been founded in the nineteenth century or had begun as recently as World War II. Moreover, the personal values and beliefs of these founding fathers were an integral part of present-day belief systems, as several examples indicate.

At Technical Products I, three beliefs were particularly important. Corporate managers believed that they must do a good job technically, keep the company on a "pay-as-you-go" basis, and make the company a stimulating and secure place to work. Both the founders themselves and the current executives traced these ideals to the founders' beliefs.

As one of the latter said:

> These goals grew out of our starting time. We believed we ought to be able to produce a constructive product that people would buy. . . . We wanted to do this without borrowing. We wanted to make this a good place to work. We had these three things, and it's hard to separate them. The people policy directed us into certain areas. We couldn't take large contracts. This kind of business requires borrowing because you have such peaks in requirements. It can also lead to layoffs.

As another executive here said: "Everything starts from the fundamental principles laid down by [the founders]. They had had to lay people off after the war, and they didn't want to do that again. They also had seen people with physical problems, and this left them with the feeling that there was a need for security and insurance." Further, the founders had had formal education in their technological field. Both the underlying values that led them to choose this specialty and the training itself shaped their commitment to technical excellence in products.

The founders were aware that others could challenge the economic rationality of some of their principles. As one said: "I suppose some could question our pay-as-you-go policy. However, we were all products of the Depression, and we did not want to borrow. By keeping ROI and growth in balance, we felt we could finance ourselves." Even though they recognized the degree of economic irrationality in their financial policy and its source in their very early experience, they remained committed to it nevertheless.

An example from another company in which managers believed in limiting long-term debt also illustrates the founders' influence on later managerial generations. In this instance the company had been founded in the nineteenth century. An executive told us this bit of company history: "It seems that one of the founders almost lost the company to the bank after a risky project failed. So financial conservatism is something that is passed down to all new generations."

Commodity Products II also reveals the impact of its founders' beliefs quite clearly. Thirty years ago one of them had written down the firm's objectives. Table 6.1 compares this statement of objectives with the corporate managers' current belief system.

Over this thirty-year period there had been only one departure from the founders' original objectives. As the italicized text indicates, the original intent had been to enter new lines of business consistent with the company's financial goals. By 1978 this intent had been altered to the admonition to "stay in the core business." As has been mentioned, the underlying reason for this shift was management's difficulty in successfully managing its one

TABLE 6.1

Comparison of Objectives and Beliefs Over Thirty Years
Commodity Products II

Original Objectives	Current Belief
Have the best team in the field.	Have the best management structure in the industry.
Foster harmony throughout the organization.	Marketing and manufacturing must work closely together.
Reward employees through adequate compensation.	Pay employees well compared to the industry.
Offer employees stock ownership in the company.	Encourage employees to own company stock.
Improve our methods and facilities so that our cost and quality will be superior to competitors'. Serve our customers so well that we will merit more of their business than competitors.	Be an innovator in products and processes. Compete on cost, service, and quality but not on price.
Expand our plant and *enter new lines of activities whenever this is consistent with the investment opportunity and the financial condition of the company.*	Expand and modernize facilities but *stay in our [core] business.*
Make an annual return better than any company in the industry.	Be the best company in the industry.

major acquisition outside of its industry. Such a shift in one principle is what we mean by "incremental change." It occurs when corporate managers have an experience that causes them to alter one principle while the basic fabric of the belief system endures, and they retain their convictions, often passed down from the founding fathers, about the other beliefs.

The Impact of Experience

Although the founders' personal beliefs lie at the heart of the belief system, corporate history also plays an important part in shaping current beliefs. As the founders and their successors manage by their principles, their experiences lead them to modify the system through the process of incremental change. At times these experiences are negative—Commodity Products II's diversification difficulties, for example, or Conglomerate II's electronics problems. However, such experiences are often incorporated into the belief system in positive ways, as Technical Products II illustrates.

During the sixties, this company's research-and-development team had come up with a product for original-equipment manufacturers. It quickly grew into an important business, accounting for a significant percentage of corporate sales. Then, in the early seventies, these customers changed the design of their own product, thereby suddenly eclipsing the demand for Technical Products II's components. The effect on the company's earnings was dramatic. It also led corporate managers to reassess their beliefs. Out of this experience they came to feel that "we should not become too dependent upon any one product or business." In all other respects, however, their belief system remained intact.

A similar process can take place when corporate managers have positive experiences, when they attempt something new, for example, and their success encourages them to develop a slightly different vision of their organization's competence. The management of Consumer Products I had just such an experience shortly after World War II. At that time they were asked by the United States Government to host a delegation of European industrialists who were developing a related business in their countries, under the auspices of the Marshall Plan. This was an eye-opening experience for these corporate managers, whose business was entirely domestic and whose headquarters were located in a relatively isolated small community. As one executive remembered:

We participated in the Marshall Plan. The government brought people here from Europe for us to teach. Three companies were spawned there from that program. One of them is a leading company there today. We heard from them that Europe was a growing market, that the time would come when products could move freely across borders.

As a result of this experience, the company began to export its product in small amounts. And by the sixties it was ready for more serious overseas expansion. As the chairman said:

> In the early sixties we were confronted by a [nationality] company who wanted to be licensees. We were looking at the Common Market. [Another executive] and I went over there to England in 1960. We had these prior contacts through the Marshall Plan. We thought we ought to get in the Common Market before the curtain dropped.

The other executive involved in this initial journey added more details about the trip, what had led up to it, and what followed from it:

> We had first hired a [nationality] salesman who picked up a few orders. We also had an English customer with whom I had a fight over the telephone. It was one of those curious things. I decided to go to England to settle the fight, and I asked [the chairman] if he wanted to go for a couple of days. He said he wouldn't go for a couple of days, but if I went for a week or two, he would. So I took him with me. On that trip we also saw our customer in [the Common Market country]. We became interested in the man and his family who were running the company and decided to buy it.
>
> Behind this was the fact that we knew there was going to be a Common Market with people [using our product]. From that point on we developed it step by step. We first went to the countries where we had people that knew the country. Our starting point was to get the right people and develop from that point.
>
> Some of us had a dream that we were going to have everybody in the world using our product. Some of us still have that dream. I still do. Don't ask me why; I don't know. [The chairman] does too.

From this small beginning, and the dream it engendered, came a major international operation that today represents one-third of the company's profits. However, for us the most interesting aspect is the emergence of the corporate executives' belief that they could succeed internationally. First, of course, was their awareness that a large potential market existed in Europe in which they would have little competition. But this awareness was reinforced by the belief, developed from their Marshall Plan contacts, that they could deal with Europeans, as well as by their belief they could produce superior products at lower costs than potential competitors. Together these led to the exploratory trip and the initial venture. Thereafter success in the early venture reinforced their conviction that they could succeed outside of the United States.

Examples such as these indicate the way in which managerial belief systems change incrementally as a result of both corporate successes and corporate failures. However, they also suggest that there is another aspect to the development of these beliefs that becomes evident as corporate managers search the external environment for opportunities that fit their beliefs about distinctive competence and appropriate risk. If an opportunity fits these beliefs, they will try it, often on a small scale, with a limited commitment of human and financial resources. If the trial fails, the belief emerges that the activity is outside the firm's distinctive competence and that future activities in this direction would be too risky. If the trial succeeds, the conviction grows that further efforts in this direction are appropriate risks.

The Impact of Financial Results

As they search for new opportunities, managers must assess more than distinctive competence and risk. They must also measure those opportunities and judge their relative success or failure against the constraints imposed by the financial goals systems and their constituencies' demands. Our evidence suggests that as long as the existing belief system leads to decisions that satisfy those financial constraints, corporate managers are likely to adhere to their beliefs. Thus one fundamental reason that managers become so committed to their beliefs is that they work. They lead to success as managers define it, personally and for the company. They also provide a practical framework within which to experiment with new ideas. If an initiative threatens the stability of the financial goals system, or fails to meet management's perception of what the several constituencies want, it will be abandoned, and managers will develop the belief that this is an inappropriate activity. Conversely, if an experiment succeeds, they will pursue it, if it can be managed within the balanced system of financial goals and if it meets constituencies' demands. Such successes expand their beliefs about distinctive competence, appropriate risk, and the way to achieve self-sufficiency.

As long as there is no major change in external constraints, this process of making decisions within the context of the existing belief system can go forward successfully. However, when changes in these conditions threaten relationships with and among constituencies or, even more fundamentally, the long-term survival of the firm, corporate management may accept a major disruption in its belief system. This topic will be discussed at length in the next chapter. But for now it must be emphasized that such disruptions in external constraints must be serious before these executives will accept a fundamental challenge to their belief system. In fact, they must seem impossible to repair within the context of the existing belief system, as a situation at Technical Products III makes plain.

This firm was seriously affected by the economic downturn of 1974. Its corporate managers were faced with the fact that the financial goals system would be seriously out of balance. This imbalance challenged the managers whose beliefs included minimal long-term debt with steady growth through new technology in their field, particularly big breakthroughs. Two executives provided their recollections about this dilemma. Said the first: "We were using our debt capacity too fast. The momentum of our capital expenditures program was carrying us out too fast especially in [a business] where the outlook had been changing negatively. We had to decide what was critical to the future of the company." According to the other executive: ". . . [in 1974–1975] survival was the name of the game. The first thing we had to do was to perpetuate the company and not let it get away from us, but [the new product] represented the future and we couldn't let that go. It would be a technological breakthrough. It was a big chip to bet on."

Various options were considered, but the choice boiled down to two: significantly expand long-term debt or cancel major research-and-development programs. In essence, one principle or the other had to give. Management decided to undertake a major long-term debt issue. Because they believed in minimizing long-term debt, they chose to borrow as little as possible and to preserve their strong credit rating. Their thoughts about this decision are reflected in their comments:

We didn't want to risk losing the company to the banks even in a severe downturn.

We were not accustomed to living as a highly leveraged company.

There was concern about losing [a high] credit rating. We learned from a contact in the credit agency we were on the knife's edge.

> We were afraid once we lost [the credit rating] we would have trouble getting it back.

> Would you want anything less than [credit rating] associated with this company's name?

Clearly these managers were uneasy about their choice, but in reality they were reshaping their beliefs about long-term debt. Now they were prepared to borrow what was needed to fund current operations and expansion provided that this debt level did not threaten their credit standing. They made this choice rather than compromise their commitment to the new products in which they saw the company's future.

Further, while holding firm to this commitment, they made sure that they eliminated any research-and-development programs that did not have a high chance of success. As one manager explained:

> There was no way we weren't going to support [one new product] project. We had a long-term future with it, no inherent problems, and we had a strong competitive position. Even though the company was in a risky position, we were going to support it. This was not so with [another new business] where we were concerned with [an operations] problem and the threat of regulatory issues.

The second program was terminated accordingly. Similarly, corporate managers wished to continue their most significant—and most uncertain—new business development. Here they decided to delay and temporize, by asking the managers responsible for the new business to conduct another market study. This would forestall any capital commitment for the time being. As one of them remembered:

> We never seriously considered not going with [the major new product]. The question was when and how much to expand. What we didn't want to do was to cut it to the bare bones. By temporizing it, we were really just "buying the next card."

> We had [the major new product] in sight even back then and we wanted to keep our options open.

However, their decision not to drop this venture was anything but obvious. Without the conviction that such products were essential to the long-term health of the company, management might have decided to terminate it. As one executive said: "[The major new product] was one where the rational man would have discouraged it."

From these examples it is clear that the nucleus of belief systems lies in the founders' personal beliefs about their company's strengths and the means to achieve success in their lines of business. As they and their successors lead the corporation through the opportunities and exigencies of its history, these belief systems may change incrementally to achieve desired results. But barring some cataclysmic event, they maintain their essential character.

They do so because the founders and succeeding generations of management recognize that what works is a pattern of principles that fit together to maintain equilibrium in the financial goals system and among their three constituencies. Like an architect designing a building, these corporate managers recognize, at least implicitly, that their beliefs and priorities must be harmonious. In the early history of the company they experiment, within the limits set by the financial goals system, their three constituencies, and their personalities. Ultimately they develop a pattern that has this harmony and therefore works. Or, as one CEO observed: "If you have a way that's working, you want to stay with it. . . . This is not the only way to run a company, but it has sure worked for us."

Emotional Commitments to Belief Systems

As has been seen, the belief system serves the company and its managers by guiding them to decisions that perpetuate the firm. Such guidance provides the most obvious reason for the commitment these corporate managers feel to their principles. That this should be so is both intuitively obvious and supported by various psychological theories on learning. But the attachment that the managers hold to these principles is particularly strong. A CEO in a company whose management believed in limited long-term debt illustrates the depth of such convictions very well:

> I have this turmoil inside of me. Others borrow money, and maybe we should. If we could go out and borrow money and work it into a profit, then we might do it. But we want to provide ourselves with a bit of discipline and provide ourselves with a benchmark. We don't want to get out on the end of a limb like we were in 1974–1975. We have two sets of influences here—those who lived through the Depression and those who lived through 1974–1975.
>
> What I am asking myself is "Are we too conservative?" But when you move

too far away from the basic principles of where the money comes from and where it goes, you may be putting future generations in a position that's dangerous. In an inflationary period we should borrow, but we must do it prudently.

As his comments suggest, this CEO feels real personal anguish in departing from his principles. In fact, his feeling is considerably stronger than the problem of abandoning a belief that works would warrant. At least two other reasons explain the depth of this commitment. One is the way in which these beliefs are transmitted from one generation of managers to the next. The other is the function these beliefs serve for the corporate managers as they perform their current jobs.

Transferring Beliefs from Generation to Generation

Since belief systems in these companies could and did remain relatively stable for more than two decades, it is particularly interesting to study how these beliefs were transferred from one generation of corporate managers to another. At first glance the process is deceptively straightforward. One generation of managers simply teaches the next by example and by talking about what they believe in one-on-one sessions, in meetings to review subordinates' plans, and in problem-solving meetings to reach decisions about corporate direction. An executive in one of the technical products companies, who was in his forties, put it very plainly and colorfully: "We [he and his peers] have all worked together twenty years. We have had two very good schoolmasters who stood in front of the class all those years."

That these younger managers learn from actions as well as talk is demonstrated by an executive in another technical company: "[The founders] didn't lead by getting up and talking philosophically. They always tended to be very pragmatic. From this we've come to know what's important. . . . The visible set of principles follows the practices which come from their very personal ideas."

The president of one of the consumer product firms provided a more specific example:

> He [his predecessor] became president about 1947. In our staff meetings he'd say, "We were caught between two giants—the retailers and our suppliers. We're the little unit in between. We need to grow so we can exercise power on both sides."
>
> I don't ever remember a staff meeting in the early 1950s when an officer didn't make some mention of this point. . . .

In these meetings, this corporate manager was getting an important lesson in what economists today would label industrial organization. He was taught the importance of growth as well as of establishing a brand franchise to give his company some power in relation to the giants around it. These beliefs persist in his company today.

Moreover, because such acceptance is rewarded, younger managers also accept their superiors' beliefs. Another consumer products executive testified to this as he spoke about what he had learned from one of his older superiors:

> He gave me three pieces of advice when I was working for him in Europe: (1) You'd better not be short of product. You're better off having too much inventory at times; (2) Don't touch anything, but [brand name]—a piece of advice I now don't believe in; (3) Don't let your price get lower than [a major competitor]. We sell for less in the States, and our image is lower, but in Europe we are equals.
>
> We got along fine as long as I followed those rules. He made sure I got whatever support I needed.

In other words, as long as he stayed within existing principles he took no flak. For competitive younger executives who are committed to advancing in their company, such treatment would be an important lesson in continuing advancement. Clearly an experience like this provides a powerful incentive to learn and to accept such beliefs. Further, it is likely that the selection and hiring of young managers facilitates this acceptance of beliefs. The newcomer may be chosen, and may choose to join the company, because his personality is compatible with the beliefs of those doing the hiring. Thus the new manager joins the firm predisposed to live by its principles.

However, current literature on adult development also suggests that there is a deeper and more important psychological reason for this educative process, one that goes beyond extrinsic rewards or the predispositions of the younger managers themselves. Young adults need a *mentor*. Teacher, advisor, and sponsor, a mentor can also be a host and guide who acquaints the younger manager with the organization's "values, customs, resources and cast of characters." In addition, he can serve as an exemplar whom "the protege can admire and seek to emulate," because of "his virtues, achievements, and ways of living."[2]

Moreover, as Levinson and associates also point out, the mentor has another important role that is developmentally critical for the younger manager. That is his ability to support and facilitate the younger person's *dream* of what he wants to become. To quote Levinson, the mentor "fosters the young adult's development by believing in him, sharing the youthful dream and giving it his blessing, helping to define the newly emerging self in its newly discovered world, and creating a space in which the younger man can work out a reasonably satisfactory life structure that can continue the dream."[3] For most adults such relationships begin in early adulthood and can extend into the late thirties. Because the mentor/protégé relationship is a complex one, involving potential rivalry as well as love and caring, it often ends with bitterness and bad feeling on both sides. But, as Levinson points out, even after such a breakup, "the younger man takes the admired qualities of the mentor more fully into himself."[4]

We did not seek to learn about such mentor/protégé relationships in our data gathering. Yet we found considerable indirect evidence that they play an important role in perpetuating belief systems. Most of the corporate managers joined their company in young adulthood. As they moved through their careers, they may well have had a series of such mentors, each of whom inculcated some of his beliefs. The fact that older corporate managers have reached a stage of life at which they are particularly concerned about generativity further supports this possibility. They could deal with this concern by engaging in the active development of the next generation of managers. Thus they would find a mentor/protégé relationship as psychologically rewarding as the younger managers working their way up toward corporate management.

When managers talk about learning from their elders, they are apt to be describing very powerful psychological experiences. The principles they have learned become a part of their concept of what it means to be an effective corporate manager in the company, and this concept is an important aspect of their dream. Clearly, therefore, this experience provides another partial explanation for why corporate managers become so emotionally tied to their belief systems. Not only do these belief systems work, but they also become an important part of each manager's concept of himself as an executive in his firm.

The Here-and-Now Functions of Belief Systems

There is at least one other reason why these executives become so committed to a system of beliefs. That is the way in which these beliefs enable them to perform jobs that are demanding and complex. The decisions these managers must make require trade-offs among the interests of various constituencies including, of course, themselves and their colleagues. Often they must choose between relatively certain profits now and uncertain growth in the future. Often, too, they must base their decisions on judgments about their organization's capabilities and their customers' and competitors' likely reactions. Yet the best data on which such decisions can be based are estimates and forecasts, whose accuracy is always open to question. In essence, then, they decide in a highly ambiguous and uncertain milieu.

Technical Products II's decision to launch a major new product and process research program was one example of this complexity. With a particular market in view, the executives in that firm were willing to bet on their scientists' capabilities to solve complex processing and product-characteristic problems. Similarly, in Technical Products III, management decided what to do about a major new product program in the face of a capital shortage. The managers were clear about the existence of the product they wanted and about their ability to manufacture it to specification, but was the market there? Was it really good enough to replace other products already on the market? Was it worth long-term borrowing to finance the program? Was it a better bet than other new ventures on the horizon? An executive in this company described what it is like to make such a decision:

> In a decision like [the one about the new product] we generally have all the data we could want. What comes out of all the data is credibility. A man can sit there, read the data for himself, and make his own judgment about what he believes. The financial problems, the necessity of choosing one project over another, judgments about the company such as when [a business] fell out of bed or when working capital demand was heavy—all these things would be considered at one time or another during the decision-making process.

Such uncertainties are not limited to the high-technology companies. Risks and uncertainties are equally present in decisions to expand capacity in a mature commodity industry or to acquire a new consumer venture. The CEO of one of the consumer products firms described how he and his colleagues made a decision of the latter sort. Several years earlier his firm had acquired a local retail operation with only a handful of outlets. Subsequently this business had been expanded into a national operation with almost three hundred outlets. How was the initial acquisition decision made? According to this CEO:

I went out to visit [the original operation] with a negative attitude because they didn't carry [certain products]. I spent part of one day down there watching operations and then went back the next day and watched the customers. I was impressed by the volume and by how quickly customers were served. I was still worried about [the missing products], but then the owner told me very few customers wanted them and that they just tied up space.

The efficiency of the system was also important to me. It took him [the original owner] twenty-five years to build it. I came away very impressed. Here was a man who knew his business. I had no idea how many we could build. I don't think anybody here did. All we believed was that this [retailing segment] would grow, and that was all we really knew. We didn't have any detailed studies of the market or anything like that.

This description emphasizes the extent to which such strategic decisions are made on the basis of the executives' beliefs about the future direction of external forces and about the capabilities of those who will carry out the decisions. An executive at Consumer Products I further illustrates this point with his description of critical decisions to expand in Europe and to narrow the company's product focus:

We knew we were the lowest cost manufacturer in the U.S., and we knew we could make a product at the lowest cost in Europe and that the market was there. Therefore we didn't have to do a detailed study of the marketing and the profits. We also knew [ten years earlier] that we had to get out [of one product] into [another product]. Then [a few years later] we knew we had to [narrow the consumer focus]. We just knew it.

When a manager says "we knew" or "we believed," therefore, what he really points to are shared beliefs about the future, about colleagues' capabilities, and about the implications these hold for corporate risk and self-sufficiency. In fact, it must be emphasized that as complex and uncertain as these decisions are, they are often made with little reference to formal studies. Either the studies are not conducted, or they are not central to the final decisions. For as the executive in Technical Products III indicated, corporate managers must still decide whether the data are credible. Are they consistent with their beliefs about market opportunities and tactics and their confidence in their subordinates? Do they believe that their firm can make a success of the venture or not?

This point was driven home to us by the chief financial officer of one of the consumer products companies. When asked about formal financial studies, he responded:

We do get detailed reports on capital expenditures. They are made up by the people downstairs. They know all about discounted cash flows and that sort of thing. These guys do a good job. Yesterday several of us were discussing a one-inch-thick report they had produced on a capital expenditure. All I asked was which page has the ROI on it; that's the bottom line. They told me so I turned to that page, and it looked high enough. So then I turned to [the president] and said, "Well, it's up to you to decide if your people can actually do what has to be done to make this money. If they can, it will be a good decision."

If you live with these things long enough, you don't go through all the cash flow and discounted cash flow analysis. You just know it in your head. It's all in your head. You don't have to look at the figures.

Or as the CEO of a high-technology company said: "It's a bit intuitive with us. We've been at this thing so long. . . ."

Our basic point about the here-and-now utility of belief systems is reiterated in such descriptions. Their beliefs provide a set of concepts that enable managers to make choices in areas where hard facts are often unavailing and where the tools of management science and economics are inadequate to the job. Without these belief systems, managers would be adrift in a turbulent sea, with no charts.

In ten of the twelve firms there was a tight consensus among the corporate managers about their beliefs. As they discussed and deliberated, these managers shared an understanding about goals and appropriate businesses, about the ways to compete and to manage internally. This did not mean that the executives always agreed on specific decisions. But such differences as did occur usually concerned assessments of likely future scenarios rather than underlying beliefs. Fundamentally they agreed on where they wanted the company to go—and how to get it there.

In sum, the belief system facilitates corporate management's job of strategic decision making. It provides tools for making complex judgments, and it does so in a manner that minimizes disagreement about fundamentals. This is one reason for the managers' emotional commitment to such practices. But there is another. When an executive in one of these companies is promoted into corporate management, he brings with him an emotional commitment to the company's belief system that has developed through his relationship with valued mentors. Generally, in these mature companies he finds himself among colleagues who share these assumptions and principles, and this sharing enables them to work together to reach decisions. For these reasons, corporate managers are likely to hold onto these beliefs as long as they produce the result they seek above all others—the long-term survival of their company. Minor threats or opportunities are handled by a process of incremental change. But these beliefs are truly a powerful constraint to the management's strategic choices.

And yet the belief system can be fundamentally altered to eliminate these internal constraints, if there is a clear consensus among the corporate managers that incremental changes are not sufficient to perpetuate the company. As important as the belief system is to these executives, as individuals and as a group, once they have undeniable evidence that it is no longer working to assure corporate survival, they will accept the challenge. How such a restructuring occurs will be the subject of the next chapter.

CHAPTER 7

Changing the Fundamentals

American business history contains many examples of companies and even entire industries that have become outmoded and disappeared during periods of economic turbulence. The Curtis Publishing Company and its most important property, *The Saturday Evening Post,* provide a case in point. At one time this magazine was an American institution. Yet its top managers were unable to respond to the changing environment of the late 1940s and 1950s. They stuck to their beliefs about editorial policy and to their vision of the company as an integrated magazine publisher despite clear evidence of fundamental changes in consumer tastes and industry economics. The result was the magazine's demise and, eventually, the parent company's. The belief system that had guided these executives in making successful strategic choices could—and did—blind them to new opportunities and dangers.[1]

Current statistics on corporate bankruptcy and failure remind us that the Curtis Publishing Company's experience is not unique. The latter half of the 1970s and the initial years of the 1980s have been unkind to many American companies. In several industries foreign competitors have taken over large shares of the domestic market. The costs of basic raw materials and labor have risen dramatically. High interest rates have increased the cost of borrowing and diminished the extent to which management could rely on short-term credit to balance the financial goals system. Customers have postponed purchase decisions, the demand for industrial products has fallen, and factories have been underutilized.

Because our study focused on twelve healthy enterprises, it is not surprising that they were not part of these statistics. Nor did we find evidence in their corporate histories of the sort of blind adherence to outmoded beliefs that characterized the top management at Curtis. However, we did discover many instances in which our executives were forced to confront the fact that their beliefs no longer led to successful strategies. What happened then? How did these executives adjust to new economic realities and overcome the constraint of their beliefs?

Answers to these questions come from two sources. One is the group of companies in which corporate management had successfully altered its belief system. The other is the pair of companies in which such a process was going on at the time of our investigation. Before examining either, however, we must turn once again to the objective economic and financial constraints under which management operates. For it is here that we find the forces which stimulate fundamental changes in management's beliefs and strategy.

Objective Forces for Change

In the preceding chapter we considered the circumstances under which management's objective constraints foster stability in both financial goals and the strategy of which they are a part. In essence, we said that a mature financial goals system balances constituent needs and interests. Further, once attained, it remains appropriate as long as: (1) constituencies remain stable; (2) the economic and financial environment does not change radically; and (3) corporate performance promises to accord with the goals management has set. However, if any of these conditions does not obtain, and, in particular, if the gap between management's expectations and reality is large and persistent, then it follows that powerful forces for change will develop. These forces in and of themselves need not evoke fundamental strategic changes. Indeed, they are more likely to give rise to the sort of incremental changes that we have already considered. And yet, as shall be seen, over time these forces can and do become irresistible.

Among the twelve companies included in the study we found examples of each of the circumstances conducive to change. Perhaps most readily apparent were those instances in which one or another of management's three constituencies was altered. For example, we observed significant realignments in investors among these firms. These realignments included the shift from private, family-dominated ownership to dispersed public ownership, the movement of large blocks of stock into institutional hands, the concerted efforts of individuals or corporations to buy up a controlling interest, and the shift in shareholder compositon as a firm evolves from a "growth industry" stage to maturity. In each case, the new investors brought new investment standards, expectations, and objectives. Such changes may be abrupt and even unexpected (as they would be were a raid to take place). Or they may be gradual and extend over many years. But in either case, managers must look beyond the issues immediately affected by the changes (price-earnings ratios, for example) to all their financial goals. Ultimately the entire system must be involved if management considers a major shift in any individual goal.

Similarly, changes in the product market arise for many reasons. Competitive relationships shift; new technologies are introduced; the government intervenes; major customers are won or lost. And here again the change may be gradual and imperceptible in the short run. However, occasionally such changes are dramatic, and their impact on corporate managers' goals and, eventually, their strategy is quite apparent, at least to those on the inside. Two examples illustrate an experience of this sort.

At Consumer Products Company IV, management was confronted with a technological breakthrough, developed abroad, that promised to open up a major new market for one of its products. The technology had recently become available to this company—and others. Should they be the first to introduce it in the United States and perhaps take up a preemptive position in the new market by doing so? Or should they wait and let other existing or potentially strong competitors do so? The capital investment was large. The near-term rate of return was low. The outcome could radically alter the competitive structure of the domestic industry.

Similarly, the managers at Consumer Products Company III had decided to diversify internally by entering a new consumer market on a national scale with a product developed by their scientists. But to do so was to go head to head with one of the largest and best-managed consumer products companies in the country. To succeed, Consumer Products Company III would have to capture and hold a substantial share of the market, some of which would have to come from this respected competitor. This would be a whole new experience for the company, which had been accustomed to a strong and dominant position in its traditional market for decades. Now it would have to be the new kid on the competitive block for five to ten years.

In both these companies, as in other similar cases, a major shake-up in the product market led management to commit substantial new funds and to increase the rate of growth of investment. Inevitably the effects of these changes were felt throughout the financial goals system as well as in corporate strategy. For one thing, such surges in investment are often accompanied by a near-term decline in the rate of return on investment, as the denominator increases immediately while the numerator does not. For another, the demand for funds puts pressure on the rest of the system as management increases debt, reduces dividend payouts, or shifts funds, at first instinctively, to balance the cash flow and later perhaps as they reexamine established beliefs. (As we have noted before, reserves can cushion this shock to some extent; but in the end they only buy a finite amount of time in which managers can realign their priorities in a more orderly manner.)

Significant changes in the organizational constituency will also affect management's goals and strategy. The most visible of these occur when a new person becomes the chief executive, the chief financial officer, or a key member of the top management team. Obviously, such a change in individual officeholders does not by itself predict a change in financial goals or strategy, given what we have said about the corporate belief system and executive selection from within. In fact, even new men from outside the company will not necessarily ensure such sweeping changes, although they are more likely to make them and may have been chosen for exactly that purpose. However, new personalities inevitably do bring some new perspective, and sooner or later this may be reflected in the goals they emphasize. How quickly a new CEO moves to put his personal imprint on corporate strategy depends on many things, including the question of whether, and to what extent, he wishes to separate himself from the past administration.

These constituency changes can be seen most clearly when a merger or a major acquisition takes place. At one and the same moment, the company may acquire a distinctive new shareholder group, a new set of competitors and customers, and a new management team. Moreover, the acquired management may, and often does, succeed to the parent leadership—sometimes within a short period of time. Consequently it is useful to recall this possibility, even though none of the twelve companies studied had such an experience. Though the consequences are often concealed from public view, mergers and acquisitions provide a most dramatic illustration of the way in which constituency changes can combine to promote radical shifts in corporate goals and strategy.

Discontinuities in the economic or financial environment of the industry or the economy can also foster changes in goals and strategy. This is particularly true when there is a sharp downward turn and hopes for a quick recovery are few. Such an event can highlight an imbalance in goals or a shortfall in performance that might otherwise go unaddressed. It can also lead to revised priorities, as the broad consensus of gloom created by a precipitous collapse provides an excellent opportunity to face up to false expectations and do something different.

The economic and financial crises of 1974–1975 and the early 1980s are recent examples of this phenomenon. Both produced a set of circumstances in which the organization's capacity to resist change was weakened and a new sense of direction was tolerated, if not welcomed. Of course, a strong economic recovery can also provide such an opportunity; but as it may occur only after several false starts, it may be more difficult to identify as an independent force for change. Moreover, the optimism recovery engenders may be more subtle and dispersed than the pessimism of collapse, while the "touch wood" syndrome may leave management reluctant to assert boldly that a new period has begun.

Finally, there are the forces for change latent in the company's failure to achieve management's goals over an extended period of time. In and of themselves, such failures are difficult to identify with specific strategic changes. Indeed, they may not even exercise a particularly strong discipline on management, for in such cases the terms of accomplishment are usually vaguely defined, left unstated, or revised to bring them into congruence with the company's performance. Management's earlier tendency to assert absolute goals (to become a billion-dollar company by 1980) gives way to relative goals, or rates of change, without reference to date of achievement. Moreover, it is rare that someone blows the whistle to announce the final score. On the contrary, hope springs eternal among top managers, particularly as performance rarely moves uninterruptedly in a given direction.

However, the question of balance in the goals system and in actual funds flows provides a more explicit and unbending discipline. Year by year, quarter by quarter, managers must balance their cash budget and calculate the bottom line. Either they make it or they don't. The company's real cash position may be less widely publicized than its profit, but it is well known to those in control. Further, the cushions available from reserves, reallocations of expenditures, and pushing on the margins of the guidelines have precise limits, and at some point the organization can no longer be shielded from the full impact of the problem. Persistent cash deficits demand a response, therefore, and they challenge even the most cherished corporate beliefs.

Nevertheless, even cash shortages may be insufficient to challenge management's beliefs in a fundamental way. Instead the executives' first response is likely to be an incremental change in beliefs and strategy. More systematic restructuring will come only when a number of such events and circumstances occur at the same time and so persistently that the corporate managers feel a clear and unequivocal discontinuity with the past.

This awareness can often take several years to develop. To an outside observer, a specific historical occurrence may appear to trigger strategic change. (Events such as a major business recession, new ownership or a new CEO, the OPEC cartel, government regulation or deregulation, war or peace, cash insolvency, or a new technological breakthrough are all likely candidates.) But one more familiar with the company's situation will recognize that the forces of change have been building for years. Specific events may provide the occasion for a moment of consensus among top management about the need to restructure beliefs and strategy. But absent these underlying forces of change—and management's belief that the forces have reached the point at which they threaten corporate survival—such events will not call forth new strategic directions and goals.

In this context it can be understood why it is difficult, if not impossible, for an involved manager to know whether a particular decision represents an incremental change in the belief system or is part of a more fundamental restructuring process. Any decision seems to be a discrete choice at the time it is made. Only as those involved review a series of such decisions does the magnitude of the change become apparent to them. Consequently, hindsight provides an excellent opportunity to study the process by which beliefs are rethought and psychological barriers to change are removed. In the following section three companies' experiences afford us this opportunity.

Consumer Products I

Before World War II this company sold utilitarian products to consumers through large, national retail chain stores. One chain bought 50 percent of their product, while three such customers accounted for 75 percent of their sales. Thus competence in marketing was not important to them, because it was handled by their large retail customers. Much more significant was management's vision of the company as an efficient and low-cost producer. This vision was bolstered by the executives' experience during the war, because the company's entire output was converted to military use. In addition, throughout the war years profits were sufficient to provide a steady acceptable income to the only capital market constituency that counted—the members of the two founding families.

However, at the end of the war the company's situation changed suddenly and dramatically. As the chairman remembered earlier events from the vantage point of 1979: "The market for [our original product] dried up overnight. We started making [our original product] after the war, fat, dumb, and happy, but the inventory backed up on us." It had done so for a reason the current president grasped intuitively: the product market was no longer the same. As he described the underlying causes: "The ultimate customers' tastes had changed. . . . They didn't want to be regimented. I sensed this at the time because I didn't want to join anything. The only thing I joined after getting out of the service was my golf club."

Management's first response to changing consumer tastes and declining earnings was to seek products that played to old strengths. It looked for items that would utilize the firm's distinctive competence in manufacturing and its financial resources but that could still be sold through the chain stores. A variety were tried during the next two years. None succeeded. As the current president said:

> We got into [another product], but unfortunately we still sold them to the chains. We had also begun to sell through wholesalers by this time, but they didn't want some of the style features we thought the consumer wanted so our products didn't match the channels of distribution we were in. So we tried selling directly to the retailer and to develop our own products. We also learned that with more style built into the product, there were not as many reorders so we still got stuck with inventory and so did the wholesalers.

In essence, then, these first decisions to try something new were consistent with top management's beliefs. They represented an incremental shift in attitudes at most.

Management's next step was to think about diversifying. To this end it acquired a company that produced a related product. But this, too, failed to produce the desired results. As the current chairman, then a vice president, told it:

I didn't want to buy [the acquisition] because I was concerned that their product would follow ours. When we got over there, it turned out I was right. The plant had been shut down for four weeks, and all the buildings over there were full of [the product]. We went over there and found an attitudinal problem on the part of the supervisors, who had been promised that if the prior owners sold out, it would be sold to them. So we had a real attitude problem on our hands. I was so mad I didn't make another acquisition for seventeen years.

Because of these difficulties, corporate executives continued to look inward for a product that would successfully replace their prior business and use their manufacturing competence. As the same executive said:

The way we happened to get into [our current product] was we were desperate to run our machines, and we said what can we get to run on our machines. This was 1947. We came up with the idea of building our brand name in competition with [three other firms]. We thought we would be beating each other's brains out, but what we were doing was changing the whole image of [the product].

We borrowed short-term money up to the excess of our net worth to do this. The bankers weren't happy, but they were willing to ride along because we had always been profitable.

By this time [one of the founding families] had departed, and I had acquired a substantial interest in the company. There was a little over-the-counter market because of the stock they had sold. I got my interest by borrowing every cent they would let me because I had so much confidence in what the company would accomplish. This was before the war. [The chairman and president, at the time] had much more capital in the company. They were borrowing even more than I.

Thus by 1947 several significant changes were occurring simultaneously: the capital market constituency was shifting; top managers were beginning to believe that they could market branded products; and the manufacturing vice president just quoted became president at the age of fifty. This executive had come up through manufacturing, and he was the architect of the company's advanced and innovative production process. His ascension to the presidency was based on his skill at what his superiors and peers believed was their company's basic strength as well as on his ownership position. It is he who is credited by his colleagues for leading the company to its current size and success. As the current president said:

[The chairman] was the man who said we needed to be bigger to negotiate with people behind us and in front of us in the channels of distribution. He was willing to take a chance and make mergers. He also scouted out areas of opportunities to build plants. He was young and dynamic. He did a lot of good intelligence research on other companies that were competitors.

An important aspect of his leadership was his ability to inculcate beliefs in his subordinates that built on the company's previous principles but modified them in fundamental ways. As we would expect from the information presented earlier, these beliefs were shaped significantly by this executive's personal experiences:

> I always wanted to succeed in business. It was my idea to go to [a business school]. But instead of going back in 1930 for the second year, I looked hard at the money I was spending. My father was a farmer, and I looked at the money and decided I had better not go back. . . . I went to work for [another company]. I ran every machine in the plant. They put me on time study and later I worked in their headquarters. They wanted me for two reasons. I didn't know anything about their business, and I could provide some objectivity about how they did things. Finally, in '35 I got the offer from [my present company]. I came here because they had a policy of no nepotism. This came about because the families didn't want to fill the company with duds.

Thus he brought with him a strong desire to succeed in business and a conviction that the company's no-nepotism policy would enhance his career. Interestingly enough, thirty years later corporate management still adheres to the principle of no nepotism. Even more important, it is still totally committed to beating its competitors. As one executive observed: "Our major goal, although it isn't expressed, is to beat the performance of [our major competitor]."

But the new president also had novel ideas about how the company could succeed, which led to an important shift in the belief system. He was convinced that the firm could be competent at marketing a branded product, and he valued growth highly:

> I had the idea [the product] was going to be a lot bigger than anyone else around. I knew we had the lowest cost in manufacturing, and if you were dealing [with big retailers], that's a big thing. We first started advertising during the war to convince our own employees to stay on the job because they could earn more money other places. In '47 we made the decision to which all agreed to build a brand name. We wanted a brand name to fit the image. We made many other innovations. . . . We had more confidence than sense. So we went ahead building a marketing competence, we were still behind there.

> Here we were in a fragmented industry, and I felt it had to evolve into bigger units to afford to build bigger and more efficient production facilities. We would have looked for new products anyway, but the war caused us to move more quickly because of the decline in [our products].

He also communicated these beliefs and underlying reasons forcefully. As one of his subordinates said: "[The current chairman] told the executives in the mid-fifties, 'Get off your butts, or we'll sell you off and let somebody else be your masters.' This became a mandate to grow or perish. But efficiency of domestic operations was still the key strategy." Thus these executives kept their faith in the firm's manufacturing competence, even as new beliefs were entering in, and they keep it still.

Related to the new president's interest in growth was another tenet, one that had to do with debt. As the current president told us: "I guess two things were in his [the chairman's] mind. One was the desire not to be crushed by suppliers and customers, and second was the heady fruits of growth. Therefore, we wanted to keep growing. He said we'd never turn down a proposal because we didn't have the money." Consequently, management became convinced that long-term borrowing in large amounts was a reasonable risk. Such beliefs were quite consistent for a CEO who had already borrowed heavily personally to build his own equity in the company. As the current president said: "He [the current chairman] wasn't scared of borrowing. We had lived through the depression, and what it taught us was to think about the return. [The current chairman] looked at other firms' balance sheets and saw they had more leverage. [The previous chairman] knew all those bankers too, and that helped."

Over a period of about five years, then, this firm's corporate management made a series of basic decisions under the leadership of its new president. Clearly the problems generated by the postwar period provided the stimulus. But the convictions of the new president also heavily influenced specific choices. Even before the war, he had been concerned about being squeezed by large suppliers and customers. His solution was to develop a brand franchise. In addition, he was highly motivated to succeed competitively, and he believed that the industry was entering a period of consolidation. Together these beliefs led to his commitment to growth, and he was willing to borrow to achieve this end. In fact, in the late fifties he took the company to the public equity market to finance growth, thereby creating further changes in the capital market constituency. Speaking of this decision, he said: "Going public was the result of estate considerations and to allow us to grow without so much short-term money. We really were not concerned about loss of control. My philosophy has always been if you are a well-run company, you will be allowed to run it."

From these events came a fundamental change in the belief system shared by all the corporate managers. In essence, they became committed to growth, to beating their major competitors. To accomplish this they were willing to develop the marketing competence essential to build an image of their brand. They were also willing to borrow and even go public. Thus their beliefs did not reflect a major concern about self-sufficiency. And yet they did not abandon entirely their earlier principles. They still believed that their distinctive competence rested in manufacturing low-cost products, and they still forbade nepotism.

As we saw in chapter 5, this basic belief system was later modified to include overseas operations. But the conduct of these operations was consistent with the principles that had worked so well in the United States. In effect, the decision to compete overseas was an incremental shift in beliefs; it did not alter basic premises about competence or self-sufficiency. The corporate managers believed that such expansion was an acceptable risk, as long as it was carried out in accordance with the new tenets developed in the post–World War II period.

Consumer Products II

Like Consumer Products I, Consumer Products II was seriously affected by World War II. But in this company the process of change extended over a much longer period of time. In fact, it was almost twenty years after the end of the war before management's new strategy and belief system were solidified.

Before the war the company produced and sold industrial products as well as consumer goods. This diversity increased during the war, as the company moved into several defense products very different from its traditional ones. This experience convinced corporate management that the company could manufacture these new items, and it was decided to market similar products to consumers after the war, thereby combining consumer-marketing competence with new skills.

This diversification effort continued for almost ten years. But it was never thought to be highly successful. At the same time, a change in consumer tastes that had begun during the war gradually gained momentum. The effects on the firm were serious: both its base consumer business and its industrial business declined. In addition, new concerns for all of management's constituencies began to emerge. As one executive pointed out, both the product market and the capital market were affected by the firm's problems:

> In the 1950s we were becoming a mature company, but there were some products with only limited potential. It was at about this point we brought in [a new president]. We were looking for stronger growth in the sixties because our principal shareholders wanted it. He [the new president] decided that we should be getting out of some businesses and into others.

Another executive described this decision in more detail, noting the organizational constituency's need as he did so:

> Our concern with growth was largely a response to investor interest, but it was a little more profound here. We could clean up the company to attract investors, but the ability to retain and attract managers matters too. While we had grown by the late fifties, we felt we needed to grow more for the creation of additional job opportunities for people. [A major shareholder] saw the need to bring in outsiders to make dramatic decisions that would ensure the viability of the business.

The new president brought a new financial officer with him. Together with the existing corporate managers, they began to ask some hard questions. An executive described these events:

> The reasons we got started in diversification was that [a major shareholder] was dissatisfied with our performance. He brought in the two new executives, and together they began to work on it. [The new financial officer] didn't know how to run things, but he got us into some good industries. The key was his willingness to face up to reality. It took somebody from the outside to do this. Our internal group couldn't have come up with a decision to close [a major business]. I was opposed to diversification at the time because I was running [the base business], but I was wrong. One of the qualities we have retained since this time is the willingness to get out and take our lumps when a business doesn't work.

This comment emphasizes a critical point: someone must "face up to reality" if a fundamental change in corporate direction is to occur. Traditional beliefs must be questioned and, if necessary, abandoned. The questions may come from within, as they did at Consumer Products I. Or they may be asked by newcomers, as they were here. But in either case, the challenge must be made.

The challenge was particularly tough for the management group at Consumer Products II, because they were discarding their commitment to their traditional product market along with their old beliefs. As a result, they had to abandon physical facilities and employees as well. As an executive who was directly involved in this divestiture told us:

> The decision had been made early under [the new president and financial officer] to get out of industrial businesses and to grow in consumer products. We wanted to get out of industrial business and into [a related consumer business]. But that didn't work out so within two years we decided to get out of all of it, period. We sold twenty-four plants and laid off seventeen hundred people. The way we did it gave the corporation the guts to face up, bang, bang, bang to divestments in [three other businesses]. [The new financial officer] pushed more than anyone else on this.

From these experiences, executives challenged their vision of the corporation's distinctive competence, and they began to develop the belief that "facing up to losers was the correct thing to do." In fact, in 1979 it was still an important article of faith at this company that the greater risk was to continue a losing venture.

In addition, the new president reached a decision about financial goals that in 1979 continued to be a widely shared principle. As one executive said:

> [The new president] was brought in to rethink our strategy. The conclusion was we were going to be a [X percent] EPS growth company, *and it still is.* This figure came off a tree, but it was consistent with what other growth companies were doing. The growth was needed to get our stock up. It provides a more exciting environment too. At some point our stock will be rewarded for our growth, and that is the belief today.

Thus the new belief system included not only a specific growth target but also the conviction that growth would eventually be reflected in higher stock prices, thereby pleasing the capital market constituency. But growth was also important for the organizational constituency as well, as executives still believed in 1979, although they also felt that the price of the company's shares did not yet appropriately reflect its growth record.

To return to the 1960s, however, these decisions had left top managers with a new set of beliefs about financial objectives and the importance of pruning back losing businesses. But they were also left with considerable cash and no clear concept of where to put it. In the midst of these changes their vision of the company's distinctive competence had disappeared. As one vice president said: "During the sixties we had four out of every five capital investment dollars going into acquisitions. There were many new venture teams going and we got into quite a number of businesses. We were searching for new business. . . ."

Eventually this search process came to include some hard self-appraisals. As another executive remembered:

> What we did in the mid-sixties was to assess the management group. We stepped back. There were several sessions with top management out of the office. It was a self-assessment. It was top management assessing itself and saying we didn't see good prospects for technology in [the basic consumer] business which we previously had hoped for. If we had anything to bring to new industries, it was our ability to think about customers, how to do market research and market planning, etc.

Thus another tenet of the emerging belief system came into focus. Despite the company's large research staff and its facility devoted to its established consumer business, the corporate executives challenged its belief in the importance of technology. Instead they chose to focus on their distinctive competence in marketing consumer products. From this point on, the company pointed its internal development and acquisition activities to build heavily on this vision. By 1979 the company was operating in a wide spectrum of consumer businesses, and it had divested its last industrial business. Further, its technical research budget had been greatly decreased.

Thus over a twenty-year period these corporate managers, stimulated and led by two newcomers, reshaped their beliefs about their financial goals, strategic means, and distinctive competence. As one executive summed it up: "You must temper everything about [the company] with the fact that it is not the same company it was before."

These two consumer-product firms underscore the conditions necessary to produce a fundamental change in top management's beliefs. Two of these arise in response to conditions outside the firm—changes in constituents' expectations and a persistent imbalance in the financial goals system. The third reflects conditions within the firms, more specifically, the presence of a new leader who will challenge old principles and help to find new ones.

Given the circumstances under which this process of restructuring takes place, it is not altogether surprising that new leadership would be an essential component. In each of these cases, as in others, corporate managers were faced with the fact that their beliefs no longer worked. The managers' traditional practices simply did not achieve the financial goals necessary to meet their constituents' demands and their personal desires for competitive excellence and company survival. And yet the recognition of this fact led to considerable confusion, as these managers wondered which principles could be adhered to. It is small wonder, therefore, that a new leader was necessary to reformulate the belief system.

Moreover, in both cases the process of fundamental change was neither short nor smooth. Both companies experienced false starts, and in both the process took years, almost twenty in the case of Consumer Products II. In each case, too, specific decisions led to new initiatives. Those that worked engendered new beliefs which gradually fit together into a new system. Old tenets were not entirely abandoned, unless such a course was essential for corporate survival. This same dynamic process is clearly evident in the third company that will be examined, Commodity Products I. But here an additional factor contributed to the change in top management's beliefs—the introduction of new strategic planning concepts by a consultant.

Commodity Products I

Commodity Products I had been a leading producer of consumable supplies for industrial customers since the late nineteenth century, when the company was founded. Early in its history it was a closely held company, with a majority of its stock owned by directors, employees, and descendants of the founders. Through the end of World War II management was committed to earning a return that would meet the expectations of these shareholders through growth in what they believed to be an expanding market for their products. The 1950s brought a rude awakening, however. Their belief that growth and ROI could be sustained in their traditional product market was challenged. As the current chairman recalled:

> Back in the fifties sometime, a member of the finance department made a study of the industry which showed that it was in a mature phase. This was the first time that the company had done such a study, and the management was shocked by its implications and particularly by the implication that the industry and therefore the company would stop growing. From that point on everyone became concerned about that problem and what they were going to do about it.

Corporate management decided to do what many other firms were doing at the time—diversify. Such a course promised to provide the growth the managers believed important to shareholders and employees. As one executive commented: "We acquired business in the sixties with no clear direction. There was no real support so it failed. We flubbed around. People said we should be in [a certain business] because it had growth, but we never picked out what segment of [the business]. And the chairman and president didn't support the program." In short, although the corporate managers' prior beliefs had been sufficiently challenged to encourage these acquisitions, no new direction had been established. Such direction would have to come from the chairman and president, but neither appeared to be behind the acquisition effort. The old belief system was in disarray, and members of the management group had doubts about its efficacy, yet no one appeared to point a new direction.

Into this vacuum came a new leader and CEO. As at Consumer Products I, he was promoted from within by the board. But for the first time he was not a member of the founding family. Moreover, he took office when the fears and concerns of other corporate managers about the continuation of the company were greatest. Two executives described this period. According to one: "There was a real concern for our jobs back then. There was a threat from the investors for new management or selling the company." The second executive said: "There was a real question of survival when [the new CEO] came in. Could the company survive? How was it to survive and what was the strategy that would restore it to a healthy situation?" Thus the new generation had ample reason to support changes, even if their predecessors had not been eager to do so. The company in which they had grown up, with which they identified, and which was important to their future was at stake. The new CEO shared his subordinate's concerns, and he pushed for bold new initiatives. As one executive analyzed his situation: "The CEO is on the spot all the time because he is not a family member. Yet he has made the boldest moves the company has ever made. He is probably motivated by personal objectives and a desire to preserve the autonomy of the company from unfriendly takeover."

As he searched for a new direction to assure corporate survival, the CEO learned about new strategic planning ideas promulgated by several consulting firms. During the late sixties he retained two of these firms to examine the company's problems. As one executive observed: "The [consulting firm's] way is a new style for the company that started in the late sixties. The approach is also a reflection of [the CEO]. Divestitures and acquisitions are his style. He was looking for a better way to run the company, and he brought in [the consultants]." At about the same time, the CEO also brought several executives into corporate management from outside the company. Insiders viewed these men as risk takers. As one said later:

> [One executive] is not conservative. He will take risks. His performance is measured in terms of getting rid of companies and acquisitions. [A second example] was a thirty-seven-year-old guy who was aggressive as hell. He was a real hustler and damn good at what he did—a broker type. He pushed acquisition candidates at them as fast as they could handle them.

One of these two, who was president in 1978, described this period:

> Shortly after I joined the company a planning committee was established which took a gross look at the corporation and its various entities acquired during the sixties. We classified these entities into three categories: build, maintain, and sell. This classification really amounted to two basic approaches, to either stay in a business or get out. The distinction between build and maintain was simply a matter of degree of emphasis. The process of reviewing the company in these terms took eighteen months.
>
> Although this had the appearance of [the consultants'] influence, it was not particularly strong at the time. We reviewed these issues primarily on historical financial data. I was able to participate in these decisions because I had no stake in the past and could help make the hard decisions as to what changes to make.
>
> I was able to make divestment decisions because I was new to the company. I had no history with the company, with the people, with the decisions. I had complete support. Top management was happy to have someone else do it.

As at Consumer Products II, we see again how important an outsider's objectivity is in enabling him to view issues without the emotional commitment of insiders who may see what should be done but find it hard to do because of their commitments to beliefs as well as to their product market and organizational constituencies. But as this same executive recalled, his review took in more than financial realities. It also included a vision of the company:

> The review and decisions were not based entirely on financial data. If the business were doing reasonably well financially but the area of activity did not fit, then the decision was made to get out. We defined [our vision of the company] to include the businesses which involved broadly distributed consumable products selling to industrial users. We considered ourselves to be very good at selling such products to industrial customers. We did not do well with capital goods, and we were lousy at consumer products.

Out of this assessment came a clear vision of the product markets in which management believed it could succeed. This vision of the firm's distinctive competence had been shaped by the earlier diversification failures. Also, even with outsiders and consultants involved, it retained an important aspect of the old belief system—the view that the company was best in dealing with consumable products. As two executives stated: "Our emphasis is on consumable products rather than capital goods. The style of business is different because so much is at stake" and "We don't like to get into high technology, but technology just high enough to make ease of entry difficult."

When this assessment had been completed, a companywide management conference took place at which management stressed both its vision of the kinds of business it wanted to be in and its financial goals. The current president described the process from this point on:

> At the time of the meeting there was only the general outline of strategic planning. It was [a year], when the strategy committee was formed, that we got down to the level of reviewing the strategies of each business. Initially strategic planning was not heavily quantified, but then the finance group began asking for forecasts and that has become a pattern ever since. The only thing that lies outside this process of strategic review by the strategy committee is the decisions about acquisitions and divestments. These are handled by the chairman's "inner cabinet." This is because of the critical need for privacy and confidentiality on these matters.

Although the reassessment redefined the scope of the company's business activity, management's beliefs about the financial goals system still reflected the conservatism of the earlier period. Diversification and growth were to be funded through retained earnings or divestment, not through new debt. As the financial officer said: "Our ROE must be greater than our growth rate to maintain the debt/equity ratio over time." Moreover, these managers thought of the company as a portfolio of businesses selling consumable products to industrial users. Consequently, they expected that the portfolio would be balanced to achieve the desired relationship between return on equity and growth. Within the portfolio, some businesses were expected to provide excess cash that could then be allocated to the more rapidly growing businesses. But the managers also expected that all businesses would have a number-one market position. A business in neither the "hold" nor "grow" category should be sold, therefore. As the president explained, because of their concern with the organizational constituency, these executives had difficulty becoming committed to the consultants' concept of "harvesting" a business: "One thing impossible for us is to truly harvest a business—to run it right down. That's more hurtful to us than selling. If you sell, people aren't always looked after, but you can rationalize that it's not your fault. We are lousy 'harvesters.'"

In response to these feelings, these corporate managers had developed the corollary belief that no business should be sold unless the manager running it wanted to do so. Perhaps this was nothing more than a rationalization: what happened to the people involved was not corporate management's fault. And yet their serious concern for the organizational constituency was consistent with a tenet from the earlier belief system to which corporate management was still committed in 1978. As the president said: "This company has a heavy emphasis on a concern for people and remaining nonunion. There is a familylike tradition in the company. We do things by evolution, not by revolution. We're conservative, and we feel comfortable with this."

Nevertheless, by 1978 there was no doubt that reliance on strategic planning was central to corporate management's beliefs. These ideas had produced results that enabled the firm to achieve the financial goals in which its management believed. Consequently they became committed to them. Every executive interviewed stressed this point:

[The chairman] placed lots of credibility in [the strategic planning] framework. It's a pretty good way to organize the business.

Strategic planning has become a religion around here. We've become very disciplined. Everyone knows what they're doing today, and there's annual follow-up to each division's strategy. This was not so in the sixties.

Corporate management is thinking more strategically about business than they had earlier. The change in character and management has been so dramatic it's hard to believe. Management today has a good understanding of their strengths and weaknesses. They have plans for each business, corporate commitment, and a strong sense of objectives.

In addition, the executives believed that this way of managing enabled them to achieve the diversity they felt the capital market constituency wanted. According to one: "Our shareholders are looking for income and staying whole with inflation. We've got to keep them happy by diversifying the portfolio."

Commodity Products I's experiences mirror those of the two companies already discussed. In each case management was confronted with constituency changes, a persistent imbalance in the financial goals system serious enough to raise questions about the company's survival, and a new and dynamic leader. However, this company is unique in that its strategic planning concepts were introduced by consultants. Given the recent popularity of strategic planning tools, therefore, what is particularly interesting here is the process by which these concepts were accepted. Ironically, it is almost identical to the way in which the managers in other companies learned new principles from their own experience.

Initially the strategic planning concepts piqued the new CEO's interest. Impressed by the consultants' reputation, he was willing to allow them to try out these concepts by analyzing his company's situation. But it takes more than a consultant's reputation to make an idea part of a corporate management's beliefs. As has been seen, the time was right for these new beliefs, because the old system had been shattered by changing constituency constraints and because they were advocated by a forceful new leader, who was able to convince others to try them. Moreover, the ideas worked. Strategic planning tools enabled the managers to achieve their primary goal, the survival of the company. As a result, management came to believe in strategic planning as a "religion."

The process through which management came to accept this belief also differed significantly from that prescribed by many consultants and academics. According to these authorities, strategic planning ought to take place in a logical sequence. First managers must establish their goals; then they must search the environment for opportunities and threats and choose the best course to their desired objectives. Such an approach is certainly intelligent, rational, and comprehensive. But the experienced and successful corporate executives studied rarely use it because it ignores several facets of the choices they must make. Given a real world in which choices are often based on uncertain, complex, or even unreliable information about future events; in which ends and means are intertwined; and in which account must be taken of any decision's impact on all three constituencies (including the organization with all its residual questions of commitment and motivation), management's actual practice is far more likely to replicate the necessarily "untidy" process we have been describing.[2]

Whether we think of these beliefs as a religion or as the corporate managers' personal theory about corporate strategy, it is clear that only the consultants' presence differentiates this company's experience from that of the two consumer-products companies. There the managers developed their new tenets by trial and error through their own deliberations. Here they were first suggested by the consultants. But in both cases the new ideas had to be accepted by the top managers as tenets in the belief system before they could be fully utilized. And this was a long, complex process in all three companies, whether the new ideas were provided by outside consultants, a new CEO, or generated within the existing management group.

In fact, we might go further, for our evidence suggests that there are two distinct, if related, phases to the process of fundamental change. The first phase involves a *challenge* to existing beliefs. Faced with economic events of sufficient magnitude and duration that they seem to threaten long-term corporate survival, the managers question and reexamine old beliefs! Are the traditional goals still appropriate? Could they be altered without infringing on the changing demands of any of their constituencies? In the three preceding examples apparently the answers to these questions were negative. In all three situations investors were concerned about past and likely future performance, while the organizational constituency was concerned about jobs. Such pressures led the managers to question beliefs about strategic means. In each case, too, corporate management was examining its distinctive competence. In light of changing product market constituencies, managers questioned how else to achieve the goals necessary to satisfy the capital market and organizational constituencies. But this questioning did not produce clear answers immediately. In fact, in each of the three companies it led to abortive attempts at new initiatives. It was not until the second phase of change that a clear new concept emerged.

This second phase is a *restructuring* of the belief system. Here a new leader (from within or without) is of paramount importance. It is he who must define the new direction as well as possess the patience and confidence to see it through. As these examples demonstrate, the process of fundamental change requires many years. False starts and failures are highly probable. Consensus builds slowly, particularly when corporate managers are implicitly rethinking such critical concepts as distinctive competence, appropriate risk, and desired self-sufficiency. The newly emerging belief system may share some common features with the old one along any of these dimensions; but it will also be different in fundamental ways. Consequently it cannot be brought into being without expert leadership within the firm.

Managing the Process of Change

The foregoing examples indicate clearly the vital importance of skilled top managers during the years in which new beliefs and strategies are being developed. Indeed, on the basis of our research we would argue that without such leadership, this process cannot go forward successfully. We do not mean by this to suggest that the CEO and the members of his management team are superhuman. On the contrary, it is our central premise that they are, in fact, very human, and that it is their humanity which makes them so committed to corporate survival and so vulnerable to the limitations imposed by their psychological and objective constraints. Yet they are human beings with unusual qualities. These qualities have brought them to their high levels of responsibility and make them capable of leading their corporations through periods of turbulence to a new strategy and system of beliefs.

The most obvious of these qualities are patience and persistence. These characteristics are essential if a manager is to deal successfully with the long lead time and inevitable failures of the restructuring process. They are also essential in dealing with the psychological constraints of the belief system. It takes time to shed old beliefs and assimilate new ones, just as it takes time to sell new ideas and prove that they work. While the evidence accumulates sufficiently to be convincing, patience and persistence are valuable assets.

The capacity for personal reappraisal and corporate self-assessment is also essential in managing the process of change. The CEO must be able to step back, both from the pressures of day-to-day activity and from others' increasing concern about survival, to understand the sources of the company's current difficulties and to assess its current and future strengths. To do this an executive must have confidence in his vision. But even more important, he must trust his own judgment, for he must be capable of making critical assessments at a time when others around him are seriously disturbed about the company's future viability.

Moreover, he must be able to draw on well-developed interpersonal skills. Top managers must be able to listen and to persuade others to try new approaches. They must also be able to deal with the conflicts likely to occur when their subordinates or peers advocate competing ideas, either by resolving those conflicts or by creating an atmosphere in which their ideas can coexist, at least for a trial period.

Finally, the executive in charge must have a personal vision of what the company can and should become. As has been seen, there is usually a great deal of confusion at the beginning of a period of strategic change, when events are challenging top management's old beliefs. At that point the firm needs a leader who has a sense of where the company can and should go next. In the end, the new shared vision may benefit in many ways from the ideas and suggestions of many other top executives. But at the outset one person must have a preliminary and tentative vision, and he must have the confidence—and authority—to try it out.

Typically that person will be new to his office. In all the companies studied, we invariably found a new leader whenever we also observed fundamental changes taking place. Two of these men were entirely new to the company, while the others had been promoted from within. In fact, the strong predominance of long-service career managers in all these companies was striking, given conventional wisdom as well as newspapers full of reports and announcements of outside executives assuming leadership roles. However, our evidence suggests that the attention paid to such changes reflects their newsworthiness, not their prevalence. The fact is that mature and successful American companies are managed at the top by experienced career managers.

Ironically, this preference for promoting from within makes the job of leading strategic change that much more difficult. Insiders are naturally committed to existing beliefs, and they are apt to find the necessary distance from these familiar principles difficult to achieve. Thus the CEO promoted from within who must make a reappraisal is faced with a particularly problematic situation. Confidence in his own ideas will help, but he must also have a capacity to step back and examine the current situation objectively, an exercise undoubtedly easier for the CEO brought in from the outside. However, the latter faces his own problem—his ignorance of the existing beliefs system. Lacking such knowledge, he may find that his new initiatives run into a barrier he cannot comprehend and that seriously limits his success at introducing strategic change.

Belief Systems in Transition

The difficulty and complexity of bringing about fundamental change in a belief system were nowhere more evident than in Conglomerate II and in Commodity Products II. Both firms had faced serious problems in meeting constituency demands and in balancing the system of financial goals during the ten years prior to the study. This experience had challenged the old belief system and opened a debate among the corporate managers as to future direction. But there was little consensus among them. In fact, these were the two companies in which corporate managers had the least consensus about their beliefs. In both firms the CEO and some corporate managers had developed a set of beliefs to which they wanted to adhere; but other powerful voices in the executive suite disagreed about important principles. A brief discussion of each situation illustrates the issues and the feelings involved.

Conglomerate II

Conglomerate II's current CEO had been brought in from outside by the board of directors when the company encountered serious financial performance problems. He identified two stages in his work with the company:

> I like to think of two phases to my activities. Phase 1 [five-year period] we were cleaning up messes. We were stopping the business losses. We fixed up the businesses we could and got out of some others which were marginal. Phase 2 is from then until now. We have been taking what we had and improving the product line through research and development.

Additionally, he believed that financial resources were not a constraint in this process: "I have not had to make choices between businesses. There is something for everyone without penalizing anyone." But some of his subordinates in corporate management differed with him. According to one: "We see ourselves as cash poor. We believe that if it isn't cash, it doesn't count. Capital expenditures are bad, we feel."

Similar disagreements surrounded their beliefs about internal management. Again the CEO had one view: "We want to run the company with an operating cast. Not because we can prove it's best but because we are more comfortable that way." Other corporate managers held another view: "Another idea here is that corporate management is deeply involved in the management of divisions, but that isn't true."

And still a third area of disagreement was pointed to by another executive: "We say we make acquisitions to grow, but then we turn around and run them as if we were trying to make a return out of them."

In short, corporate management disagreed about means as well as about the appropriate balance between the goals of growth and return on investment. These disagreements seemed to be related to differences among the executives about how much risk should be taken in spending on research and development for future growth. The CEO and those who agreed with him believed that research-and-development spending was a key to the company's future. But another senior manager held the sharply contrasting view that "risk is bad."

It may seem that such disagreements are the result of a CEO's failure to convince his subordinates that his ideas are viable. But such an explanation is too simplistic. Old beliefs die hard, and new ideas are often greeted with skepticism and lip service. Until they have been proved effective over a sustained period, the new ideas are unlikely to convert all corporate managers no matter how effective a leader the CEO is.

Nevertheless, the CEO's involvement in introducing fundamental change in direction is critical. The company's performance problems and managers' commitment to corporate survival can lead to a challenge of the old set of beliefs. But someone must take a leadership role in developing new directions. The CEO at Conglomerate II was in the midst of this process; so was his peer at Commodity Products II.

Commodity Products II

At Commodity Products II the debate about principles had been in process for several years. It had its inception in capital and product market events dating back almost twenty-five years. As the executive vice president told us:

> In '55 a wave swept the industry to acquire within the industry. We acquired all kinds of smaller companies. This lasted through the sixties. In the late sixties we expanded our industry capacity internally and acquired outside the industry. There were two reasons for these acquisitions in the sixties—to get debt capacity and to make us too big to swallow. In the current situation a fear of Metzenbaum and Kennedy has stirred up the medium-sized companies, and they are all running for cover looking for somebody to acquire them. We turned them down.
>
> This frustrated our chairman, who is an acquirer. He and I have different philosophies. [The president], on the other hand, is a liquidator. I'm closer to him than [to the chairman]. From [the president's] perspective you can scale back assets and keep the high-profit generation and get a high ROI and receive a big reward from the financial community. The problem is people want growth as well as ROI. There is a balance in the equation.

As at Conglomerate II, one issue being debated was the appropriate balance between the goals of growth and return on investment. The company had grown in size during the period of industry consolidation, but the return on investment had not grown. This had led to the acquisition outside the industry the executive vice president mentioned. As the same executive said:

Our industry wasn't doing well in the seventies. We got into trouble ourselves. Under those conditions you'd expect groping transitions. There was a lot of talk up and down the hall that we ought to get out of [the base business] and be like [a well-known conglomerate]. There was slow growth in the industry, and little growth for us in that. This feeling is clearing now, and we are spending dollars to build new businesses and advanced systems in our industry.

This executive believed that the diversification issue had been resolved. The company would not diversify further. But the chairman and president felt that as long as growth and ROI goals were still being debated, no consensus about diversification was possible.

According to the chairman:

The last four to five years there has been a tug of war going on between [the president] on one hand and [the executive vice president] on the other. He [the president] is less growth-oriented, less risk-oriented than I am. If our industry hasn't yielded a satisfactory growth rate over time, then the company will have to find new areas for investment. There are other fields that we can manage well.

But the president saw things differently:

So much depends on the CEO. He's a builder, a grower. His view was only ten companies would survive, and we had to be a big company so we could survive. He loves debt. He'd borrow 200 percent. [The executive vice president] is a super operator. I think what you will see over the next ten years is we will get back to one industry.

Perhaps most interesting were the comments of the executive vice president, the youngest of the three. As he indicated, he felt more in accord with the president, while the chairman placed him in his camp. His own statement supports his view that he was closer to the president:

We didn't have a coherent strategy a couple of years ago. We do have a strategy today, but it's not so clear. It's falling into place. We won't buy anything else until we get a strong sense of direction. We're saying let's husband cash and spend it in areas we know something about. It's not a brilliant strategy, but it's better than we had before.

Presumably a brilliant strategy would be one that resolved the divergent beliefs about growth and return on assets, about diversification and success in the base business. When such an idea emerges, it will clearly allow a reformulation of the corporate belief system. In the interim, however, the executives were able to live with these disagreements about fundamentals. As one executive stated it: "There is not a consensus at all about the role of [the base business] and the role of the diversified business. It's still an open question. We will look at our actions over time and try to make the most money. We will do what will compound our stockholders' investment. It's as simple as that." Or as the chairman said: "The CEO has to be capable of using diversified people with different views and make it work. [The executive vice president] and [president] are very different. [The executive vice president] is more risk-oriented; he is more offensively-oriented. [The president] is needed to be more of a devil's advocate.

It is impossible for us to say whether these statements rationalize some deeper concerns about these disagreements. Clearly such perspectives do allow the executives involved in these fundamental changes to work together during the period of restructuring in spite of their differences. Also, while there was disagreement about these critical tenets, it is important to recognize that there was also a strong consensus about other beliefs and, most important, a deep conviction that come what may, the survival of the enterprise was critical. These executives were well aware that "they must all hang together or they will hang separately."

It may seem surprising that these executives did not show a greater sense of urgency in resolving these issues. However, they had no need. Despite their internal debate, the company was now performing well enough so that the financial goals system was in balance, and they were meeting the demands of all three constituencies. Because of this, they had the luxury of continuing to disagree.

But even from our limited observations, it was clear that in these two companies the executives' world is filled with strife and conflict. There were more struggles for power here than in any of the other companies. Lacking a coherent system of beliefs, these managers were regularly faced with disagreements on fundamentals. And these disagreements in turn sparked factions that sought to further their own views.

As a CEO works to rebuild a consensus around new strategies and beliefs, therefore, he faces a critical internal management problem. He must hold the corporate management group together during the long years of transition. We have no way of knowing whether, and to what extent, such disagreements existed in Consumer Products II, Consumer Products II, and Commodity Products II during their restructuring phase. However, it is reasonable to expect that they went through some degree of internal turmoil. What is perhaps most remarkable is that in all these firms, top managers' dedication to the survival of the company maintained their cohesion during their search for new direction.

Once again, the CEO's skill in managing relationships within top management is clearly of critical importance in this phase. The CEO at Commodity Products II emphasizes this when he speaks of the importance of using "diversified people." The CEO must be able to lead subordinates who disagree with each other, and with him, while he retains his own convictions about the desirable direction for the corporation. This conviction may be tested over several years by the skepticism and dissent of other senior officers. But if the CEO and those who agree with his ideas for new direction are persistent, and if they are correct in their decisions, so that improved results become apparent to others, then gradually they can rebuild a consensus about the "rightness" of the new ideas and these will be incorporated into management's beliefs.

From this evidence about fundamental change in belief systems it is clear that the reshaping of corporate direction involves reshaping the underlying belief system. Basic changes in corporate strategy can and do happen; but they require a long lead time, a great deal of excellent administrative leadership, and above all, a shared personal conviction that the survival of the firm is the critical goal. Indeed, this last is the single most important element in top managers' willingness to undertake the process of redirecting their corporate strategy. If these managers believe that corporate survival is at stake, they will extricate their strategy from their beliefs and make appropriate changes—however painful the process. Lacking that commitment, however, they are unlikely to develop a coherent or successful strategy whatever the objective economic and financial pressures to do so.

CHAPTER 8

Strategic Choice Under Managerial Capitalism

Leading large corporations is a complex, demanding job. The managers who succeed at it have experience, judgment, skill, and stamina as well as an intense dedication to their firm's long-term health. The possibility of failure always exists, even for large, mature, industry leaders such as the firms we have studied. Industries mature; new competitors enter markets; the entire economy can take a severe downward turn.

The quality of corporate leadership is critical, therefore. A "source of permanence, power and growth," in Alfred Chandler's words, these executives direct the large business enterprises that are so prominent in the American economy. Thus they are central to the economic system Chandler has aptly labeled "managerial capitalism" (that is, a system dominated by firms controlled by salaried managers rather than owners or bankers).[1] Through their corporate managers' strategic decisions and through their collective importance, these firms affect the economy in significant ways. Their success is as vital to our national well-being as their failure would be detrimental. Consequently, their managements' corporate strategies and goals are—and should be—a matter of interest and concern well beyond the executive offices in which they are formulated.

The Ultimate Objective

The first and foremost of those goals is organizational survival. As has been seen, this theme has guided top management's plans and actions time and again. Thus our evidence strongly supports Chandler's contention that "in making administrative decisions, career managers preferred policies that favored the long-term stability and growth of their enterprises to those that maximized current profits."[2]

Further, these corporate leaders meant much more by survival than mere existence or the avoidance of bankruptcy. Desirous of leaving their personal imprint on the organization for succeeding generations, they want their companies to be vibrant and growing. Managerial independence is an essential element in this effort. As has been discussed, the desire to perpetuate their organization's unique economic and human potential causes top management to seek as much corporate independence as possible. Like the goal of survival, independence has a personal dimension as well as an organizational one, and the individual manager may have difficulty—and little interest—in distinguishing between the two. But its effects are apparent not only in top management's concern with governmental regulation and intervention but also in its desire to keep its various constituencies at arm's length and to defend against control by rival organizations or individuals.

Self-sufficiency enables these managers to deal successfully with the often conflicting objective constraints imposed by their constituencies. Experience teaches them that no company, however large and mature, can afford to take for granted the continued cooperation and support of its constituencies. An unexpected change in circumstances may turn a mutual interest into a conflict in which the vital interests of each party are at stake; and these challenges can come from any quarter: from the many external organizations and institutions upon which the firm depends or from within, from the organization itself. In either case, at such times top management's only protection comes from the capacity to act independent of its constituencies.

Of course, such independence is a matter of degree, because few managers can reconcile their aspirations for corporate survival with the principle of total self-sufficiency. (To cite one example, one need only think of the ways in which absolute financial independence would restrict the growth essential to satisfy the demands of the product market and the organization itself.) Nevertheless, these corporate managers did give priority to their ability to survive on the firm's own resources, if necessary, and to emerge from a test of self-sufficiency with their essential capabilities intact. Their corporate strategies reflected that priority. They achieved balanced funds flows and financial self-sufficiency to avoid capital market constraints and interference. They diversified in varying degrees to free themselves from the competitive imperatives of any single product market. They adopted internal management practices designed to insulate the firm from the arbitrary consequences of a mobile and volatile market for personnel.

Closely connected to survival in these managers' minds was their desire to succeed in what was often an uncertain, or even hostile, environment and to be seen by others as successful. Whatever other elements of society may think about the power and influence of the corporate establishment, these managers see themselves as engaged in a continuous struggle against vigorous and powerful competitors at home and abroad. They compete for customers, for money, for skilled employees and managers, and the outcome is always uncertain. Thus the personal compulsion to "win," and to continue to win, against specific, respected competitors, by objective and commonly recognized standards, becomes fused in their minds with the goal of survival.

To some this characterization of the modern industrial corporation may appear to be seriously lacking in social content and purpose. Given the fact that the immediate social function of the business firm lies in the "value added" in goods and services, they would argue that few benefits are to be expected from firms dominated by the objective of self-preservation for owners, employees, and especially for the managers in control. But we believe that this inference fails to take sufficient account of the complexity of modern industry and the difficulty of developing strong organizations. In order to provide goods and services most efficiently on either a national or a multinational scale, management must create an organization capable of large, complicated, and interdependent tasks. Such organizations take years, even decades, to develop, and they are always vulnerable to changing events. From a national point of view, therefore, they are an important and scarce resource.

Thus there is an economic benefit to society in the competitive struggle to develop and to preserve the very best of these organizations. This is not to say that competitive excellence or superiority can always be equated with the capacity to survive. Nor does it mean that the strategy and tactics that promote an individual firm's survival will invariably be in society's best economic interest. To take one obvious example, a monopolistic position that would ensure a particular firm's survival would also have a detrimental effect on the economy as a whole. A vigorous competitive environment provides the primary defense against such eventualities. Consequently, an economic system that permits—and even encourages—a corps of professional managers to place organizational survival ahead of product or capital market priorities must, at the same time, assure an effective competitive environment in the markets from which those organizations derive their essential resources.

The Creation of Corporate Wealth

In a world of uncertainty survival, self-sufficiency and success are relative, not absolute, concepts. Thus it is natural that the operational surrogates found in the corporate financial goals system are also relative concepts—ratios and rates of change in which the standard is comparison with competitors' or the firm's past performance, better or worse. Moreover, top managers' own desire to excel leads them to establish organizational goals that are never fully attainable and that remain forever just beyond their reach.

To most managers, the key to organizational survival in an economic sense is the accumulation of corporate purchasing power or wealth by which they can command the goods and services essential to their mission. To "assure" survival, self-sufficiency, and success, these top managers strive continuously to conserve and augment corporate wealth. Thus they have a natural inclination to amass resources, including the financial resources that give them a significant measure of independence from the capital market constituency. (As we have explained, these senior executives find little comfort in having access to the capital market's rich resources because they may be denied that access at a time of critical need.) In general, therefore, these ultimate objectives are consistent with the traditional economic view that top managers seek the maximization of wealth: the more wealth, the greater the assurance of the means of survival and all that this implies competitively.

However, this conclusion must be qualified in several important regards. First, our definition of wealth takes in corporate wealth in its entirety—that is, the technical, market, and human resources under management's direct control as well as the firm's financial resources. Consequently, it goes beyond the wealth measured by conventional financial reports to include the firm's market position as well as the knowledge and skill of its employees in technology, manufacturing processes, marketing and distribution, and administration of the enterprise.

As is apparent, this definition differs considerably from the economists' traditional concern with shareholder wealth. The goal of maximizing corporate wealth also differs from the familiar notion of maximizing profit. Corporate wealth passed on to shareholders in the form of dividends may be consumed or reinvested in competing organizations. But corporate wealth retained and reinvested for the organization that generated it will add to the resources under management's control. From the point of view of a shareholder who is indifferent to the particular source of his wealth, it may or may not represent the most efficient usage.

Further qualifications concern the concept of maximization. Traditionally this concept connotes an ultimate value. It implies that management has attained the full potential of its resource base. Yet managers have no maximization meters in their offices, nor does such a concept mesh with their reliance on financial criteria that measure relative performance. As we have indicated, their only test of success is a comparative one.

Moreover, the resource regeneration and retention essential to organizational survival have a qualitative as well as a quantitative dimension. An ever-larger resource base does not improve competitive strength and financial viability unless that resource base is employed as the financial goals system directs: to maintain a vigorous and continuous flow of funds over the long run. Large aggregations of wealth restricted to a moribund industry by economic, technological, or competitive realities, or by management's belief system, are doomed to go down with the industry, sooner or later. Consequently, some degree of diversification in the source of earnings and the mobility of resources is an essential element of corporate wealth maximization.

Indeed, since wealth has many dimensions and potential beneficiaries, the importance of which may change with time, managements may be observed to be engaged in both maximization and what Herbert A. Simon calls "satisficing."[3] The need to reconcile the interests of the external competing constituencies and to distinguish them from those of the organization as a distinctive and ongoing entity clearly implies trade-offs. To maximize one dimension of wealth necessarily implies the possibility that other dimensions may be limited to that which is necessary to assure continued cooperation and loyalty. A persistent concern for corporate survival may be expected to focus attention on a corporate rather than a constituent definition of the wealth to be maximized.

The Silent Priority

Given our emphasis on top management's commitment to corporate survival, it seems ironic that the executives interviewed did not discuss this subject often. Once a specific crisis point had passed, they might refer to it in terms of survival. But more typically their concern was shared but unstated. In fact, once top management had reached consensus about important financial goals and had developed a sense of commitment to them, there was little discussion about these objectives either. Instead they were incorporated into the beliefs that guided management's specific choices.

The daily experiences of these top managers provide an explanation for this phenomenon. For one thing, questions about ends and means soon become intertwined in the real world of corporate decision making. Managers may well ask what the effects on the earnings stream will be if a particular business is developed, or what the consequences will be if a business continues to decline. But unless such specific questions threaten to create a serious negative imbalance in the flow of funds, they are unlikely to provoke a comprehensive reassessment of the financial goals system.

Similarly, as has been seen, the thought process of strategic change is not often clear and explicit. Rather than being a simple matter of detailed staff studies and careful analysis, important decisions are often matters of judgment based on past experiences and shared assumptions about likely future events. Often top managers will seize opportunities because they represent an obvious fit with their vision and beliefs. And even when a careful analysis has been done, the senior managers may treat it with caution and even skepticism, because they recognize that there are many imponderables and uncertainties in future events. In addition, they know that the subordinate line and staff managers who have carried out the analysis have their share of biases as well. Thus they may rely less on the analysis itself than on the credibility of those who have prepared it, reinforced by their own experience.

Then, too, there is often an experimental quality to a particular piece of an emerging strategy. Managers will try out a new product or make an acquisition because it accords with their vision. But if this attempt does not succeed, they are unlikely to jump to the conclusion that their strategy is flawed. Instead they will continue the search for other options, or even put the ideas on the back burner until by chance or through creative effort another possibility appears.

In short, from top management's day-to-day perspective, strategic turning points are infrequent and indistinct, except perhaps in retrospect. Rather, top managers are engaged in a long series of choices and decisions that over time may add up to a significant change in strategic direction. In this sense even major change is an incremental process. True, on occasion there are dramatic management crisis points or significant board of directors' meetings. But often these events ratify the results of many informal discussions and decisions that have preceded them. They are the milestones that mark the achievement of countless forgotten steps.

Strategies for Survival

Nevertheless, crises and turning points do occur. If the corporate journey is to continue, top management must be able to develop strategies that fit its changing economic and financial environment. In particular, the executives must be able to adapt to change and incorporate new visions of their organization's distinctive competence into their goals and strategy.

The strategies that we have seen emerge from this process have a common characteristic: an internal consistency and harmony. Not surprisingly, this harmony was also present in the underlying belief system that had guided the individual choices of the companies' CEOs and their key lieutenants. Like other creative thinkers, these men were able to deal with many variables concurrently, reduce them to their essential components, and understand their interrelationships. In times of change, they were able to fashion a series of choices that meshed together into a harmonious strategy and that gradually, over time, left them with a new, coherent belief system.

This consistency and harmony was vital in view of the length of time—often a decade or more—normally required to effect a meaningful change in corporate direction. In some of the companies we studied the issues that had preoccupied management at the beginning of the period under review were still around, awaiting closure, ten or fifteen years later. It made little difference whether the issue was one internal to the firm (such as a new business development), or whether management was looking outward toward the path of acquisition. Nor was the time significantly reduced if management was able to achieve a coup through intelligence or good fortune. Acquisitions that promised a dramatic alteration in the corporate earnings base commonly brought with them fundamental conflicts in personalities, organizations, and culture that took years to harmonize. And as might be expected, most acquisition strategies produced some successes and some failures. As a rule they were followed by a lengthy period of consolidation and shake-out before further acquisitions were undertaken.

This extended time line increases the difficulty of planning for change. As should be obvious, there is an inherent incompatibility between the time required to bring about fundamental strategic change and the customary financial planning cycles. Because management is well aware that its capacity to forecast the future in detail is severely limited, budgets are usually set on a yearly basis. The five-year cycle used for most financial planning is longer, but it too is dictated by human constraints, specifically the span required to implement significant funding and investment projects. Yet even the five-year planning cycle proves to be inadequate to see fundamental strategic changes through to fruition. Rather than be fully realizable within the planning horizon, the changes implicit or explicit in one plan's goals will reappear in successive plans until they are accomplished or superseded by a new strategic direction.

The prospects for successful strategic redirection depend significantly on a benevolent economic and financial environment. Externally this means that economic and industry trends should be free of extended disruption or even—ideally—moving smoothly upward. Yet realistically there is little that management can do to influence these external trends. Therefore corporate managers must pay particular attention to those aspects of the firm's internal finances and economy they can control. They must be able to sustain a balance in the funds flows and financial goals system and thereby avoid the stress of either a funds-flow deficit or an embarrassing surplus. They must also be able to devise strategies to minimize their constituencies' constraints. In these ways they can maximize their own potential for independent choice.

As has been seen, most of these top managers chose to follow a policy of financial self-sufficiency. They did so because they had learned that the only truly loyal money was money over which they had direct control. Such a strategy does not eliminate the need to be concerned with how the firm is perceived in the capital market, but it does extend the range of choice within which management can act independently and confidently.

A high degree of financial self-sufficiency gives the professional corporate manager the opportunity to assert corporate financial priorities over those of his capital market constituency and to contravene the behavior of transient shareholders or short-sighted portfolio managers that he considers counterproductive. To the career manager loyalty means everything and desertion is a punishable offense. That a shrewd and perceptive investor can derive as much benefit from corporate failure as from success is obviously repugnant to him.

Further, financial self-sufficiency gives management greater leverage to resist the capital market pressures likely to occur during periods of change. By definition, periods of change are times of heightened uncertainty during which the information gap between management and the external investor widens. Consequently, to the degree that change can be implemented with funds firmly within management's control, the risks inherent in misinformation or misunderstanding on the part of the arm's-length investor cease to be a threat to the organization.

The desire of top executives to put some distance between themselves and their particular product market constituencies was likewise evident in their product market strategies. As has been seen, most of these managements were keenly aware of the long-term vulnerability created by a one-industry, one-product, one-market strategy. Not all were equally prepared to do what was necessary to reduce that dependence and vulnerability, however. For some, a genuine search for an alternative income base was inhibited by the inevitable uncertainty surrounding the maturation and decline of an industry or market as well as by their particular vision of their firm's distinctive competence. But most of these top managers were actively engaged in exploring alternative revenue-producing activities compatible with their beliefs. These explorations were not always continuous; but the pattern they created was clear and unmistakable.

In discussing diversification, whether internal or through acquisition, it is important to distinguish between the unrelated acquisition commonly associated with conglomerates and the deliberate search for new income sources compatible with perceived organizational strengths and abilities that has been under discussion here. Inevitably the latter sometimes takes on the appearance of the former, since it must be somewhat experimental at first and may even appear opportunistic. However, in the companies under consideration (with the obvious exception of the conglomerates), the intent behind diversification is clearly different. The corporate managers of these firms have beliefs about their limitations as well as their strengths, and they look for businesses they can manage successfully. They weigh the work that must be performed as well as the technological, economic, financial, and organizational demands it will impose. Moreover, as they succeed in their search for new opportunities, their vision will also be changed: there will be a new strategic focus, a shedding of peripheral and less promising alternatives, and the emergence of one or a few newly dominant income streams that, in time, will also mature and need to be replaced.

The effects of such corporate diversification on the product market constituents in the base industry are marked. Customers, suppliers, labor unions—the power of each is weakened by a successful diversification strategy. Less immediately apparent but also significant are the effects of diversification on the capital market constituency, particularly the professional investor. For this constituency diversification may provide no value-added whatsoever, because such an investor can achieve diversification in his or her own portfolio with greater speed and efficiency. In fact, diversification may even lead to an actual loss of value to the investor, since the merging of separate product market activities reduces the amount of specific information on individual product market performance. Thus share value may decline as a hedge against increased investor uncertainty.

Nevertheless, from management's perspective the firm's value has been increased through diversification because the uncertainty about its viability and ultimate survival has been reduced. Indeed, nowhere is the drive for corporate survival more evident than in the managers' interest in entering new businesses. True, their choices are limited by their vision of the company's distinctive competence; but within this limit they generally seek to perpetuate the company by moving out of declining businesses and diversifying into those that they believe hold more promise. Thus we have been led to conclude that the drive to survive through fundamental strategic change demands the opportunity to diversify. Otherwise the constraints of a dying product market may also spell the death of the firm.

This fact points to a difference between the American corporation and some major international competitors that has not received particular attention—the relative ease with which the corporate earnings base of American firms can be shifted from one industry to another, through the purchase of control in the open equity market. Obviously such ease is not always a blessing. In some instances corporate leaders have abused this freedom by behaving like stereotypical portfolio managers and switching out of competitive situations that do not respond quickly to immediate action. Such managements have little or no industry loyalty or identity, and they have adopted financial performance as their ultimate—and only—objective. In our experience, most American industry leaders do not fall into this category, and they consider such practices unprofessional. Certainly the managers in the companies under consideration were more deliberate in their thinking about diversification and more circumscribed. Their visions led them to a persistent identification with particular skills, knowledge, and expertise, and they were attracted to those industries in which such attributes offered a distinctive advantage. Further, they were more likely to stay overly long in a deteriorating industry than to cut and run, because they had become committed to it by their vision combined with their powerful drives to compete and excel. Thus even though the freedom to move into new and different industries can be abused, we conclude that it is an important strength of the United States' economy. It enables managers to further their company's survival by preserving the valuable financial, human, technical, and organizational resources that have taken decades to accumulate.

Strategic Myopia

This concern with corporate survival is the major reason for our discomfort with those who charge that American industry has given excessive priority to short-term profit or return-on-investment objectives to the neglect of long-term technological development, productive efficiency and capacity, and competitive leadership. The corporate goals, priorities, and strategies we examined included short-term results; but they looked far beyond them as well. In those instances in which we observed managers "underinvesting" in declining businesses, they were actually relocating resources because, in their judgment, corporate survival demanded a shift to more promising product markets. Therefore we believe that this popular criticism oversimplifies and overstates more complex realities.

That there are considerable short-term pressures on these companies is undeniable. The reporting of corporate performance has focused with increasing relentlessness on year-to-year and quarter-to-quarter profit performance, with particular emphasis on continuity and growth, and there has also been an increase in the attention given to return on investment. Yet we found little evidence to indicate that management was preoccupied with these measures. At times financial exigencies dictated a disruption of long-term expenditure patterns in both operating and capital budgets. However, we did not observe chronic neglect. On the contrary, the foundation of future earnings was a persistent preoccupation of management.

One possible explanation for this fact lies in our focus. As we have often emphasized, these are *successful* companies. Their managers enjoy the relative affluence that is the fruit of success. Thus they are not threatened by the week-to-week and month-to-month financial demands that increasingly preoccupy the managements of failing or marginal companies. On the contrary, their success affords them the opportunity to think beyond the exigencies of immediate results and to respond to the needs of the more distant future. Thus the cause-and-effect relationship between corporate success and the planning horizon is in practice difficult to untangle.

Further, we would argue that these short-term priorities originate primarily in one segment of the capital market constituency and that they do not represent the natural priorities of professional management. In recent years a number of financial concepts initially developed and found useful in the management of financial assets (securities) have been extended to the management of real assets, without a clear recognition of the major differences that exist between the capital and the product markets. The relative efficiency of the capital markets and the speed with which major structural change can be effected with a minimum of friction have led to the emergence of a "now generation" of professional portfolio managers who are expected to generate, and who therefore expect, instant results from the corporations in which they invest. The notion of waiting five or ten years for competitive excellence to mature is beyond the limits of their patience, or that of their investment clients. But managements that strive to meet these expectations to the exclusion of other priorities are likely to be their own worst enemies, since time is a crucial ingredient of success in managing the real-asset portfolios for which they are responsible.

The corporate managers in this study recognized this fact. As we have reported, they complained often about the tyranny of quarter-to-quarter profit growth standing in the way of investment for the long term. They saw the pressure for persistent near-term performance as incompatible with the natural cycles of investment and return on investment, particularly in capital-intensive industries. They also tended to perceive professional fund managers and investment analysts as hostile to the true interests of their corporations (even though many of the latter do take the long view and cannot be fooled by earnings that cannot be sustained).

Beyond the statments of the managers themselves, this study contains evidence that runs counter to the image of myopic American industrial leadership. One piece is provided by the financial goals system itself, which reflects the entire spectrum of short- and long-term priorities. It is, of course, true that in balancing the system of financial goals, corporate managers frequently require some product market general managers reporting to them to generate short-term earnings, which can then be used to fund other growing businesses. Indeed it may well be that some of the complaints about myopia cited by critics emanate from these lower-level managers. But these actions are necessary from time to time to balance the financial goals system while maintaining financial self-sufficiency. They are not applied across the board, nor are they representative of management's overall corporate goals.

We should also point out that we find nothing which indicates that the reward system in these companies is dominated by short-term results. On the contrary, the financial incentive systems were usually designed to anticipate trends beyond the current year. It does not take long for a manager to figure out that today's achievement becomes tomorrow's benchmark. Moreover, and more important, managers, unlike investors, typically live out their entire working lives with one company. Thus they must live with the consequences of decisions made years, or even decades, earlier.

Finally, we must return to the fact that these managers' overriding concern for corporate survival underlies all their strategic choices. Like Winston Churchill, the leaders in these companies have no intention of presiding over the dissolution of an empire—even though, like Churchill, they may end up doing so because of events they cannot control. In fact, what is most striking to us about these corporate managers' decisions, when viewed with the advantage of hindsight, is the persistence with which they continued to strive for corporate survival in the face of both objective and psychological constraints.

We suspect that this description applies more generally to the executives in other major successful American companies as well. Consequently, to the extent that American firms such as those we have observed are falling behind foreign competitors at this stage of their existence, we conclude that we must look for reasons beyond a preoccupation with short-term profitability or the limited horizons of financial planning and corporate strategy. Our inclination is to look at the constraints on choice created by top managers' own beliefs and by the constituencies from which they derive their corporate resources. Therefore, to the extent that these companies have failed to meet the challenge of domestic or foreign competitors the explanation appears to lie in myopia of a different sort: either top managers have failed to perceive environmental changes correctly; or having perceived them, they have been incapable of adjusting to them because they are locked in by objective constraints and a set of beliefs about themselves and their capacities that are incompatible with the direction of change.

Unlimited Ambition, Limited Choice

Top management's freedom to set strategic direction in the mature industrial corporation is significantly constrained. The necessity to protect a competitive position commits the enterprise to a rate of growth and of investment largely defined by the industry (or industries) in which it operates. The capital markets impose limits on the ability to retain earnings and to use debt as a supplement to internal funds. The need to attract and hold superior personnel requires organizational expansion and change that may dictate a rate of continued growth not satisfied by the current industrial base. And all of these demands must be balanced and reconciled within a goals system that managers believe must be inherently self-sustaining in order to provide the assurance of long-term survival.

This description clearly contradicts the popular notion of the senior corporate executive as a man who can move mountains with a memo. More important, it also reminds us of the ways in which top managers continue to be subject to the external forces of a competitive market environment. Thus we must differ with Alfred Chandlers's contention that "in many sectors of the economy the visible hand of management [has] replaced what Adam Smith referred to as the invisible hand of market forces."[4] We would argue instead that those market forces have been internalized through the corporate financial goals system and that they are alive and well as a discipline on management's choices. Moreover, senior managers view these objective constraints through the filter of a well-entrenched belief system, which has its own set of limitations. Nowhere are those beliefs more evident than in top managers' sense of their organization's distinctive competence. In fact, it is no overstatement to say that, in the main, management chooses industries, not goals, and that these industries—and their related capital and human resource markets—impose the requisite financial goals that discipline resource allocation and strategic choice.

So potent are these beliefs that managers who are concerned with their capacity to make strategic change would do well to make them as explicit as possible. To this end, a periodic audit of the company's belief system could be a useful part of the planning exercise. While corporate managers can attempt to carry out this assessment themselves, personal adherence to their beliefs may make them difficult to isolate and identify. Therefore, the outside members of their board of directors can play a unique role in this assessment process. On one hand, these directors are well versed in management's strategic thinking. On the other, their own beliefs and experiences give them sufficient distance to make a more objective evaluation.

In any case, the basic purpose of such an audit would be to make management's beliefs explicit. It would not (and should not) remove management's adherence to those beliefs that underpin a successful corporate strategy. But it would help to guard against the possibility that they may become a barrier to essential strategic change.

This is not to say that management has no choice in defining a meaningful financial goals system and strategy. For one thing, we have noted that there is a degree of "play" in the goals system arising from the relatively crude measures of performance, imperfections of information, uncertainty, and corporate and market inertia. For another, corporations are rarely fully efficient in utilizing resources, and management's judgment as to the necessary degree of financial or organizational slack will vary with time and circumstances, even within a stable belief system.

And yet, on balance, we remain most impressed by the constraints on top managers' choices. Their freedom to set goals and strategy can be pushed only so far before they come into direct confrontation with the objective reality of the financial goals system and the psychological constraints of their beliefs. Ironically, the more efficient a management is in the full utilization of its resources—the more it has used up all the tricks of the financial trade—the closer it is to having reached the limits of what it considers acceptable choice. Thus it is also closer to being the captive of its unique constituency environment, at least in the short run. For should some new challenge or demand arise, the goals system will necessarily be driven by that constituency on which the firm most depends.

The movement of a business organization across the decades, as it seeks to escape one increasingly hostile industry environment and relocate in a more benevolent one, can be likened to the journey of an interplanetary spaceship. Having made the decision to relocate and chosen the new base of operations, it takes enormous energy and sustained thrust to escape the gravitational pull of the existing environment. At first economic, organizational, and psychological forces tend to resist the move; the parameters of the financial goals system in the firm are dictated by the existing corporate environment just as the parameters of flight are dominated by the forces exerted by the spaceship's existing planetary environment. But the guidance system of the spaceship is indifferent to the alternative environment to be selected or the time frame within which it is to be accomplished. That is the responsibility of the human beings who operate it. So too for the corporate managers: they must anticipate when the existing environment will become incapable of supporting life as they wish to live it and what new environment holds the prospect of better conditions. With that decision made and the flight underway, the forces of the existing environment will gradually lose their hold on the vehicle and the forces of the new environment will begin to dominate the journey.

Like spaceships, corporations can only travel toward their objectives if they have skilled pilots at the controls. By dealing with the objective and psychological constraints they face, these executives are able to create the window for independent action and for the strategic choices that ensure their organization's health and survival. Unless corporate managers understand these constraints and develop the distinctive corporate thrust necessary to overcome the limitations they impose and to set a new course, they cannot hope to assure the passage of the enterprise into the next century.

APPENDIX A

Methodology

Several considerations governed our selection of the twelve companies to be studied. Perhaps most obvious was long-term corporate success. As we have noted, all of these firms are major forces within their respective industries. Thus they are comparable as a group, even though their characters and particular corporate histories differ, as do the industries in which they are primarily based. By further limiting the sample to industrial companies, we could also assure comparability among the financial documents that are a primary source of evidence. We could rely on standard traditions of reporting and evaluation, and we could compare financial statements as well as budgets and plans.

Access and confidentiality were also significant considerations as we defined the sample. Obviously research such as this could not go forward without the disclosure of all relevant information. Consequently, no study was undertaken unless the company agreed in advance to give the research team unrestricted access to its documents and management personnel, present and past. In return, we promised to hold all information in confidence. Last, we weighed the issue of government involvement and decided to exclude all regulated industries. No business is entirely free of regulatory influences, of course, but government involvement in questions of pricing, investment, or rate of return would have impinged on the very heart of this study.

Once these guidelines had been established, twelve major industrial firms were chosen. This sample was small enough to allow the intensive investigation necessary, while large enough to diminish the possibility that the unique experience of one company or set of managers would dominate the findings.

Research began once a chief executive officer had confirmed his organization's willingness to participate. With management's assistance, we collected the primary documents on which the study rests. These are the company's written records: prospective and retrospective, public and private. Documents available to us included annual planning reports, budgeting manuals, project analyses, special studies, records of conferences and speeches, and interoffice reports and memos. Also included were the detailed records of financial and corporate performance ordinarily reserved for internal use, as well as facts and interpretive information on the company, its competition, and the firm's economic environment. These documents allowed us to capture top managers' thoughts and intent, as they spoke among themselves, off the record and free of retrospective filters. They also allowed us to test the executives' accuracy and consistency, as we compared them with one another and over time.

Some of this information is summarized in appendix C, a statistical record of goals and performance against goals for the period 1968–1978. As we would expect, the companies differed in the number and nature of their financial goals. However, beginning in the seventies, we found a clear trend toward more specific and detailed statements of financial goals. A few companies continue to be satisfied with simple statements of corporate purpose, but the large majority now have a clear and comprehensive set of financial goals that are an integral part of the financial planning and resource allocation process. Moreover, as these statements became more detailed and comprehensive, they became more and more similar in their general content. Thus they indicate clearly the influence of the funds-flow discipline.

An extensive series of interviews supplemented these written documents. Two subjects were of particular importance. The first was the way in which financial goals were established within the company. The second was the history of two or three major decisions of the sort described in the text: to diversify through acquisition; to introduce a major new product developed internally; to undertake large capital expenditures for new plants; to expand activities internationally. However, the sessions were largely nondirective as befit the temperament of the successful executives involved and our own desire to minimize bias in their response. Wide-ranging and open-ended, these discussions often served the additional purpose of identifying new issues unknown to others, or forgotten by them, which could add to the data.

During the course of these interviews we met with the financial, planning, and operating executives who constituted the top management team. We also spoke with some of the divisional managers who were subject to the discipline of the planning and goal-setting process, as well as with past and present chief executives.

Usually two interviewers were present at each session to ensure a complete and accurate record. Whenever possible, we met with each respondent individually, so that remembered plans and events could be cross-checked for accuracy and detail from several participants' perspective. Thus we strove to guard against the possibility that we would miss important clues because our informant did not mention them or that we would hear only what a particular manager wished to be heard.

We were also careful to guard against allowing our prior expectations to color what we heard. From our initial interviews on, we found that corporate managers talked constantly about what they "believed" in their company. Yet we were slow to label these statements "beliefs," because we suspected that they might reflect nothing more than management's way of speaking about the economic realities that the firm faced. Nevertheless, as the investigation continued through the twelve companies, we became convinced that there was indeed a unique pattern of beliefs among the managers in each company. We further recognized that for each firm, these beliefs had a major effect on how its corporate managers interpreted the demands of their three constituencies and therefore on the decisions they made.

Appendix D presents these corporate belief systems in summary form. As can be seen, we have reported an elaborate system of beliefs for most of the firms studied. However, in a few the beliefs reported are more limited, and they provide a simple skeleton. Our own success in collecting data may well account for some of these variations. (In fact, our data for the two conglomerates are less complete because the relationship we were able to establish with these two companies was more limited.) But a more significant explanation lies in the degree of consensus found among the members of a particular management team, a subject discussed in detail in chapter 7.

APPENDIX B

The Diversification Index

A complete index of diversification should be sensitive to at least two aspects of diversification: (1) The *number* of different markets in which the firm is engaged; and (2) the *distribution* of its cash flows or productive activity among those markets.

Traditionally used methods have been inadequate to capture these two dimensions of diversification. Counting product lines addresses the first dimension but not the second. The ratio of a company's sales in its primary market to its total sales partially measures the distribution of the company's cash flows (as between primary and secondary markets), but it neglects the number of different markets in which the firm is involved. A "compromise" solution—measuring the concentration of activity in the firm's two or three largest product markets—partially measures both the number and the relative dominance of the firm's major activities. However, this solution is unsatisfactory in that firms that differ greatly in their degree of diversification could have identical indices of unity. (For example, a single-product firm and a dual-product firm could generate the same index, despite differences in their actual degree of diversification.)

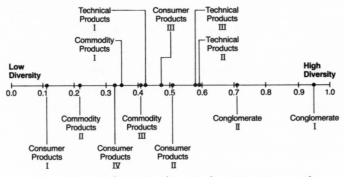

Figure B.1   Relative Product Market Diversity, 1978*

*Closely held companies are written above the diversification line, while widely held companies are shown below the line.

The index we have devised addresses these problems. It is defined by the formula:

$$D = - \log \sum_{i=1}^{n} s_i^2$$

where: n equals the total number of different product markets in which the firm is engaged; Σ equals a sum over all n product markets; and s_i equals the proportion of a firm's total dollar sales accounted for by the ith product market. The index takes a value of zero for a single-product market (i.e., no diversity whatsoever) and may, in principle, increase indefinitely thereafter, depending on the number and size distribution of a firm's product markets. As a practical matter, however, it would be unusual to see the index rise much above 1.0. (To give a specific example, a company in ten different product markets, with sales divided equally among all ten markets, would have a diversification index value of one.)

This diversification index is a variant of an index of industrial concentration originally developed by Orris C. Herfindahl.[1] For our purposes the important part of the index is the term Σs_i^2. This term represents a weighting scheme for a firm's proportions of sales by product markets, where the weights are simply the fractions of sales themselves. The log transformation is employed for statistical reasons and in no way changes the ordinal ranking of levels of diversification derived simply from Σs_i^2.[2]

The index is sensitive to the *number* of activities in which the company is engaged because we sum over *all* of the firm's fraction of sales by product market. The index is also sensitive to the *distribution* of sales among product markets because each sales fraction squared is the proportion of total sales accounted for by a corresponding product market. Finally, by taking squares of each fraction of total sales, we ensure that our sum will never equal unity except in the case of a single-product company. Thus we avoid having an identical value of the index for firms with truly different degrees of diversification.

The Data

The data used to construct the diversification index were the company's reported sales by major product line. Several caveats should be mentioned in connection with the use of sales data of this type. First, the use of sales data obscures the fact that a company's actual cash flow from a particular product market may be quite different from its fraction of total cash flow (i.e., cash flow from a market can be negative, but sales cannot be). Thus an index constructed on the basis of sales data may belie the actual success of a company's diversification program. Second, the use of sales data renders the index sensitive to exogenous forces beyond management's control that change the composition of sales despite their consistent allocation of productive assets to each line of business. Thus changes in the index over time cannot wholly be ascribed to management's diversification goals. Third, comparability between firms is impaired to the extent that they vary in the detail with which they report sales by line of business.

Despite such drawbacks, reasons of convenience and availability dictated the use of sales by product line. Except in very recent years, assets by product line were usually not reported, and companies never compiled such data themselves until new federal reporting requirements forced them to do so. For better or worse, therefore, sales by product line are the data available over a useful length of time.

APPENDIX C

Goals and Performance of Research Sample Companies

Complete data on the key elements of the financial goals system were available for nine of the twelve companies. For the other three one or another element was unknown or had to be inferred. For example, Consumer Product I's top management, particularly the chief financial officer, resisted formal analysis and planning at the time of our study. Managers there preferred to be "flexible," and they refused to be pinned down to a specific dividend payout and debt equity ratio. In contrast, the management of Commodity Products II, a single-industry company, was very specific on its debt and dividend policy but remained vague on growth and ROI targets. (The failure to attain a satisfactory ROI over many years may explain this reluctance.) In essence, therefore, the company was driven by a rank in industry competitive goal, and its growth and ROI numbers reflected that fact, coupled with management's clear-cut debt and dividend policies. Finally, Technical Products I had a goal of zero debt and zero dividends. (In fact, it paid a small dividend.) The managers refused to adopt an explicit share of market and growth rate objective on principle; but since they clearly adopted the concept of financial self-sufficiency, a specific growth target could be imputed.

	Consumer Products I	Consumer Products II	Consumer Products III	Consumer Products IV	Technical Products I	Technical Products
A. *Current Financial Goals*						
Growth Rate of Sales	17%	12%	15%	14%	—	14%
Return on Net Assets	27%	14%	14%	19%	18%	14%
Earnings Retention Ratio	—	.65	.67	.48	—	.67
Debt/Equity Ratio	—	.82	.33	.54	0	.33
After-Tax Interest Rate	3.8%	4.5%	5.4%	3.2%	—	4.4%
B. *Implicit Financial Goals*						
Growth Rate of Sales	—	14%	11%	13%	18%	11%
Return on Net Assets	—	12%	18%	20%	—	17%
C. *Actual Performance* 1968–1978						
Growth Rate of Sales	18.0	15.5	15.1	11.9	20.0	9.8
Return on Net Assets	14.9	12.7	16.3	11.0	16.3	10.6
Earnings Retention Ratio	.74	.66	.46	.44	.88	.53
Debt/Equity Ratio	.24	.75	.16	.29	.01	.22
D. *Industry Performance* 1968–1978						
1. Growth Rate of Sales						
Industry	—	9.3%	10.8%	10.2%	—	9.7%
Selected Companies						
Mean	—	13.0	12.3	13.0	—	11.8
Range	—	11.7–14.7	9.5–16.8	6.6–20.8	—	10.2–15.8
2. RONA						
Industry	—	NA	NA	NA	—	NA
Selected Companies						
Mean	—	17.6%	20.0%	13.6%	—	15.5%
Range	—	14.7–24.7	13.5–30.0	12.2–14.9	—	12.8–18.3
3. Retention Ratio						
Industry	—	.65	NA	NA	—	NA
Selected Companies						
Mean	—	.61	.48	.61	—	.58
Range	—	.38–.79	.43–.54	.49–.77	—	.35–.68
4. Debt/Equity Ratio						
Industry	—	NA	NA	NA	—	NA
Selected Companies						
Mean	—	.45	.24	.38	—	.31
Range	—	.08–.72	.01–.43	.30–.46	—	.13–.52

Technical Products III	Commodity Products I	Commodity Products II	Commodity Products III	Conglomerate I	Conglomerate II
8%	15%	—	10%	8%	10%
17%	18%	—	13%	16%	9%
.50	.65	.52	.70	.60	.75
.38	.67	.54	.54	.50	1.00
5.0	5.1%	4.9%	4.5%	4.4%	5.3%
11%	17%	—	12%	13%	10%
13%	16%	—	11%	10%	9%
11.0	11.5	11.5	9.3	7.5	7.2
11.2	8.4	7.2	8.6	12.4	8.6
.38	.54	.56	.43	.59	.79
.17	.23	.28	.52	.31	.68
9.3%	8.8%	—	10.2%	9.0%	9.0%
11.0	10.0	—	10.8	11.6	11.6
7.6–15.3	8.5–12.7	—	9.8–12.0	6.6–18.1	6.6–18.3
16.4%	NA	—	14.4%	13.9%	13.9%
17.2%	18.8%	—	13.8%	14.8%	14.8%
15.6–21.0	10.7–23.2	—	11.9–15.7	9.7–17.6	9.7–17.6
.54	NA	—	.59	.48	.48
.42	.48	—	.46	.73	.73
.37–.51	.46–.52	—	.39–.52	.50–1.00	.50–1.00
.34	NA	—	.46	.73	.33
.55	.26	—	.43	.71	.71
.42–.76	.10–.42	—	.35–.48	.46–1.35	.46–1.35

APPENDIX D

Corporate Managements' Belief Systems

Corporate Managements' Beliefs About

Company	Establishing Financial Goals	Establishing Means	Internal Organization
Technical Products I	Stay on a pay-as-you-go basis.	Do a good job—technically superior products.	Our major resource is our people.
	Make a profit.	Minimize acquisitions because you don't acquire good managers.	Avoid being a hire/fire company.
	Don't diversify except where our technology can be applied.	Compete with many unique products.	Make company a stimulating, fun, and exciting place to work.
		Innovate in bite sizes.	We are all one big interactive team of 40,000 people.
		Be innovative in technology but conservative in marketing.	People should make a long-term commitment to the company because we are not a hire/fire company.
		Market share comes through technically superior products.	We grow to give people a challenge.
		Don't buy market share. Products should show a profit from the start.	We encourage people to own shares of the company.
			We include everyone in profit sharing.

Corporate Managements' Beliefs About (continued)

Company	Establishing Financial Goals	Establishing Means	Internal Organization
Technical Products II	Be measured against the best. Be at the top of everything.	We can always find a technological market opportunity.	The real problem is how to use good people efficiently. The dollars will follow the people.
	Our mission is technology, profit market.	We must be what we are: We don't want to grow by acquiring somebody and taking the acquisition route.	Compensation based on corporate results to build commitment. It takes managerial team building.
	We must be masters of our fate [less cyclical].		
	We must not be dependent on one major product line.	Do not lose the mystique of being a technology company even if we have to accept a certain cyclicality.	People [in the local city] have few alternatives for places to work and therefore should be insulated from severe employment fluctuations.
	We must be conservative financially. There are not more good opportunities than we have generated funds internally.	Payoffs will always come from inventions [in technology].	People wish to grow with stable careers.
	We must grow in volume and ROI.	Technology is our driving force—in fact and perception.	We should give all our employees the experience of an opportunity to grow with a stable career.
	To run the company for the long run, for exotic future growth.	Go anywhere but only where you have a technological advantage.	
	Over the long run, if we do a good job, market price of stock will follow.	We develop unique technical solutions to large market needs, or we find the large market to fit the technology.	
		After solving the technical problem of high-volume users, we must work down the learning curve and keep others from backward integrating.	
		Bet on the long ball [a major R&D effort].	
		We must maintain product excellence.	

Technical Products III	We must grow as fast as the industry, plus the rate of inflation.	We must manage well what we have right now.	Don't shove targets down people's throats.
	ROI is no good unless you have a strong competitive position in the market.	Follow new technology and stick with products based on [technology] because you are better off doing what you can do best.	Don't manage like a detached investment banker.
	We must maintain a conservative financial structure.	Support weakness from within.	Leave initiative with the bottom. Let top management respond to what division managers say.
	Flexibility for the future is needed more than financial safety now.	Stick with potentially big technological breakthroughs.	We must strive to make division managers see that they are playing in a bigger ball game.
	We must take a long-haul view and worry about the integrity and survival of the corporation above all else.	Get the strongest leadership position in each business and hold it even in the short run.	We have a cohesive culture.
		Today one must ride technology-based products longer rather than letting competitors have it as soon as it becomes commoditylike.	We believe in paying higher than average wages.
			We don't believe in firing a manager if he makes a mistake, like at ITT.
			No unions.
			We believe in hiring the best people and keeping them.

Corporate Managements' Beliefs About *(continued)*

Company	Establishing Financial Goals	Establishing Means	Internal Organization
Consumer Products I	We must be in the upper three-quarters of companies in our industry but above all must outperform [a competitor].	Get every consumer in the world to use [our product].	We get good people and keep them.
	Superior ROI will over time provide superior stock performance.	We are a [product] company.	We must breed our own management.
		We must grow outside the United States.	We believe in above-average people for a given job in our industry.
	Be careful about our current ratio because we are a working capital company.	There are major overseas business opportunities.	A stake in the company will motivate employees and executives.
	We can't run a lot of businesses we don't know anything about.	It's risky to be a style leader.	We want to maintain a nonunion work force.
		Profits grow with share of market.	We do not believe in nepotism.
	You have to grow to survive and be prepared to issue equity and long-term debt to grow.	It's important to have a known brand name.	Stable employment is a basic employee right.
	Dividends must increase faster than inflation.	We must be flexible in a dynamic uncertain industry.	
	We must be a well-run company so we will be allowed to run it.	We must maintain flexibility overseas because of political uncertainty.	
		We must be a leader in manufacturing methods to keep costs down and quality up.	

Consumer Products II	We want to be in the upper 25 percent of *Fortune* 500 companies.	Our diversification must be into branded consumer products.	We need growth opportunities to attract good managers.
	We want to be an all-weather company.	New lines of business must be comfortable to our management, in consumer products and in United States	We believe in a lot of participation in planning.
	Achieving [our financial goals] satisfies our institutional investors and allows us to be well paid as managers.	We should acquire new small lines of business with growth potential, which are fully competitive and have strong management. No turnarounds.	We want each operating manager to sponsor his own efforts.
	We should avoid thinking of equity as a means of financing.	We must also be willing to get out of unsuccessful businesses. Take your lumps and stay current.	If we are to pay managers well, we must perform well.
	We want to maintain a leverage situation but with [a less than AAA] rating because we don't want to manage debt to achieve higher rating.		
	We want to pay out [X percent] of earnings.		
	While we are an all-weather company, we are not a conglomerate because we must have a clear strategy with which people can identify.		

Corporate Managements' Beliefs About (continued)

Company	Establishing Financial Goals	Establishing Means	Internal Organization
Consumer Products III	Preserve the company as a private concern for the next generation.	Diversification should be in consumer products.	We do not want any unions.
	We must be profitable but sustain the growth tempo to maintain vitality.	We must continue to do business in only good clean honest businesses.	We're people oriented.
			We believe in making decisions informally.
	We must diversify beyond traditional areas to spread risk because growth has slowed and to leave something for the next generation.	Only launch true "product pluses."	We take pride in being ahead of everybody in profit sharing.
		Stay with high-gross margin products.	We believe in higher pay.
	While long-term debt of [X percent] is acceptable, we don't want more so we can maintain quality of life for management by keeping free of bank restrictions.	Launch for leadership in six months.	We believe in womb-to-tomb-type security.
		But don't abandon losers [either products or geographic markets]. Stay with them until they become winners.	Growth is necessary to provide opportunities for employees.
	Maintain reliable payout of dividends to keep family happy.		We must make the world a better place for us having been here by:
			Improving or maintaining quality of life for employees.
	We don't have to be the biggest company in the world, but we must be the best!		Enhancing quality of life for host community.

Consumer Products IV

We must sustain investor interest.

To do this we must improve return on assets.

We need an internal flow of funds so that we can preserve our lines of credit and avoid new equity.

We believe in minimizing risk, because that's what analysts want.

Stability is highly desirable because it's important to investors and management.

Since practically speaking it's impossible to maintain steady earnings, we want some growth. We believe either you grow or fall back.

We want to be: balanced 50/50 between [major business] and between United States and overseas.

Pursuing our basic strengths is key.

We should move cautiously into new products and with new products.

We must maintain our brand images, as long as it doesn't negatively impact RONA.

The quality of our products is our number-one concern.

Advertising is our strength in building brand image, and we believe in few trade deals.

Large organizations are less flexible.

We must be a decentralized organization.

We rely on inertia to guide the organization.

But the CEO should make the major decisions.

We promote from within.

Corporate Managements' Beliefs About (continued)

Company	Establishing Financial Goals	Establishing Means	Internal Organization
Commodity Products I	Higher price/earnings ratio than the Dow Jones Average.	Be number one in all of one's business segments.	We must be willing to delegate responsibility to separate business.
	We want high sustained growth in EPS and a return on equity of [X percent].	"Expense invest" when entering a new business in order to establish number one position.	We allow managers the freedom to act and don't overcontrol.
	Diversify out of [traditional products] and don't be too dependent upon the industry cycle.	We try to gain market share even in case of economic downturn.	We are concerned for our people and the integrity of management.
	Diversify the portfolio of businesses but keep it balanced in cash flows and cash needs.	We won't harvest a company and will only sell one if the manager running it wants to go.	We must remain nonunion.
	Limit diversification to noncapital equipment and stay away from high-technology and capital-intensive products.		[The company's] first responsibility is not to shareholders but to employees.
	Debt/equity should be at [X percent] except if more is needed to finance a major acquisition.		
	We must keep dividend payout at [X percent].		

Commodity Products II

Be the strongest top-ranked participant in the [industry].

We shall stay in [industry] and not make any major diversification out of it.

Be in the upper one-third of all manufacturing companies.

This means having return on equity of [X percent]; steady improvement in market share; constant innovations in product and process; having the strongest management structure in the industry.

Dividends are never to be cut and should be [X percent] of earnings.

Maintain [X] credit rating by keeping debt less than [X percent] of capital.

Our geographical location provides us with a cost advantage.

We must offer better service to our customers.

We must expand plants for the long pull.

Major customers like big suppliers committed to the industry.

We must improve profit position through lower costs, not higher prices.

Market share is important but through low prices.

We must compete on innovation in processes and basic products not in price.

Foster harmony and preserve a family feeling within the company throughout all levels of employment.

Encourage personnel to play full part in the affairs of their community.

We must keep the employees who believe in our industry happy because the industry is what we are good at.

Preserve the drama and emotion of the industry.

We want to keep management "open door" and participating.

Top management must include at least one person who understands manufacturing operations and processes.

Good coordination between sales and manufacturing gives us the ability to serve customers better than competitors.

Corporate Managements' Beliefs About (continued)

Company	Establishing Financial Goals	Establishing Means	Internal Organization
Commodity Products III	We must be profitable as measured by return on net assets.	We don't fund projects; we fund strategies.	Keep [the traditional industry] people happy first.
	We must grow at an [X percent] per annum rate to survive and get the best people.	We're good at two things—manufacturing and distribution.	Pay constant attention to management development.
	Since we must have an [X] credit rating, we must do nothing to improve or jeopardize it.	You must be cost effective to compete in [basic industry].	We believe the CEO should have a long development period and a long term in office.
	Enter new businesses where we think we can win.		Treat every idea with respect. We can afford to have failures.
	But first optimize what we have.		
	Achieve market share objective and you will achieve RONA and growth goals.		
	We want a dividend payout of [X percent] because we can make better use of the money than the shareholders.		
	Don't let cash accumulate because it could make us a takeover candidate.		

Conglomerate I	We want a return on equity of [X percent] because that's what the better *Fortune* 500 companies are doing. This includes above-average growth in earnings and dividends. We want to allow the widest range of diversification through acquisition and internal development. We want to achieve a stream of opportunities to be exploited which leads to stability of earnings and capital base.	We want to obtain dominance in each market segment. Each division should compete in whatever way is best for it. Each division must be the most efficient producer in its industry. Product market portfolios are not operative here. We want superior performance *based on products and services of excellence and quality.* This will benefit shareholders, employees, customers, and society in general.	Our priorities will be people development, internal growth, and expansion into new areas of opportunity. We allow divisions autonomy except in control of cash flows. We want to create an exciting environment for management by growing. Our managers manage a wide range of industries.
Conglomerate II	RONA is the key goal. We want to grow through diversification to get better margins, but will also stay in [the core business]. We want to maintain our present bank rating. We want to maintain our present dividend payout and try to have frequent improvement. We believe that cash is good.	We can manage in a range of industries. We must stay out of electronics. R&D will allow us to compete in industries where we do not have a strong position.	Management education is very important. We manage by the numbers. People here identify with their individual business. It's hard to build a corporate identity.

Notes

Chapter 1

1. Richard P. Rumelt, *Strategy, Structure, and Economic Performance* (Boston: Harvard University, Graduate School of Business Administration, Division of Research, 1974), p. 32.

2. Alfred D. Chandler, Jr., *Strategy and Structure* (Boston: MIT Press, 1962); Oliver E. Williamson, *Corporate Control and Business Behavior* (Englewood Cliffs, N.J.: Prentice-Hall, 1970).

3. Leonard Wrigley, "Diversification and Divisional Autonomy" (DBA diss., Harvard Business School, 1970); Rumelt, *Strategy, Structure, and Economic Performance,* pp. 50–51.

4. *Wall Street Journal,* 11 June 1980.

Chapter 2

1. Ideally our data about both perspectives would be complete. However, the practicalities of field research made this an impossible goal. For example, a 1976 study indicated that the CEOs of *Fortune* 500 companies spent a median of fifty-six hours per week at work. A more recent study of general managers at several levels increases this average to fifty-nine hours per week. Our own experience, as we scheduled interviews with these corporate managers, suggests that our group was at least this busy. Even though we had arranged our sessions several months in advance, with executives prepared to be fully cooperative, a single interview of one to two hours was the most we could consistently manage. And even then we could

devote only a limited portion of each interview to personal characteristics, given the broad scope of the topics we had to pursue. Therefore the data we have assembled about each of these managers are limited and sometimes fragmentary. Nevertheless, when they are examined in conjunction with other available studies, a clear pattern does emerge that provides insight into the managers' personal motivations. Charles G. Burck, "A Group Profile of the *Fortune* 500 Chief Executives," *Fortune* (May 1976): 172; John P. Kotter, *The General Managers* (New York: Free Press, 1982), p. 81.

2. Burck, "A Group Profile," pp. 173–177.

3. "Korn/Ferry International's Executive Profile: A Survey of Corporate Leaders" (New York: Korn/Ferry International, 1979).

4. Frederick Herzberg et al., *The Motivation to Work* (New York: Wiley, 1959); Edward E. Lawler III, *Pay and Organizational Effectiveness: A Psychological View* (New York: McGraw-Hill, 1971).

5. Daniel J. Levinson et al., *The Seasons of a Man's Life* (New York: Alfred A. Knopf, 1978); George E. Vaillant, *Adaption to Life* (Boston: Little, Brown & Company, 1977).

6. Michael Maccoby, *The Gamesman: The New Corporate Leaders* (New York: Simon and Schuster, 1976), p. 49.

7. Among the most useful of these are Levinson et al., *Seasons of a Man's Life;* Vaillant, *Adaption to Life;* Roger Gould, *Transformations: Growth and Change in Adult Life* (New York: Simon and Schuster, 1978); Neil J. Smelser and Erik H. Erikson, eds., *Themes of Work and Love in Adulthood* (Cambridge, Mass.: Harvard University Press, 1980); and Erik H. Erikson, *Identity: Youth and Crisis* (New York: W.W. Norton & Company, 1968).

8. Levinson et al. *Seasons of a Man's Life,* pp. 72–84; Neil J. Smelser, "Issues in the Study of Work and Love in Adulthood," in Smelser and Erickson, *Themes of Work and Love,* pp. 1–26.

9. Levinson et al. *Seasons of a Man's Life* pp. 191–200.

10. Abraham Zaleznik and Manfred F.R. Kets de Vries, *Power and the Corporate Mind* (Boston: Houghton Mifflin, 1975).

Chapter 3

1. The academic literature in corporate finance reflects the long-standing disposition of academics to identify corporate financial goals with the creation of shareholder wealth. Invariably financial theory prescribes good management practice in terms of its positive impact on the market value of owners' equity. While serious scholars of business practice recognize that other goals and other criteria exist in the real world, they tend to treat these as aberrations that can be corrected by appropriate compensation packages or other forms of shareholder discipline. The ultimate authority is seen to lie in the power of the public capital markets to allocate or withhold corporate purchasing power. For a clear summary of this point of view, see James C. Van Horne, *Financial Management and Policy,* 5th ed. (Englewood Cliffs, N.J.: Prentice-Hall, 1980), pp. 8–11. For a concise survey of the recent academic literature on this subject, see Neil Seitz, "Shareholder Goals, Firm's Goals and Firm Financing Decisions," *Financial Management* 11 (Autumn 1982): 20–26.

Notes

Chapter 4

1. The concept of a model or equation of corporate financial self-sufficiency, even though inconsistent with the currently popular efficient capital markets theory, has existed for some time in academic literature in different forms. For a recent development, see Robert C. Higgins's articles "How Much Growth Can a Firm Afford?" *Financial Management* 6 (Autumn 1977): 7–16 and "Sustainable Growth Under Inflation," *Financial Management* 10 (Autumn 1981): 26–40.

2. See, for example, Richard Brealey and Stewart Myers, *Principles of Corporate Finance*, part 2 (New York: McGraw-Hill, 1981), pp. 10–105.

Chapter 5

1. That beliefs impact on management's decisions has been recognized in the literature on organizations for some time. In *Leadership and Administration* (New York: Harper & Row, 1975), Philip Selznick wrote about "organization character." Eric Rhenman, building on Selznick's work, discussed its impact on long-range planning in *Organization Theory for Long-Range Planning*, trans. Nancy Adler (London: John Wiley & Sons, 1973). "Strategies, Structures, and Processes of Organizational Decision," (*Comparative Studies in Administration*, ed. James D. Thompson, et al. [Pittsburgh: University of Pittsburgh Press, 1959], James D. Thompson and Arthur Tuden indicated that one of the critical elements of organized decision making is whether a consensus exists among decision makers about beliefs concerning cause-effect relations and the organization's technology. Richard Michael Cyert and James G. March, in *A Behavioral Theory of the Firm* (Englewood Cliffs, N.J.: Prentice-Hall, 1963), discuss decision premises that underlie managers' critical decisions. In *Value Systems and Social Process* (New York: Basic Books, 1968), Geoffrey Vickers first used his term appreciative system to describe essentially the same phenomenon.

More recently organization theorists have concluded that this important topic is poorly understood. This conclusion has resulted in a deluge of theoretical papers. In *Organizational Strategy, Structure, and Process* (New York: McGraw-Hill, 1978), Raymond E. Miles and Charles C. Snow write about "management philosophy." John P. Kotter, Edward Baker, and Phelps Tracy write about "organizational culture" in "Managing Organizational Culture" (working paper, Harvard Business School, 1980). Jeffrey Pfeffer, in "Management as Symbolic Action: The Creation and Maintenance of Organizational Paradigms" (Research Paper No. 503, Graduate School of Business, Stanford University), borrows Kuhn's phrase and writes about "organizational paradigms," as does Alan Sheldon in "Organizational Paradigms," *Organizational Dynamics* (Winter 1980): 61–79.

Authors concerned with strategy formulation have also been aware of this phenomenon. In *The Concept of Corporate Strategy* (Homewood, Ill.: Dow Jones-Irwin, 1980), Kenneth R. Andrews continues to use the concept of values, which is consistent with work in the field of business policy. Chandler, in his early study entitled *Strategy and Structure*, described how manager's belief in the viability of their traditional functional organization delayed the formation of divisionalized structures at companies like Sears and Du Pont long after the realities of diversification suggested the need for such change.

We have used the concept of *belief*, rather than one of the myriad terms already coined by others, because we wanted a term as simple and as descriptive of the phenomenon we were observing as possible. Terms like paradigm and character, while more fashionable, seemed

198

too imprecise and broad. The concept of "culture," while in vogue among managers and some social scientists, has its roots in the field of anthropology, where there is considerable conceptual confusion about its meaning. The term values was rejected because, as Vickers has pointed out, what we are concerned with is not just the question of what is valued but also the convictions about reality that decision makers hold.

Admittedly, a concept as broad as beliefs does mix together convictions about normative matters (such as values and desired goals) with those about decision rules—cause-and-effect relationships in product markets, for example. However, corporate managers hold equally strong convictions about both types of beliefs. While it is certainly true that the beliefs about decision rules can be verified more readily through experience, there is no evidence that such beliefs are more or less susceptible to change than those about normative matters.

2. Michael B. McCaskey's 1982 work, *The Executive Challenge: Managing Change and Ambiguity* (Boston: Pitman), which is a review of the work of John Dewey and John D. Steinbruner, provides an explanation of why this may be so:

> Dewey's observations on human nature are strongly supported by a recent review of work in cognitive psychology during the last several decades. Steinbruner (1974) found that, while researchers might disagree at the frontiers of knowledge about how the mind works, there was general agreement on five basic principles. Researchers found: (1) The mind is an inference machine that actively imposes order on highly ambiguous situations. (2) The mind works to keep internal core beliefs consistent and unchallenged. (The stress literature also shows that the mind will deny, distort, or ignore signals which contradict core beliefs.) (3) The mind prefers simplicity. (4) The mind is constrained by reality (here the objective side of reality) in important ways. (5) The mind prefers stable and enduring relationships among its core beliefs. The five principles are all of interest to managers facing ambiguity but the first principle is perhaps the most important; and the other principles all stem from it. *The mind is an inference machine that strives mightily to bring order, simplicity, consistency, and stability to the world it encounters.* In other words, where nature is ambiguous, people develop strong beliefs and act upon them. (p. 25)

Since corporate managers are dealing with complex and often ambiguous information, they develop core beliefs that, for them, are orderly and consistent. Therefore, they are no more likely to question a normative belief than they are a belief about decision rules.

3. This belief is consistent with organizational theory. See, for example, Tom Bruns and G. M. Stalker, *The Management of Innovation* (London: Tavistock Press, 1959); Paul R. Lawrence and Jay W. Lorsch, *Organization and Environment* (Boston: Harvard University, Graduate School of Business Administration, Division of Research, 1967); and Jay W. Lorsch and Stephen A. Allen III, *Managing Diversity and Interdependence* (Boston: Harvard University, Graduate School of Business Administration, Division of Research, 1973).

4. Fred K. Foulkes, *Personnel Policies in Large Nonunion Companies* (Englewood Cliffs, N.J.: Prentice-Hall, 1980).

5. James Brian Quinn, *Strategies for Change: Logical Incrementalism* (Homewood, Ill.: Richard D. Irwin, Inc., 1980).

6. Thomas J. Watson, Jr., *A Business and Its Beliefs: The Ideas That Helped Build IBM* (New York: McGraw-Hill, 1963), p. 5, italics added.

Chapter 6

1. As organizational scholars remind us, managers must deal with two types of external change. One is the set of regular and predictable changes they expect and with which they are prepared to deal—for example, seasonal changes in demand for their product or cyclical fluctuations in economic conditions. Rhenman has labeled these "cyclical" changes, while Sheldon calls them changes within the existing paradigm. The second type of change is more dramatic: it is the unexpected event that requires a fundamental change in strategy. These Rhenman calls "structural" changes, while Sheldon suggests that they require fundamental shifts in the organization's paradigm. The change we call an incremental change in strategy lies between these two extremes. It is not so regular as to be built into management's belief system, nor is it so traumatic that it challenges the fundamental premises of the system. Such change is implicit in the term dynamic equilibrium. See Rhenman, *Organization Theory*, pp. 15–19; Sheldon, "Organizational Paradigms"; and Quinn, *Strategies for Change*.

2. Levinson et al., *Seasons of a Man's Life* p. 98.

3. Ibid., p. 99.

4. Ibid., p. 101.

Chapter 7

1. *The Saturday Evening Post*, "HBS Case Services 9-373-009 (Boston: Harvard Business School, 1972).

2. In his paper "On the Science of 'Muddling Through,'" (Public Administration Review [Spring 1959]: 81), C. E. Lindblom gives us a typology of decision making:

Rational-Comprehensive (Root)	Successive Limited Comparisons (Branch)
Clarification of values or objectives distinct from and usually prerequisite to empirical analysis of alternative policies.	Selection of values, goals, and empirical analysis of the needed action are not distinct from one another but are intertwined.
Policy from data is therefore approved through means-end analysis. First the ends are isolated, then the means to achieve them are sought.	Since means and ends are not distinct, means-end analysis is often inappropriate or limited.
The test of a "good" policy is that it can be shown to be the most appropriate means to desired ends.	The test of a "good" policy is typically that various analysts find themselves directly agreeing on a policy (without their agreeing that it is the appropriate mean to an agreed objective).
Analysis is comprehensive: every important relevant factor is taken into account.	Analysis is drastically limited: 1. Important possible outcomes are neglected. 2. Important alternative potential policies are neglected. 3. Important affected values are neglected.
Theory is often heavily relied upon.	A succession of comparisons greatly reduce or eliminate reliance on theory.

Lindblom has labeled the method advocated by strategic planning experts the "root method." What he has called the "branch" approach is clearly closer to the reality we and others have found. It recognizes that ends and means are interconnected; that the real test of a decision is that the decision makers agree that it is the right policy; and that, necessarily, certain outcomes and alternatives are not fully explored. However, while our data indicate that this is a more accurate description of top management decision making than is the root method, we must modify and refine these ideas in several respects.

While ends and means are intertwined in the strategic decisions of top managers, there is an underlying pattern to this relationship. It derives from the fact that the personal motives of these men cannot be separated from their decisions as corporate officers. They want the company with which they identify personally to succeed competitively, and they want to perpetuate it. To achieve these broad ends, they must balance the financial goal system and meet constituency demands, within the context of their beliefs about self-sufficiency and appropriate risk. They choose means that are consistent with these beliefs as well as with their vision of the firm's distinctive competence.

With this perspective, ends can be distinguished from means, because it is the corporate managers' belief system that ultimately directs their strategic decisions by restricting the outcomes, values, and options considered. These beliefs are the "root" of decisions that might otherwise appear to have been made on the basis of inadequate or inappropriate information or, as Lindblom states, because the managers find themselves agreeing on a particular course of action.

We would also modify Lindblom's contention that this process reduces reliance on theory. Clearly this is so if one means, by theory, the ideas contained in texts on economics, organization theory, and strategic planning. In this case managers' adherence to theory is limited unless it becomes incorporated into the belief system. But if we follow Webster's dictionary and define theory more broadly, as "an idea or a mental plan of the way to do something," then there is plenty of theory involved in these decisions. However, it is theory derived from the collective experience of the managers and their predecessors as it has been incorporated into their belief system, rather than from books. In fact, the belief system *is* the operative theory of management for the top managers in each company.

Chapter 8

1. Alfred D. Chandler, Jr., *The Visible Hand: The Managerial Revolution in American Business* (Cambridge, Mass.: Harvard University Press, Belknap Press, 1977), pp. 8, 9–10.

2. Ibid., p. 10.

3. Herbert A. Simon, "On the Concept of Organizational Goals," *Administrative Science Quarterly* (June 1964): 1–22.

4. Chandler, *The Visible Hand*, p. 1.

Appendix B: The Diversification Index

1. Orris C. Herfindahl, "Concentration in the U.S. Steel Industry" (DBA diss., Columbia University, 1950).

2. In *Industrial Market Structures and Economic Performance* (Chicago: Rand McNally, 1970), p. 52, Frederick M. Scherer has pointed out that a statistical peculiarity of s_i^2, known as the Herfindahl index, is that its distribution in studies of industrial concentration tends to be strongly skewed to the low end of the admissible range. Whether this is of any theoretical importance in our study is debatable. It depends on whether we believe that the cross-sectional

distribution of our companies' degrees of diversification is truly skewed or that the skew is an artifact of the formula. Since nearly all of our subject firms are involved in five or six major product lines or fewer, the degree of skew observed may not be as severe as in the concentration studies that used the Herfindahl index. Nonetheless, since we make comparisons of indices across companies for relative degrees of diversification, it would seem useful to remove some of the skew by taking the log of s_i^2. Since the log of a fraction is less than zero, the resulting figure is multiplied by minus one to revert the index into a positive range.

Index

Accountability; 34–35; to constituencies, 37–40

Acquisitions, 4–6; beliefs about, 89–90, 92–94, 107–8; capital market dominance and, 71; change through, 137–38, 144, 146, 154, 155; constituency changes and, 134–35; strategies for, 165–66; unrelated, 167–68

Adult development, 26, 27, 125

Affirmative action, 41

Age: of CEOs, 16–17; of corporate managers, 18; financial incentives and, 21; psychological impact of, 25–30

Allen, Stephen A., III, 199*n*3

Andrews, Kenneth R., 6*n*, 198*n*1

Atlantic Richfield, 14

Autonomy of divisions, 107–8

Baker, Edward, 198*n*1

Balance-sheet ratios, 53

Bankruptcy, 131

Belief systems, 9–10, 79–109, 185–95; challenges to, 151; change and, 139–41, 143–44, 146–58; of commodity products company, 104–6; of conglomerates, 107–8; consistency and harmony of, 165; of consumer products company, 100–102; corporate strategy and, 111; emotional commit-

ment to, 110–11, 115, 123–30; goals and, 34, 80–87; here-and-now function of, 126–30; of high-technology companies, 102–4; impact of experience on, 118–20; impact of financial results on, 120–23; periodic audit of, 172–73; restructuring of, 151; risk and, 66; roots of, 115–18; stability of, 114; strategic decisions and, 99–100; strategic means and, 87–96; transferred from generation to generation, 124–26

Board of directors, succession process and, 30

Bradshaw, Thornton, 14

Bruns, Tom, 199*n*3

Burck, Charles C., 197*n*1

Business climate, continuity in, 113

Capital, cost of, 50–51

Capital market, 49; belief systems and, 85, 101, 106; change in, 133, 140, 142, 143, 149; competitive position in, 43; as corporate constituency, 38–40; corporate survival and, 31; dependency on, 10, 67; discipline of, 7; dominance of goals by, 68, 70–74; effects of diversification on, 168; goals associated with, 42, 44–46; independence from, 50, 162, 166–67; internal, 51–57; profits and, 137; short-term priorities and, 170; stability and,

Capital market *(continued))*
  112, 114; strategies for independence from, 77
Capital programs, 94–95
Career expectations: accountability and, 39; personality development and, 26–27
Career histories, 15; of CEOs, 16
Career opportunities, 7
Chandler, Alfred, 159, 160, 172, 198*n*1
Change: fundamental, *see* Fundamental change; incremental, 118–20
Character types of managers, 25
Chemical industry, process cost in, 4
Chief executive officers (CEOs), 12, 15–16; beliefs of, 123–24, 165; change and, 140, 146–47, 150, 151–58; constituency dominance and, 78; corporate goals statements and, 41; corporate survival and, 30–31; of customers, 102; delegation and, 97; demographic characteristics of, 16–18; diversification decisions of, 87, 90; drive to excel of, 22–24; financial goals and, 36; governmental dealings of, 13; monetary motivation of, 21; new, 134; new product decisions of, 110; organizational constituency and, 40; psychological impact of age on, 25, 27–30; uncertainties and, 127–28
Chief financial officers (CFOs), 28; financial goals and, 36; long-term debt advocated by, 5; new, 134
Chief operating officers (COOs), 28
Churchill, Winston, 171
Commitment, 7; to belief systems, 110–11, 115, 123–30; length of service and, 18; of shareholders, 45; psychological impact of age and, 25; *see also* Loyalty
Commodity Products I (study company): belief system of, 89, 96, 98, 192; financial goals system of, 60; goals and performance of, 183; response to change in, 145–51
Commodity Products II (study company): belief system of, 83, 84, 88–89, 92–97, 99, 104–6, 117, 118, 193; corporate goals statement of, 41–43; goals and performance of, 181, 183; product market dominance of, 68; response to change in, 153, 155–58
Commodity Products III (study company): belief system of, 84, 89, 96, 194; goals and performance of, 183; product market dominance of, 68
Commodity products industry, 11; manufacturing expertise of corporate managers in, 19; psychology of managers in, 22–23; uncertainties in, 127; *see also* Commodity Products *study companies*
Common Market, 119
Company man character type, 25
Compensation, 13; of CEOs, 17; as motivator, 20–22
Competence of corporation, *see* Distinctive competence
Competitive position, 7; beliefs about, 83, 105; in capital market, 43; capital programs and, 95;

change in, 133; corporate goals statement on, 41; demand-related goals and, 46–47; drive to excel and, 22–24; expansion and, 4; financial goals and, 35, 63; geographic location and, 96; innovation and, 91; modernization and, 5–6; product market dominance and, 68–70; short-term considerations and, 7–8; stability and, 114
Computer industry, 3–4
Conference Board, 13
Conglomerate I (study company): belief system of, 88, 96, 98, 107–8, 195; financial goals system of, 63; goals and performance of, 183
Conglomerate II (study company): belief system of, 88, 89, 96, 97, 118, 195; goals and performance of, 183; response to change in, 153–55
Conglomerates, 8, 11; *see also* Conglomerate *study companies*
Constituencies, 37–40, 49–50; beliefs about, 84; change in, 133–35; change in relationship with, 120–21; constraints imposed by, 79, 80; demands of, 66–78; independence from, 160; "satisficing" and, 163; stability of, 112, 114; trade-offs among interests of, 126–27; *see also* Capital market; Organizational constitutency; Product market
Consulting firms, 146–47, 150–51
Consumer Products I (study company): belief system of, 83, 90, 97, 118, 128, 188; corporate versus divisional goals of, 46; goals and performance of, 181, 182; product market dominance of, 68; response to change in, 136–41
Consumer Products II (study company): belief system of, 89–90, 96, 98, 189; goals and performance of, 182; response to change in, 141–45
Consumer Products III (study company): belief system of, 84, 89, 90, 92–93, 97, 98, 100–102, 106, 190; corporate goals statement of, 42–43; financial goals system imbalance in, 60, 62; goals and performance of, 182; response to change in, 133–34
Consumer Products IV (study company): belief system of, 90, 97, 115, 191; goals and performance of, 182; response to change in, 133
Consumer products industry, 4–5, 11; financial studies for, 128–29; marketing expertise of corporate managers in, 19; psychology of managers of, 22–24, 27–28; transfer of beliefs from generation to generation in, 125; uncertainties in, 127; *see also* Consumer Products *study companies*
Corporate managers, 15–16; demographic characteristics of, 18–20; drive to excel of, 22–24; monetary motivation of, 20–22; psychological impact of age on, 25–30; work of, 12–14; *see also* Chief executive officers
Corporate strategy: belief systems and, 111; definition of, 6*n*; stability of, 114; *see also* Strategic change; Strategic means
Corporate survival, 160–62; accountability and, 37; beliefs about, 84; change and, 145, 146, 152; change in external constraints and, 121; financial

goals system and, 62; goals related to, 48; maximization of wealth and, 163; organizational dominance and, 75; psychology of managers and, 30–31; as silent priority, 164–65; strategies for, 165–74

Corporate wealth, maximization of, 7, 162–63

Costs: of capital, 50–51; lowering of, 41; of raw materials, 8, 131–32

Craftsman character type, 25

Credit limits, 44–45

Credit ratings, 32, 34; beliefs about, 83, 105; management accountability for, 35

Curtis Publishing Company, 131, 132

Customers: accountability to, 37–40; loyalty of, 45, 47; *see also* Product market

Current earnings, financing from, 5; *see also* Internal capital market

Cyclical changes, 200*n* 1

Cyert, Richard Michael, 198*n* 1

Debt/equity ratio, 53; organizational dominance and, 74; target, 57

Debt financing, 51; conservative, 52, 53; *see also* Long-term debt; Short-term debt

Default, risk of, 53*n*

Delegation, 96–97

Demand for funds, 44; belief systems and, 80; goals related to, 46–47, 55, 57, 64, 75

Dependency, general theory of, 66–67

Dewey, John, 199*n* 2

Distinctive competence: assessment of, 120; beliefs about, 80–81; change and, 118, 137, 140, 143–44, 148, 165; diversification and, 107, 108; new product introductions and, 101, 102, 110; strategic means and, 87, 88, 94; technological, 103, 104

Diversification, 6, 8, 10; acquisition decisions and, 107; beliefs about, 80; capital market dominance and, 71; change through, 137–38, 141–48, 156; in conglomerates, 11; corporate wealth maximization and, 163; delegation and, 96; funding of, 63; independent goal setting and, 68; index to, 178–80; internal, 133; organizational dominance and, 74–75; organizational structure and, 12–13; product market dominance versus, 70; strategic means and, 87–96; strategy of, 77, 167–69

Divestiture, 4–5; beliefs about, 90, 92, 93; change through, 143, 146

Dividend payouts, 6, 51; beliefs about, 86, 105–6; capital market dominance and, 72; cutting, 5; as financial goal, 44; new products and, 101; reinvestment of earnings versus, 53, 56; target, 57

Divisional organization structure, 12; autonomy in, 107–8; goals in, 46

Dominance, constituency, 67–68; by capital market, 70–74; by organization, 73–76; by product market, 67–71

Drive to excel, 22–24

Du Pont Corporation, 198*n* 1

Dynamic equilibrium, 200*n* 1

Earnings: acquisitions and, 107; division of, 6; reinvestment of, 53; retained, 7, 74; stability of, 98, 104

Earnings coverage ratios, 53

Earnings per share (EPS), 34, 35, 44; beliefs about, 83

Earnings retention ratio, 57

Economic constraints: changing, 132–36; stability promoted by, 111–15

Educational background: of CEOs, 16; of corporate managers, 18–19

Electronics industry, 3–4, 88

Employees: accountability to, 37–40; belief system and, 86, 96; committed and loyal, 10, 45; expectations of, 7; impact of divestiture on, 5; monetary motivation of, 21; psychological contract with, 97–99; social goals and, 42; unionized, *see* Unions; *see also* Organizational constituency

Energy-intensive industries, 32

Entrepreneurial spirit, 36

Equity base, dilution of, 44

Equity financing, 51–53

Erikson, Erik, 26, 29–30

Ethical behavior, 41

Ethnic background of CEOs, 16

Excellence: beliefs about, 84, 101, 103, 107, 108; change and, 145; corporate survival and, 31; drive for, 22–24; stability and, 114

Expansion, 3–4; international, *see* International expansion; organizational structure and, 12

Experience, impact on belief systems of, 118–20

Failure, corporate, 131; to achieve goals, 135; investor benefit from, 167; possibility of, 159

Family life, personality development and, 26, 27

Financial assets, 7

Financial goals, 32–50; belief systems and, 80–87, 120–23; capital market dominance of, 70–74; change and, 132–36, 143, 148, 149, 154; classification of, 43–48; consistency in, 59–61; constraints imposed by, 79, 80; creation of corporate wealth and, 162, 163; data on, 181–83; discipline of, 61–64; discretionary limits of management in setting, 76–78; diversification and, 87, 93, 107–8; divestiture and, 4–5; hierarchy of, 41–43; and illusion of unlimited resources, 50–51; imbalance in, 121–22; internal capital market and, 51–57; internal management practices and, 98; internalization of market forces through, 172; managerial choices and, 66–68; modernization program and, 5–6; nature and function of, 34–37; organizational dominance and, 73–76; perception of risk and, 64–66; product market dominance and, 68–71; public image and, 33–34; self-sustaining growth and, 57–59; short- and long-term priorities in, 170–71; stability of, 111–15; strategic choice and, 166; ultimate beneficiaries of, 37–40

Foreign competition, 8, 131

Index

Forest products industry, 5

Fortune 500 companies, 6n, 11; CEOs of, 16–17; competitive position of, 23, 24; return on equity of, 107; survey of senior managers of, 19

Founders, belief systems of, 115–18

Freud, Sigmund, 26

Fundamental change, 131–58; in commodity products company, 145–51; in consumer products companies, 136–45; in conglomerate, 153–55; managing process of, 151–53; objective forces for, 132–36; planning for, 166

Funds flow, 35, 50; belief systems and, 80; boundaries of management initiative and, 76; change and, 134–36; diversification and, 87, 107–8; goal of self-sufficiency in, 63; impact of financial goals on, 43–48, 55; internal capital market and, 52–54; limits on, 50–51; perception of risk and, 64–66; planning model for, 61–64; qualitative interrelation of goals and, 64; self-sustaining growth equation and, 57–59; stability and, 112, 114; strategic choice and, 166

Future: assessment of, 152; stability and, 113

Future generations, concern for, 28–29

Gamesman character type, 25

Generational transfer of beliefs, 124–26

Generativity versus self-absorption, 29–30

Geographic origins: of CEOs, 16; of corporate managers, 18

Goals: beliefs about, 80–87; *see also* Financial goals

Government agencies, 13

Gross national product, 6n

Growth: beliefs about, 83, 86, 100, 101, 103, 104, 107, 155–56; change and, 140, 141, 143; choice between profits and, 127; corporate survival and, 31; diversification and, 92; in earnings per share, 44; as financial goal, 35; goals for, 52; industry rate of, 69–70; organizational dominance and, 74, 75; power and, 125; rate of, 6; risk and, 65; self-sustaining, 50, 57–59, 70; stimulating work environment and, 97–98; target rate of, 57

Higgins, Robert C., 198n 1

High-technology companies, 11; delegation in, 96; product market dominance of, 69; psychology of managers of, 23; technical expertise of managers of, 19; transferring beliefs from generation to generation in, 124–25; uncertainties in, 127; *see also* Technical Products *study companies*

High-volume customers, 103

Host communities: accountability to, 38, 42; belief systems and, 101

Human assets, 7

IBM, 3, 108

Identification with company, 25

Incremental change, 118–20

Independence: managerial, 160; need for, 30

Industrial organization, 125

Inflation: borrowing and, 5; funds flow ratio and, 57–58

Initiative, boundaries of, 76–78

Innovation: beliefs about, 91; commitment to, 105

Interest rates, 132

Internal capital market, 6, 51–57; independent goal setting and, 68; organizational dominance and, 75; self-sustaining growth and, 57

Internal management practices: beliefs about, 82, 84, 96–99; change in, 154; diversification and, 108

International expansion, 6, 8; beliefs about, 90, 92, 118–20, 128; change through, 141; corporate managers and, 13; psychological factors in, 29

Interpersonal skills, 152

Jungle fighter character type, 25

Kotter, John P., 197n 1, 198n 1

Kuhn, 198n 1

Labor, rising costs of, 131–32

Lawrence, Paul R., 199n 3

Length of service: of CEOs, 17; of corporate managers, 18; psychological impact of age and, 25

Levinson, Daniel J., 26, 27, 125–26

Lindblom, C. E., 200n 2

Long-term debt, 5–6; beliefs about, 80, 82–83, 94, 101, 102, 116–17, 123–24; expansion of, 121–22; to facilitate change, 140; financial goals and, 32, 33; innovation and, 91

Lorsch, Jay W., 199n 3

Loyalty, 45; independent goal setting and, 68; organizational dominance and, 74; stability and, 112; strategies producing, 77

McCaskey, Michael B., 199n 2

Maccoby, Michael, 25, 26

Management philosophy, 198n 1

Managerial capitalism, 159

Managerial practices, *see* Internal management practices

Manufacturing facilities, improvement of, 104–6

March, James G., 198n 1

Market segmentation, 69

Market share, 35; increase in, 41; target growth rate and, 47

Marketing: beliefs about, 89, 105; change and, 139, 144; drive to excel in, 22; expansion and, 4; of new product, 101, 102

Markets, 6; competitive position in, *see* Competitive position; international, *see* International expansion; *see also* Capital market; Product market

Marshall Plan, 118–20

Maximization, concept of, 163

Measurement systems, 13

Mentor/protegé relationships, 125–26

Mergers, constituency changes and, 134–35

Midlife transition, 27, 28
Miles, Raymond E., 198*n* 1
Mintzberg, Henry, 6*n*
Modernization: beliefs about, 104–6; financing of, 5–6
Monetary motivation, 20–22
Morale, impact of negative decision on, 4
Mortality, acceptance of, 27, 28
Motivation, financial, 20–22
Multidivisional organization structure, 12, 46, 107–8

Nepotism, policy against, 139, 141
New products: commitment to, 122; decision not to approve, 110; introduction of, 100–104
Nonunionized companies, 99, 102

OPEC crisis, 32
Operating general managers, 12
Organization character, 198*n* 1
Organization theory, 198*n* 1, 199*n* 3
Organizational constituency, 38–40, 49; beliefs about, 84, 96–99; change in, 134, 142, 149; dependency on, 67; diversification and, 92; dominance of, 68, 73–76; goals related to, 47–48; quality of life for, 101; strategies for independence from, 77
Organizational culture, 198*n* 1
Organizational structure, 13; multidivisional, 12
Ownership patterns, 11

Patience, 152
Payout ratio, 44
Performance: data on, 181–83; funds flow and, 59; past, competition against, 69; short-term measures of, 169, 170; stability of, 113–14
Persistence, 152
Personal background: of CEOs, 16; of corporate managers, 18
Personal goals, changes in, 25–26
Personality theory, 26
Personnel: impact of divestiture on, 5; recruiting and upgrading, 41; *see also* Employees; Organizational constituency
Petroleum industry, process control in, 4
Pfeffer, Jeffrey, 198*n* 1
Planning, 13; belief system audit and, 172; change and, 149–50, 166; financial goals and, 36, 41; funds flow ratio and, 57, 64; reserves and, 53–54; stability and, 113
Power: appeal of exercising, 30; growth and, 125
Price-earnings ratio, 5; change and, 133; target, 35
Privately held companies, 11, 17; belief systems of, 100, 102; psychology of managers of, 29; shift to public ownership of, 133
Process control, 4
Product line capacity, 41
Product market, 38–40, 49; beliefs about, 84; change in, 133–34, 137–39, 142, 145, 148; delega-

tion and, 97; dependency on, 67; dominance of, 67–71; funding of, 50; goals related to, 46–47; growth in, 51; self-sufficiency in, 53, 55, 59, 63; strategic means and, 87, 88, 92, 95, 96; strategies for independence from, 77, 167–69
Production, increase in, 41
Products, 6
Profits: beliefs about, 91; choice between growth and, 127; discrimination among opportunities for, 69; of *Fortune* 500 companies, 6*n;* impact of OPEC crisis on, 32; long-term growth of, 4; from military production, 137; new products and, 101; rate of growth of, 6; short-term, 169, 170
Progress, tangible evidence of, 113, 115
Promoting from within, 153
Psychological constraints, 8, 10; financial goals and, 34; objective constraints versus, 79–80; *see also* Belief systems
Psychology of managers, 20–31; corporate survival and, 30–31; drive to excel in, 22–24; impact of age on, 25–30; monetary motivation and, 20–22; and transfer of beliefs from generation to generation, 125–26
Public image, 33–34

Quality: beliefs about, 83, 105; as goal, 114; preservation of, 41
"Quality of life," 41; beliefs about, 101

Rank in industry, 69
Raw materials, rising costs of, 8, 131–32
RCA, 14
Recession, expansion during, 3
Regulations, government, 13
Research and development, 4; beliefs about, 154–55; commitment to, 102–3; diversification and, 88, 90, 91; drive to excel and, 23; expenditures for, 6; growth and, 86; in high-technology companies, 11; impact of external constraints on, 121, 122; incremental change and, 118; new products and, 100, 102
Resource allocation, financial goals and, 41
Retail chain stores, sales to, 136
Retained earnings, 7, 74
Return on equity (ROE), 5, 58, 63; capital market dominance and, 72–73
Return on investment (ROI), 39; beliefs about, 83, 86, 103, 154–56; discipline of capital market and, 7; diversification and, 89; evaluation by methodology of, 50–51; as investor-related goal, 45; natural cycles of, 170; near-term decline in, 134; short-term, 169; target, 57, 63, 75
Return on net assets (RONA), 58, 60, 62, 63; capital market dominance and, 73; target, 63
Rewards system: corporate goals statement on, 41; long-term, 171
Rhenman, Eric, 198*n* 1, 200*n* 1
Risk: assessment of, 106, 120; belief systems and, 81, 127–28, 155; change and, 147; of default, 53*n;* in

Index

Risk: *(continued))*
 diversification, 87, 108; in new product introduction, 101, 102; perception of, 64–66; of single-industry company, 105, 106; of single product market, 94; taken by CEOs, 17–18;
  technological, 103, 104

"Satisficing," 163
Saturday Evening Post, The, 131
Scale, economics of, 69
Scherer, Frederick M., 202*n*2
Sears Roebuck, 198*n*1
Security of employment, 97
Segmentation of market, 69
Self-absorption, generativity versus, 29–30
Self-sufficiency, 50, 55–56, 59, 63, 77; beliefs about,
  80, 81; capital market dominance versus, 70, 73;
  corporate survival and, 160–61, 166–67; diver-
  sification and, 108; dividend policy and, 53;
  model of, 198*n*1; new product introduction and,
  101, 102, 104; of nonunion companies, 99; or-
  ganizational dominance and, 74–75; product
  market dominance and, 68; test for, 62
Self-sustaining growth, 57–59; product market
  dominance and, 70
Selznick, Philip, 198*n*1
"Settling down" process, 26
Shareholders: accountability to, 37–40; corporate
  goals and, 42; financial goals and, 33, 34; funds
  flow and, 44; loyalty of, 45, 47; shift in composi-
  tion of, 133; wealth of, 7, 163; *see also* Capital
  market
Share-of-market strategy, 47, 69
Sheldon, Alan, 198*n*1, 200*n*1
Short-term considerations, 7–8
Short-term debt, 86; cost of, 5, 132; to facilitate
  change, 138
Short-term earnings, 4
Short-term objectives, 169
Simon, Herbert A., 163
Single-industry companies, 11; dependency of, 67;
  product market dominance of, 68, 94
Smith, Adam, 172
Snow, Charles C., 198*n*1
Social goals, 37, 42
Stability, financial and economic constraints pro-
  moting, 111–15
Stable employment, 97, 98
Stalker, G. M., 199*n*3
Steinbruner, John D., 199*n*2
Stock: current market value of, 21; price of, 5
Stock market; external and emotional forces in,
  35
Stock ownership: by CEOs, 17; by corporate

managers, 18; patterns of, 11; *see also* Sharehold-
  ers
Strategic choice, 165–74; belief systems and, 99–
  100; limits to, 172–74; myths and reality of,
  6–10; risk-taking and, 17–18
Strategic means; beliefs about, 82, 84, 87–96
Strategic planning, 149–50
Structural change, 200*n*1
Success, desire for, 161
Succession process, 30
Suppliers, accountability to, 38
Supply of funds, 44; belief systems and, 80–81;
  goals related to, 44–46, 55, 57, 64, 75

Takeovers: shareholders' cooperation in, 40; unfriendly, avoidance of, 30, 31
Target growth rate, 35; externally defined, 47
Technical Products I (study company): belief system of, 83–86, 91, 96, 98, 116, 185; goals and
  performance of, 181, 182
Technical Products II (study company): belief system of, 83, 84, 91, 96, 98, 102–4, 106, 118, 127,
  186; financial goals system of, 63; goals and per-
  formance of, 182
Technical Products III (study company): belief sys-
  tem of, 83, 84, 90, 91, 96, 97, 99, 121–22, 127,
  187; capital market dominance of, 70–73; finan-
  cial goals system of, 63; goals and performance
  of, 183
Technology: beliefs about, 84, 90–91, 144; *see also*
  High-technology companies
Tenure, *see* Length of service
Thompson, James D., 198*n*1
Tracy, Phelps, 198*n*1
Truman, Harry S., 16
Tuden, Arthur, 198*n*1

Unconscious goals, 26
Unions: accountability to, 38, 40; belief systems
  and, 106; companies without, 99, 102
Unlimited resources, illusion of, 50–51
Unrelated diversified firms, 11

Values, 198*n*1
Van Horne, James C., 197*n*1

Watson, Thomas, 108–9
Wealth: corporate, creation of, 162–63; responsi-
  bility of management for enhancement of, 38;
  shareholder versus corporate, 7
Work environment, stimulating, 97–98, 107
Working conditions, 40
World War II, 141; conversion to military produc-
  tion during, 137